living with fear

understanding and coping with anxiety

second edition

By the same author

Patterns of Meaning in Psychiatric Patients

Fears and Phobias

Fears, Phobias and Rituals

Clinical Anxiety
(with M. H. Lader)

Nursing in Behavioural Psychotherapy

Psychiatric Nurse Therapists in Primary Care

Behavioural Psychotherapy: Pocketbook Aid to Clinical Management

Anxiety and its Treatment
(with J. Greist and J. Jefferson)

Cure and Care of Neuroses

Mental Health Care Delivery: Innovations, Impediments, Implementation
(edited with R. Scott)

Problem-centred Care Planning: A Primer for Mental Health Care
(with S. Toole)

Self-help for Nightmares
(with M. Burgess and M. Gill)

BTSteps – Behavioural Self-Assessment and Self-Care for OCD
(with J. Greist and L. Baer)

Cope: Cognitive-behavioural self-help for depression
(with D. Osgood-Hynes, L. Baer and J. Greist)

Isaac M. Marks M.D.

living with fear

understanding and coping with anxiety

second edition

THE McGRAW-HILL COMPANIES

LONDON · BURR RIDGE IL · NEW YORK · ST LOUIS · SAN FRANCISCO · AUCKLAND

BOGOTÁ · CARACAS · LISBON · MADRID · MEXICO · MILAN · MONTREAL · NEW DELHI

PANAMA · PARIS · SAN JUAN · SÃO PAULO · SINGAPORE · SYDNEY · TOKYO · TORONTO

Published by
McGraw-Hill Publishing Company
Shoppenhangers Road, Maidenhead, Berkshire, SL6 2QL, England
Telephone 01628 502500
Fax: 01628 770224
Web site: http://www.mcgraw-hill.co.uk

British Library Cataloguing in Publication Data
A catalogue record for this book is available from the British Library

Sponsoring Editor: Elizabeth Robinson
Desk Editor: Alastair Lindsay
Produced by: Steven Gardiner Ltd, Cambridge
Designed by: Claire Brodman Book Designs, Lichfield, Staffs
Cover by: Kate Hybert

McGraw-Hill

A Division of The McGraw·Hill Companies

McGraw-Hill books are available at special quantity discounts. Please contact the Corporate
Sales Executive at the above address.

ISBN 0 07 709758 0

1 2 3 4 5 BB 5 4 3 2 1

Printed in Great Britain by Bell and Bain Ltd., Glasgow

contents

part 3

the treatment of anxiety   135

preface

This book hopes to help you understand fear and how to overcome it. Worry is an everyday trouble for everyone. There is no clear divide between normal fears and obsessions which we all have and can cope with by ourselves, and disabling anxiety problems that need systematic help when they begin to restrict our lives. Guides are needed to the origins and forms of nervous tension and what to do about it when it gets on top of us. It helps to know what troubles other people have and how they cope with those.

Many people feel that they are the only ones to have their problems. This book contains vignettes of problems you may have that have also troubled others. It describes the main patterns of anxiety found in normal life and in the clinic, be they fears of dying, of injury, of contamination, of AIDS, or of going mad. Many problems are more common than most people realise. If you recognise some of these problems in yourself, you will find that you are not alone in having them. This book enables you to learn what can be done, and what you can do yourself, to relieve nervous suffering.

The treatment of anxiety has advanced impressively and many sufferers can now be helped for the first time. A radical change in thinking has led to effective new treatment methods. You don't have to look back at your childhood to get over these worries. That approach often made people feel helpless, because we cannot reconstruct our life histories, and blaming parents achieves little beyond inducing burdensome guilt. Many therapists used to believe in the need to uncover something in order to help. Along with this went the myth of symptom substitution, the belief that if one reduced a fear without dealing with its supposed 'underlying' problem, then another trouble would pop up in its place. Research has shown time and again that this notion is largely groundless. People who lose their phobias or rituals, far from developing fresh symptoms, usually improve also in other areas of their life once they are freed from the shackles formerly imposed by their fears.

There is now abundant evidence that behavioural and cognitive treatments work for many, and could for you if you have a problem described in this book. Phobias, obsessions and rituals, post-traumatic stress and sexual difficulties can all respond well, and improvement usually continues in the years after active treatment. Not everyone can be helped. For success you need to be clear about what you want to change and how you'll be better off if you overcome your problem. You have to be prepared to tolerate some discomfort and help evolve and actively participate in the treatment plan, including doing a fair amount of 'homework' on the problem. When phobias and rituals implicate family and friends then they need to lend a hand as co-therapists working with you. For most sexual difficulties your partner should be involved in some way.

This volume explains the principles of treatment and takes the mystery out of it. Certain problems may be best handled by professional therapists, especially if medication needs to be added at times, e.g. if you feel depressed as well as anxious, but you can help professionals help you if you understand your difficulty a bit better and get some idea of how to cope with it. Moreover, many anxiety problems respond to systematic self-help along behavioural or cognitive lines.

More and more self-help is becoming possible as treatment principles are worked out and simplified. This is a recurring theme in health. Malnutrition was more common before scientists worked out the balanced diet we need for normal development and function. Nutritional principles are now common knowledge through what we learn at school and from popular books and the media and the internet, and most people can keep themselves normally nourished, although they are often pushed to eat excessive salt, sugar and saturated fats. Severe diarrhoea used to kill innumerable infants until it was discovered how important it is to maintain the body's fluids and salts in proper balance. This was done mainly by doctors or nurses giving intravenous fluids. But then it was found that babies with gastro-enteritis can take boiled salt water in the right dilution by mouth without vomiting, thus avoiding the need for intravenous fluids. Now a parent can give a baby with gastro-enteritis the correct fluid by mouth. This the child will not vomit, and so its stomach can absorb the liquid and its life is saved. As doctors discovered the principles of treatment and simplified management of the problem, they could fade out of the treatment and let the parents themselves do much of the management.

A similar process is beginning with behavioural and cognitive treatments for various types of anxiety. People want to be empowered, and research on self-help is producing the scientific approach to will-power which is necessary for success. Emphasis is shifting toward sufferers carrying out much of their own treatment, with the therapist just setting the course and giving a touch to the rudder at intervals. The last chapter in this book gives some guidance on self-help for those who are so inclined to try to help themselves. This book is a guide to both self-help and the professional methods now available for the relief of nervous suffering.

The book is dedicated to the thousands of sufferers, colleagues and students all over the world whose wisdom made this work possible. Their co-operation and penetrating insights have steadily increased our knowledge and pointed the way to ever more effective techniques of easing nervous tension. Although this book is primarily written for the lay person, it can interest many health care students and professionals, including doctors, psychiatrists, psychologists, nurses, counsellors, teachers, social workers, and probation officers. Many professionals round the world have told me that they recommend their anxiety patients to read this book.

Readers may wish to know a bit about the author. I'm a psychiatrist interested in anxiety and its management. I've done 35 years of research into the causes of tension and ways in which it can be effectively relieved. Most of this work was done at the Bethlem-Maudsley Hospital and Institute of Psychiatry of London University, usually in collaboration with wonderful colleagues in the UK and abroad. In randomised controlled trials, anxiety-disorder sufferers improved as much when doing self-treatment guided by this book or by appropriate computer systems as when it was guided by a clinician. This research into self-help culminated in my opening in 2000 of the Stress Self-Help Clinic at 303 North End Rd, London W14 9NS, as part of Charing Cross Hospital and Imperial College of London University.

The research led to my publishing 12 books and over 400 scientific articles and to lecture on every continent. The need became evident for a popular guide to modern ideas on anxiety. The first edition seemed to meet such a need to some extent, given the thanks for it received from sufferers and colleagues in many countries and its translation into many languages. It is now a self-help manual for the TOP (Triumph Over Phobia) networks of self-help groups in Britain and Australia.

This second edition is timely due to further advances since the first edition in 1978. Its many changes include research into the evolutionary background of our fears, newer labels for anxiety problems such as panic disorder, social fears and body dysmorphic and post-traumatic disorders, recently-introduced medications, progress with computer-guided and other self-help, cognitive therapy, up-to-date case histories, and neuroimaging. The book is designed to help you help yourself. Good luck if you decide to try.

Thanks and acknowledgements

The author is deeply indebted to the legion of authors and sufferers cited in this book. The authors include Dr Douglas Bond (*The Love and Fear of Flying*, International Universities Press Inc., New York, 1952), the late Dr Leonard Cammer (*Freedom from Compulsion*, Simon & Schuster, New York, 1976), Joyce Emerson (*Phobias*, National Association of Mental Health, London, 1971), the late Professor Carney Landis (*Varieties of Psychopathological Experience*, ed. F. A. Mettler, Holt, Rinehart and Winston Inc., New York, 1964), Mary McArdle (*Treatment of a Phobia*, Nursing Times, 1974, pp. 637–639), Dr Don Meichenbaum (*Cognitive Behavior Modification*, Plenum Press, Plenum Publishing Corporation, New York, 1977), Dr Colin Parkes (*The First Year of Grief*, Psychiatry, vol. 33, pp. 444–467, 1970), Dr John Price (unpublished paper on aversions), Dr S. Rachman (*The Meaning of Fear*, Penguin Books Inc., 1974), Dr Gerald Rosen (*Don't Be Afraid*, Prentice-Hall Inc., 1976), the late Dr Claire Weekes (Peace from Nervous Suffering: Self-Help for Your Nerves, Angus & Robertson, 1972).

Special thanks are due to Dr John Greist for helpful comments on the first edition's final manuscript and for subsequent fruitful collaborations regarding computer-guided self-help to Dr John Greist, Dr Lee Baer, Dr Raja Ghosh, Dr Richard Parkin, Dr Susan Shaw, and Stuart Toole.

Extensive citations in this book are culled from among the thousands of sufferers round the world in whose treatment the author has been involved over the past 35 years, and from his previous books on the subject including *Patterns of Meaning in Psychiatric Patients* (Oxford University Press, 1965), *Fears and Phobias* (Heinemann Medical Press, 1969), *Clinical Anxiety* (Heinemann Medical, 1971, co-author M. H. Lader), *Nursing in Behavioural Psychotherapy* (co-authors R. H. Hallam, J. Connolly, R. Philpott, 1977; Royal College of Nursing), *Fears, Phobias and Rituals* (Oxford University Press, 1987), *Behavioural Psychotherapy: Pocketbook Aid to Clinical Management* (John Wright, 1986), *BT Steps Workbook – Behavioural Self-Assessment and Self-Care for OCD* (with J. Greist and L. Baer 1995).

Patients' names used in this book have been changed to preserve anonimity.

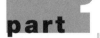

the nature of fear and anxiety

Really, I consider total absence of fear, in situations such as mine,

to be the mark not of a valiant fellow but of a dolt.

ERASMUS, IN THE FIFTEENTH CENTURY, ON FLEEING FROM THE PLAGUE

recognising normal and abnormal fear

Anxiety affects everybody

Like all of us, you get worried sometimes. You would be abnormal if you didn't. Anxiety has always been part of the human condition and will remain with us for the foreseeable future. The caveman worried where his next meal was coming from, the Roman Emperor brooded on the next attempt to be made on his life, the airline pilot in the twenty-first century bites his nails when his landing system is faulty, and you live with plenty of worries: your threatened job, your children's health or education, your faltering marriage, or just things that go bump in the night. Although the things we worry about change as our styles of living alter, the tensions continue.

Anxiety is normal in that it is widespread and affects almost everyone. What makes people anxious may vary from one person to the next, but certain things put most of us on edge. Anxiety is part of everyday life. It can be brought on by our daily routine which often involves some danger. On crowded roads we must be constantly alert; near misses are quite common and the unexpected is always happening. The insecure assistant worries over his job, the top executive dithers over decisions, and the call centre operator is harassed by frantic callers. Rising prices make the housewife struggle to stretch her tight budget to feed her family. Husband and wife bicker, parents and children find themselves at odds. It is almost impossible to live without some kind of anxiety.

Because anxiety is an inevitable part of life, we have to learn to live with it. Much of this book will describe common and rare worries. Understanding their main patterns allows us to better judge what we are experiencing and when we need help. The words of actual sufferers will be used to show their feelings and problems. The last part of this book will show you how to deal with fear and bring it down to normal proportions.

What is anxiety?

Anxiety is what we feel when we get into a tight corner. We may feel threatened even if we may not always know the reason for this. The feeling of anxiety is related to that of fear and similar emotions. Our language is rich in terms describing anxiety and similar emotions. Look at this list: *apprehension, uneasiness, nervousness, worry, disquiet, solicitude, concern, misgiving, qualm, edginess, jitteriness, sensitivity, discomfort, unease; being pent up, troubled, wary, unnerved, unsettled, upset, aghast, defensive, disturbed, distressed, perturbed, distraught or threatened; consternation, trepidation, scare, fright, dread, terror, horror, alarm, panic, anguish, agitation.* These words tell us about subtle nuances of emotions similar to anxiety. When society develops a rich vocabulary for certain feelings we can be sure that they are common and important.

In general, anxiety and fear are much like one another. If the cause of our worry is obvious, as when facing a robber at night, then we tend to call the feeling *fear* (old English *faer* meant sudden danger). If we worry about a minor exam months ahead we are called *anxious* (from the Latin *anxius*, meaning troubled about an uncertain event, and a Greek root meaning to press tight or strangle).

Almost all of us have minor fears of one kind or another. Children are afraid of parents leaving them, of strangers, animals, and unusual noises and situations. Adults may be frightened by heights, lifts, darkness, airplanes, spiders, mice, taking exams, and superstitions such as being haunted by ghosts, passing under ladders in the street, and so on. Such minor fears do not lead to total avoidance of the triggers and are often overcome by explanation. They do not need treatment.

Fear is a normal response to an active or imagined threat. The emotion changes our actions and body in ways that we feel and that others can see. What we sense as a pounding heart is felt as a racing pulse by someone holding our wrist. An onlooker might notice our sweaty brow. Other changes may be more subtle and detected only by delicate instruments, for example rise in the electrical conductance of our skin or blood flow in parts of our brain.

Two of the most obvious changes in behaviour during fear are in striking contrast. One is a tendency to freeze and remain motionless and mute. Rape or mugging victims often say that they froze automatically when assaulted. A form of this in animals is feigning death or playing possum. The opposite tendency is to become startled and to scream while running away. Both these patterns of behaviour are seen during fear, and we may change rapidly from one to the other, freezing and then suddenly scurrying for shelter.

Charles Darwin, who taught us about natural selection, drew a vivid picture of fear.

"The frightened man first stands like a statue motionless and breathless . . . the heart beats quickly and violently . . . the skin instantly becomes pale . . . perspiration immediately exudes from the skin and as the surface is then cold [we have what is termed] a cold sweat . . . the hairs also on the skin stand erect and superficial muscles shiver . . . in connection with the disturbed action of the heart, the breathing is hurried . . . the mouth becomes dry . . . one of the best marked symptoms is trembling of all the muscles of the body and this is often first seen in the lips.[1]"

As fear gets more intense we feel an awful terror or panic. Darwin goes on:

"The heart beats wildly or may fail to act and faintness ensues; there is a death-like pallor; the breathing is laboured; the wings of the nostrils are widely dilated . . . there is a gulping of the throat, protruding eyeballs . . . dilated pupils, rigid muscles. [In the final stages] as fear rises to an extreme pitch, the dreadful scream of terror is heard. Great beads of sweat stand on the skin. All the muscles of the body are relaxed, utter prostration soon follows, and the mental powers fail. The intestines are affected. The sphincter muscles cease to act, and no longer retain the contents of the body.[2]"

We can add to Darwin's list of bodily changes during strong fear: rise in blood pressure; a readiness to be startled; dryness and tightness of our throat and mouth; constriction of our chest; a sinking feeling in our stomach; nausea; desperation; irritability and a tendency to lash out; a strong desire to run or hide; tingling in the hands and feet; feelings of being unreal or far away; paralysing weakness of the limbs; and a sensation of faintness and falling. If fear or anxiety goes on for a long time, even healthy people become tired, depressed, slowed down, restless, and lose their appetite. They cannot sleep, have bad dreams, and avoid further frightening situations.

When we are frightened our body chemistry changes too: chemicals such as adrenaline are secreted by our adrenal glands and noradrenaline at tiny nerve endings throughout our body, to mention just two of many changes. Many of these occur not only in fear and anxiety but also during other emotions.

Can an onlooker recognise anxiety?

We can usually see if family or friends are frightened rather than happy or surprised, and people across cultures judge facial expressions of fear, anger, contempt, disgust, sadness and surprise in similar ways.[3] There are some cultural differences. Westerners often find it hard to read subtle degrees of feelings of Chinese or Japanese, and vice versa. With intense feelings recognition might be easier. Babies' emotions are harder to judge than are those of adults, who show a wider range of feelings. Whilst it may be simple to tell contentment from terror, fear is less easy to disentangle from surprise, anger, or disgust. Similarly the cries and tears of great joy on a photograph can be mistaken for those of anguish and grief.

Tension can be pleasurable

Paradoxically, people do not always try to avoid anxiety even though it is usually thought of as unpleasant. In fact, many people actively seek tension and get a charge of pleasure by mastering dangerous situations. Racing drivers, bullfighters, and mountaineers willingly expose themselves to awesome hazards. Hundreds of millions round the world love to experience at second hand the tension of watching dangerous sports or thriller films or reading books about them. Drivers in demolition Derbys enjoy deliberately crashing each other's cars to destruction.

The game of peek-a-boo that babies love to play also involves mild anxiety. They enjoy seeing Mum or Dad disappear for a few moments behind the corner of a room, only to emerge again a few seconds later. While its parents are hidden the youngster may look tense, and it squeals with joy upon their reappearance. If Mum or Dad take too long to reappear this unease mounts to fear and the child may cry.

When is anxiety helpful and when is it not?

Extreme fear can paralyse us, and severe anxiety hinders performance. In contrast, mild anxiety and fear are actually quite useful. They lead to rapid action in the face of threat and alert us in difficult situations. Actors and politicians often feel slight fear before their performance and say this keeps them on their toes. Fear normally accompanies activities like writing examinations or parachuting. Fighter pilots say that feeling afraid makes them better fighters.

An optimum amount of fear seems to be required for good performance; too little and we risk being careless, too much and we may become clumsy or paralysed by fear. When tested, veteran parachute jumpers showed only mild fear, whereas novices were more frightened, especially before the jump, although this fear subsided soon after landing. Experience of danger, however, can teach a healthy respect for danger that promotes survival. Inexperienced soldiers who were closely observed displayed little fear and disregarded safety measures. After battle experience they became more watchful, began to express fear, and made fewer careless errors.

A little fear seems to help people deal with problems. One research worker found that patients who appeared fearless before major surgery suffered more post-operative discomfort, pain, anger and resentment than did patients who had been moderately fearful pre-operatively. The latter group coped better and showed less pain and fear after the operation. Patients who had been highly anxious pre-operatively also had a lot of fear, pain and discomfort after surgery. Thus, although moderate fear may be useful, extreme degrees of fear are not beneficial and can be very destructive. Trainee parachutists do less well if they are too frightened, and even trained paratroopers may become so afraid that they lose their nerve and become unable to jump.[4]

In acute panic during a fire or earthquake, people might flee blindly in any direction and forget their usual responsibilities, as did a mother who ran out of her burning house without taking her baby with her. Soldiers under bombardment may vomit, defecate, become paralysed with fear and fail to take shelter or move others they should lead into shelter. Actors or public speakers may become so terrified that they forget their lines and become speechless.

Less intense anxiety can also resist attempts to reduce it. Anxious patients often report episodes of panic that strike repeatedly out of the blue, last for a while, and then subside regardless of what those patients are doing. Sufferers may attribute upsurges in anxiety to whatever they happen to be doing at that time and thereafter avoid that situation. For example, someone who has just started on a new drug may mistakenly attribute his panic to it and stop the drug forthwith even though he had had identical panics repeatedly long before he ever took the drug.

Anxiety that follows when the emergency is over

In a sudden crisis when we have to act quickly without thinking to avoid disaster, we may feel fear only after the worst danger has passed. After a near miss while driving a car one driver reported:

> ❝I was driving up a hill and saw a 6-year-old boy standing next to the road close by. He looked as though he'd seen me and was waiting for me to pass. Just before I reached him he made a sudden dash across the road right in front of my car. Automatically I jammed on the brake and stopped abruptly with a screech of tyres and a smell of burning rubber. I missed the lad by millimetres. It seemed like a scene in a film until a few seconds later, when I resumed driving on, my heart began to thump rapidly, I broke out in a sweat, felt shaky and my fingers and toes began to tingle with fear as I realised the calamity I'd just averted. This lasted for about 15 minutes and then died down slowly.[5]❞

This delay before anxiety starts can take hours. In war combat it is common. One bomber pilot was on his sixth mission. At the start of a bomb run, his co-pilot's face was shot off by flak, killing him instantly. The pilot did not realise this and kept trying to replace the oxygen mask. The mission was very tricky and required three separate runs on the target and several 360-degree turns directly over it. The pilot completed his mission very coolly and successfully and was complimented for his performance on returning to base. On the ground, while changing his clothes he began to tremble, went to a sympathetic doctor, and broke into a sobbing panic.

People with many duties in an emergency often cope well at the time and only later feel any emotion. Another war pilot painted a dramatic picture:

> ❝Then the gunner came up and said 'Terry's dead'. I said 'Are you sure? Maybe I can do something for him.' I went back there and looked at the back of his head; it was completely blown off. The plane was covered with blood. I opened his heated clothing; couldn't hear his heart. [Were you scared?] Hell, I wasn't scared of nothing yet! If I'd been scared I'd have just jumped out. I lifted up his eye; nothing there! If he is still alive he must be breathing. Looked at the diaphragm on the oxygen system; not moving! Poor guy. 'You're dead, you've had it'. So I went up front. How could I be scared when I have to get my navigator back? I didn't feel scared until I got on the ground. Then I began to shake like a leaf.[6]❞

After this assignment the pilot stopped flying planes for a year.

Am I normal? Do I need help?

These questions bother many of us. Normal troubles which do not require help and abnormal worries which do are on a continuum and shade into one another at some point. In threatening situations it is abnormal *not* to feel fear. Erasmus captured this beautifully in the fifteenth century. He fled from the plague as people died of it in swarms and wrote to a fellow fugitive: 'Really, I consider total absence of fear, in situations such as mine, to be the mark not of a valiant fellow but of a dolt.' We are all a bit wary at the top of a cliff or when meeting a lot of strangers in a new place. Such anxiety is protective, common, and normal. However, very few of us have to stay away from work because we are so afraid of the bus ride to get there. This is uncommon, handicapping, and abnormal. It is a *phobia* if you panic in and want to avoid or run out of situations that other people regard as harmless.

Although we all get frightened at times, this can reach the point where we wonder, 'Am I going crazy?' Anxiety does not drive one mad. Usually we can deal with troubles successfully, perhaps with help from relatives and friends. If, however, we remain plagued by endless worries about having AIDS or cancer despite thorough and repeated medical examinations and tests, we then have an illness phobia which needs active measures to deal with it.

Phobias which are so intense that they need help differ from normal fear only in degree, not in kind. Scared patients often ask: 'Am I normal, doctor? Am I going round the bend?' The answer is that *they* are normal even if their fears are not. Worries can be so intense or handicapping that they may be 'abnormal' in a statistical sense, but the people who happen to suffer these worries are perfectly 'normal' in all other respects. Developing agoraphobia is not the first step to going insane; it simply shows that a normal person's common fear is becoming so bad that it handicaps his daily activities.

Other questions many anxious people ask are: 'Will I ever be free? Can I pass it on to my family? What happens if I can't hug my kids or prepare their meals? Will I injure my family if I have these obsessive thoughts?'

With the right treatment by a therapist or undertaken yourself, most phobias can be overcome fairly readily. The last two chapters of this book describe what you need to do. Sometimes fears rub off on other relatives, but with effective treatment this need not happen. If family members already share some of your fears, they can master those fears in the same way as yourself. If your fears prevent you from acting lovingly like a normal parent, your children could get all the love they need from your spouse or another relative until you deal with your hang-ups and resume being a warm, affectionate parent. Most people who worry endlessly about harming others have very little chance of succumbing to their impulses (see p. 110).

Many quirks are adaptive, and far from their being bothersome, you may be proud of them. If you are precise, orderly, and a perfectionist, you may approve of your conscientious discipline and attention to detail, which probably benefits your work. It is quite a different story when these habits get out of hand so that you spend most of your day plagued by indecision and self-doubt, resisting intrusive thoughts, endlessly checking the locks on your doors and windows, and driving everybody around you crazy with your odd ways. At that point, pride is likely to be replaced by loathing of your obsessions and rituals, which have become burdensome, time-wasting, and unpleasant.

Minor fears and tension do not need treatment, although professional advice might be reassuring. There is comfort in learning to understand one's troubles and knowing that other people have similar worries. We can usually overcome everyday anxieties on our own, perhaps using some of the methods described in this book and with the aid of friends and relatives. However, help is worth seeking when our lives begin to be constricted by our fears. When fear of sex prevents us from establishing a normal marital relationship or when we are so worried about dirt that we spend six hours a day washing our hands till they are raw and bleeding, then treatment is indicated and can be of great value.

Most nervous tension can be treated without admission to a hospital. This book will describe many of the ways in which sufferers can learn to deal with their problems. Often people can conquer their tensions by themselves. To this end the principles of self-help are outlined on pp. 168–196. Self-help is especially feasible when the problem is in its early stages. Nevertheless, even long-standing worries can be eased surprisingly quickly if you follow a few basic principles. When the difficulties are widespread, you may be unable to apply these principles without professional help, and we will see later what forms this help can take.

The spectrum of fear

Some definitions

To avoid misunderstandings later, let us define anxiety and some similar terms. *Anxiety* is the unpleasant emotion associated with a sense of impending danger that is not obvious to an observer. *Fear* is a closely related feeling that arises as a normal response to a realistic threat. *Timidity* indicates a lasting tendency to show fear easily. *Panic* denotes a sudden upsurge of acute terror. *Phobic anxiety* is fear which is only triggered by particular situations or objects.

Although the distinction between fear, anxiety, and phobia must be arbitrary at some point, the three terms are best kept separate, because they usually describe rather different things. A *phobia* is a special kind of fear which exceeds demands of the situation, cannot be reasoned away, is beyond voluntary control, and leads to avoidance of the feared situation. Phobic patients usually recognise that their fear is unrealistic and that other people would not be unduly afraid of the same things. Because they cannot quell their phobia, it is considered irrational, although rationalisations may be offered for the fear.

The disproportion between a phobia and its stimulus

The disparity between a phobic reaction and what brings it on is obvious in phobias of things like feathers or moths. Such disproportion is also seen in more complex phobias like those of leaving one's home or of AIDS.

An example of this disproportion is Ella who was terrified by moths and butterflies. She kept her windows tightly shut at home in summer and several times left buses and trains on discovering moths or butterflies there. Her phobia caused several accidents. When she was riding a bicycle and saw a butterfly, she fell off and brought down her friends who were riding behind her. Twice she fell backward into a stream when avoiding large butterflies which had flown across her path. On another occasion she stood on a chair to clean a wardrobe, by mistake picked up a large dead brown moth, fell off the chair in her surprised fear, and sprained her ankle. She never entered a room containing moths or butterflies and always checked for their absence before entering. Interestingly her fear did not extend to 'creepy-crawlies' like spiders, earwigs, stag beetles, or furry caterpillars. 'I'd rather deal with a boxful of black widow spiders than one large English moth', she insisted.[7]

Extreme phobias cripple people's lives. 'To go outside to me was fear', said one woman.

> ❝If I went outside I couldn't breathe, I had trembly legs. So I stayed in; I stayed in for four years, and never went out. It was very gradual at first. I noticed that in crowds I couldn't breathe or I got panicky and if I went shopping for food and the shop was full I used to walk out. On a bus, I used to want to get there quicker than what a bus generally takes to get there. All these things were gradual at first, you see, but they got worse. I was always crying because I wanted to go out and I missed it when my husband took my son out for the day, but I kept the tears until my son had left the house and then I cried. I was so lonely that I used to take a drug and crawl to bed and sleep.[8]❞

People with phobias are overwhelmed by anxiety on encountering whatever brings it on. They also rehearse their frightening experience in their mind until they are in an agony of fearful anticipation about the next time they will meet their phobic object. This fear of fear becomes a fresh source of threat.

Phobics avoid the triggers of their fears

To escape their anxiety, sufferers avoid their phobic situations and restrict their activities. They are always on the lookout and acutely sensitive to the presence around them of anything remotely connected with their phobia. A spider phobic will glance round any room she enters for signs of spiders before she will sit down happily. A bird phobic will avoid those streets in the town where she is likely to encounter pigeons and confine her walks to areas less frequented by birds. In order to be able to avoid whatever brings on their panic, phobic people continually search for the trigger, find it in obscure places, and see it with their peripheral vision. One sign of improvement during treatment is decreased awareness of the phobic object in the surroundings.

Many situations that bring on phobias are common and cannot be avoided easily. The life of someone with phobias of cats, crossing streets or bridges, being in a crowd, or travelling in a bus or train can be seriously disturbed. Even uncommon events like thunderstorms in cool countries cause much misery to sufferers.

Angie aged 48 had had this phobia for 28 years.

❝I just can't carry on with my housework during a thunderstorm. I sit and wait for it to happen. When and if it does I sit in a darkened cupboard until it's over; all night if necessary. I also clamp right up as regards talking and get aggressive. I listen to every weather forecast, which I know is silly. I wish to God I could cure myself. I know I make my husband and daughter fed up with me.[9]❞

Thunderstorm phobics may phone the weather bureau endlessly for forecasts and if storms are predicted will not leave home that day. One man became so frightened when he heard a forecast of storms that he took the train 200 miles from London to Manchester to escape the weather.

Lay people find phobias hard to understand

The more common and familiar the phobic object, the greater the incomprehension and lack of sympathy which the phobic encounters in other people. Most cannot understand how anyone can be scared of a playful puppy, a fluttering bird, or going outside his home. Many think that the phobic pretends or exaggerates and should pull himself together or be forced to do so.

It is hard to grasp the panic and handicap caused by phobias. 'I find that people generally tend to brush these phobias aside. The attitude seems to be: "Don't be silly, they can't hurt you." What people don't realise is the difference between being afraid of or not liking something, and having a phobia which is absolute cold fear and stark terror of the object concerned.'[10]

Lay people would find it easier to sympathise if they knew more about the deep fear of everyday things which phobias cause. One woman dreaded wigs and false hair so much that she only visited her hairdresser after he had hidden all wigs away. She would not go near anyone wearing a wig in a store and would rush past false hair and avoid having a meal opposite anyone wearing one. She nearly rushed through a glass window when someone walked into a room wearing a wig. She felt ashamed and embarrassed by her fear.

Lay people may wonder how on earth such strange fears start. While we often do not know why such fears begin in the first place, we can understand how they spread thereafter. Each time we run away from a fear, it becomes more likely that we will want to escape next time as well. If we do nothing to deal with fear, but instead spend all our energy running away from it and rearrange life to avoid contact with any possible trigger for the fear, the chances are it will spread. This is all the more likely if we keep our worries secret so that we do not find out from friends how they deal with similar problems.

Shame and concealment of phobias

The lack of understanding by others makes many phobic people ashamed of their fears. They fear being ridiculed for having these anxieties and so suffer in silence and hide their panic as long as they can. Even when the fears can no longer be hidden, phobics may not outrightly confess what they are frightened of but complain instead of headaches, palpitations, diarrhoea, or tiredness. They may also have a secret fear that they are going insane. Their secrecy hides their phobias from the casual observer. Housewives who are agoraphobic (afraid of going out) can be housebound for years without acquaintances or relatives noticing that there is any problem. For example, many new cases of agoraphobia were discovered in the course of a rehousing scheme. Poor families who had been living in single rooms were rehoused and followed up by social workers. It soon became clear that many of the women had been agoraphobic and remained phobic in their new environment. Some would not sleep without close contact with their children or might invite a sister or friend to come and stay. Although the new flats had several rooms, only one room might be used. Many of these women turned out to be afraid of travelling or doing anything alone.

Phobias can be concealed for a while in times of extreme hardship. In a Nazi concentration camp in which 120,000 people died or were sent east to extermination camps, people hid their fears so they would be allowed to work rather than be killed. Several months after liberation and return home, some people who did not complain while in the camp again revealed their anxieties.[11]

Problems which can be confused with phobias

Certain phenomena resemble phobias yet differ from them. *Superstitious fears* and *taboos* are an example. These are beliefs about bad and good luck which are shared with other members of one's cultural group, for example, the idea that someone walking under a ladder will be harmed, or that good luck comes from crossing one's fingers.

Obsessions are insistently recurrent and unwanted thoughts which are hard to resist; for example, a mother may be plagued by urges to strangle her baby. 'Obsession' comes from the Latin *obsidere*, to besiege, and sufferers indeed feel besieged by their intrusive thoughts. Commonly they also feel compelled to carry out *compulsive rituals* repeatedly against their will, such as washing their hands 90 times a day because they feel dirty despite all evidence to the contrary.

Preoccupations are repetitive ruminative ideas without a sense of resistance against them, for example, the incessant worry of an adolescent that he is sexually inadequate. *Sensitive ideas of reference* are fears that actions and words of other people refer to us when in fact they don't, such as the idea that a roomful of people are talking about us as we enter. *Paranoid delusions* can include a fear that somebody is against one for no good reason.

Counterphobias

Counterphobic behaviour is the attraction people may have to their phobic situation or object so that they seek it out. This might happen when a phobia is mild or when the phobic is trying to master the problem. A woman who was originally so afraid of heights that she avoided lifts eventually mastered her fear by becoming an airline stewardess. Counterphobic behaviour can help us to overcome fear by spurring us to become gradually so familiar with the phobic situation that it loses its frightening aspects. Delight in mastery of the problem may lead someone who fears the sea to turn into an enthusiastic swimmer and sailor, or a stage-fright sufferer may seize every opportunity for public speaking.

Counterphobic behaviour resembles the way that children enjoy playing frightening games, or that some adults engage in risky pursuits such as high-speed racing or dangerous climbs. Not all such activities are counterphobic, however. Often people engage in these recreations without at any point experiencing fear, only excitement, challenge, or pleasure.

Aversions

Quite a few people strongly dislike rather than fear touching, tasting, or hearing things which most people are indifferent to or may even enjoy. The horrible feeling of such aversions differs a bit from that of fear. Aversions set our teeth on edge, send shivers down our spine, make us suck our teeth, go cold and pale, and take a deep breath. Our hair stands on end, and we feel unpleasant and sometimes nauseous, but not frightened. Sometimes there is a desire to wet or wash our fingers or cover them with cream. Some aversions are made worse when our skin is rough or the nails are unevenly clipped so that our fingertips catch as they pass over a surface.

A famous man intensely disliked fuzzy textures such as those of the skins of peaches, new tennis balls, or certain carpets and would not enter a room containing a new carpet with that particular texture. When playing tennis, he would wear a glove to handle the ball until the fuzz wore off. Other people find it hard to handle old pearly buttons, cotton wool, velvet, and similar articles. Some may like the *sight* of velvet in a shop even though they dislike its touch. Similar discomfort is produced by the squeak of chalk on a blackboard or the scrape of a knife on a plate.

These aversions may sound trivial but can be disabling. One woman disliked the sound of chalk scraping on a blackboard so much that she gave up a cherished ambition to be a teacher. Another found velvet so unbearable that she could not bring herself to go to children's parties. A third said 'All kinds of buttons make me squeamish. I've been like this since I was a young baby and my uncle had the same thing. I can only wear clothes with zip fasteners and hooks, not buttons.'[12]

There are endless kinds of aversions. In a UK radio broadcast Dr John Price invited listeners to write in about aversions they might have. The letters poured in. Most described more than one touch aversion, and several people were fascinated by the surface they could not touch, especially those who could not touch shiny buttons.

The commonest revulsion was of touching cotton wool, wire or steel wool, or velvet. Also frequent were taste or smell aversions causing avoidance of foods such as onions. Many of the letters expressed the agony of children who were made to wear velvet party clothes and whose mothers could not understand why their offspring did not appreciate them.

> Ever since I've been able to remember, I've been quite unable to touch velvet. My mother tells me it was all the rage to have a velvet party frock (age about 3 years) with a white lace collar and cuffs that she'd made for me in a very pretty blue. When the time for the party arrived I was duly dressed in this creation, and to her horror, I just stood with my arms six inches from my sides, with fists clenched, and would only say 'it's nasty' and my opinion has never altered (I am in my late forties now).
>
> Last summer, when shopping for some dress material, I made my way to the velvet display (I've always liked the look of it), telling myself 'this is ridiculous; you're a big girl now; be brave; handle it; it won't bite'; I think I stood there for quite two minutes, persuading myself that it really was lovely stuff. I stretched out my hands and grabbed a handful; but the effect was the same! Teeth all on edge! Sheer horror! Isn't it just ridiculous?
>
> I've now given up hope that I shall ever be able to sail into a party or theatre in a lovely jewel-coloured velvet dress! Of course, if I visit anyone with velvet scatter cushions, I make sure they come nowhere near my bare hand or arm![13]

A girl of 15 had a horror not only of velvet but also of suede, cotton wool and fluffy ties:

> Immediately I come in contact with any of these fibres my body tingles from top to bottom. When I was a young child my mother had no idea what I felt like when she put me in ghastly velvet dresses or gave me fluffy ties. A thing which stopped me smoking is the fact that the tip of a cigarette is velvety and I can't bear it.[14]

Some of the aversions ran in families:

> 66My father wouldn't allow my mother to wear velvet, plush or brushed nylon as he couldn't bear to touch it (when dancing). I've inherited this phobia now. Also my daughter (age 27) follows with this dislike, even as a baby, of plush toys with furry sides, so it's a case of three generations (I am 54) hating the same materials, for no reason.[15]99

What exactly feels aversive may differ a bit from one family member to another, and our teeth may feel set on edge even if we have no teeth.

> 66Most of my family 'suffered' from this kind of torture. My mother hated saucepans being scraped by a spoon and felt her 'teeth going on edge' when, in fact, she was *completely toothless and wore dentures top and bottom*. A brother hated blocks of cooking salt being cut up, also fingernails scraping down a wall. My dislike is children making balloons squeak with fingers, or squeaking and polished floors; the thought makes me feel horrible as I write. I can't bear to touch cotton wool, which makes a scroopy feeling in my fingers. Nor can I bear the feel of wire wool or pads. My eldest daughter can't stand me filing my fingernails, and the youngest daughter hates touching velvet.[16]99

Interestingly, as with fear, aversions subside when confronted repeatedly. A woman felt so shivery when touching cotton wool that she decided not to study nursing. Then, 'as modern methods use forceps for most dressings, I applied to do nursing. At first the irritation was quite severe but as the cotton wool was placed in a cold methylated spirits or cleaning solution this awkwardness of touching the wool disappeared. Today, although I don't like touching it, it doesn't send the shiver up me quite so much.[17] The same was noticed in another family. 'My husband can't stand cotton wool anywhere near him, our son is the same, our daughter likewise when small. For her I left pieces of it around the house and so cured her but her fear is returning at age 27.'[18]

Suede, wet wool, peach skin and rubber

A man wrote:

> 66I've had an aversion all my life to touching suede, or items of a similar texture. If I accidentally brush against a suede coat I instantly get covered in goose pimples, my hair tingles, cold shivers run up my spine and I recoil as if I've been burnt! Even the thought of it causes a skin prickling! I've never enjoyed tennis as much as I would've liked because of the ball's texture. Card tables mean brushing the tips

of my fingers over the nap of the cloth so I don't play cards. Having to clean a carpet with shampoo makes me grit my teeth and sweat, not from effort but physical abhorrence of the feel of the wet rug tufts. I can't wipe a wet wooden spoon.[19] "

Another explained 'I can't bear the feel of wet wool or synthetic woollens, and after handling them in the wash can't even stand the touch of my own fingers against each other until they're thoroughly dry. My teeth feel set "on edge" and I put my tongue between my teeth to cushion the feeling.'[20]

Aversions can stop people from peeling peaches. Those who love the fruit may get others to do the job. The aversion can become extreme. 'I have a very acute aversion to the skin of peaches, and to a lesser degree apricots. To see anyone bite the skin of a peach produces immediate revulsion and even after several hours the recollection of such an act can make me shudder violently.'[21]

On the effect of rubber: 'As a child I used to dread having to play games with balloons at birthday parties, and often I tearfully tried to convince my mother not to make me put on Wellington boots. I didn't mind wearing them as long as somebody else put them on for me. . . . At the touch of these two objects I get goose pimples and shivers down my back, my teeth begin to chatter and I get short of breath . . . as if I'd been plummeted into cold water. I *can* bear to touch these things when it is necessary for my own children, and my reaction is not quite so violent as when I was a child, but I still have to take a deep breath in order to overcome the shivery feeling.'[22]

As Dr Price pointed out, these aversions are more the pinpricks than the burdens of life but may in a few cases affect choice of career, for example, nursing or teaching, and chores in the home. People who say they cannot wash dishes, pots and pans because of their touch may not be malingering. Only rarely, however, do aversions reach the extreme described in this final letter.

" Our son of 8 has a vast and ever-increasing list of tactile and oral aversions. . . . this only started at about age six. It would be almost easier to list the things that don't give him 'the shivers' . . . all synthetic materials, many kinds of wool, brushes, paper tissues, the sound of skipping, floor scrubbing, sand, the beach! He goes pale, sucks in his lips, shivers and in extreme cases his hair stands up. [His sister shows no such aversions]. My husband and I have one or two minor aversions. He is still very attached to a soft toy, a smelly, tattered dog, who gives him enormous pleasure both to touch and smell.[23] "

Linus's blanket: soterias

The tattered toy dog brings us to Linus, that adorable child in the *Peanuts* cartoon strip. He often carried round with him the great solace of an old blanket. Linus's blanket is a soteria, an object to which one gets attached. Soterias are the opposite of aversions and phobias. They are things that comfort some of us. Examples are toys and stuffed animals which young children carry around and talismans (charms) worn by adults. Many children take everywhere their beloved blanket or stuffed toy animal until it gets so worn that it is no more than a dirty old rag trailing behind them. Mum tries to remove it at her peril. Its loss may provoke a spasm of grief. Phobic people get comfort from carrying around sedative tablets even though they never take them.

Historical aspects of fear

Fears have not changed much over the ages. Two millennia ago Hippocrates described a man who was terrified at the first note of a flute played at night though by day he did not mind hearing it, and a height-phobic man who would not go near a precipice or bridge or even stand beside a shallow ditch. In 1621 Robert Burton described a phobic reaction: 'Many lamentable effects this causeth in men, as to be red, pale, tremble, sweat . . . They that live in fear are never free, resolute, secure . . . no greater misery, no rack, no torture, like unto it.'[24] Burton distinguished fear from depression and mentioned famous phobic figures such as Tully and Demosthenes who had stage fright and Augustus Caesar who would not sit in the dark. Burton wrote of a man who would

> ❝not walk alone from home, for fear he should swoon, or die. A second fears every man he meets will rob him, quarrel with him, or kill him. A third dare not venture to walk alone, for fear he should meet the devil, a thief, be sick . . . another dares not go over a bridge, come near a pool, brook, steep hill, lye in a chamber where cross-beams are, for fear he be tempted to hang, drown or precipitate himself. . . . At a sermon, he is afraid he shall speak aloud, at unawares, something indecent, unfit to be said. . . . In a close room, he is afraid of being stifled for want of air, and still carried bisket, aquavitae, or some strong waters about him, for fear of deliquiums [fainting], or being sick; or if he be in a throng . . . where he may not well get out . . . he is so misaffected.[25]❞

When syphilis struck Europe syphilophobia came with it just like AIDS phobia today. 'If but a pimple appears or any slight ache is felt, they distract themselves with terrible apprehensions . . . and run for help . . . an honest practitioner generally finds it more difficult to cure the imaginary evil than the real one.'[26]

Fame does not fend off fear. King James I of England was terrified at the sight of an unsheathed sword.[27] King Germanicus could not stand the sight or sound of cocks. Cats frightened Henry III of France and the Duke of Schonberg. A famous Russian general was so upset by mirrors that the Empress Catherine always gave him audience in a room without any. The Italian writer Manzoni feared fainting on leaving home alone and so carried everywhere a small bottle of concentrated vinegar. Feydeau, the French playwright, only went out at night to avoid the daylight. Sigmund Freud feared travelling when in his thirties.

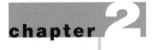

normal anxieties and fears

Like other species, human beings are predisposed to fear certain situations. This inbuilt tendency has survival value. Completely fearless people are much more likely to enter dangerous situations. Survival requires a judicious blend of courage and caution. We have to steer a path between cowardice and foolhardiness.

Fear and anxiety develop through the interaction of three influences – genetic, maturation of the nervous system, and learning from one's own and others' experience. The human infant's limited range of innate fears alters as he matures and learns by experience.

An enduring tendency to react in a frightened way is called *timidity*. Genes determine this in part in all species. Experience, too, influences timidity in species with more complex brains, especially humans. Some animal species are very timid, which increases their chances of survival. Rabbits are more timid than tigers. In addition, however, some rabbits are more timid than other rabbits. The same applies across humans. Identical-twin infants tend to resemble each other in the amount of fear they show towards strangers over the first year of life. Adult twins are also like one another in the number of neurotic symptoms which they show.

Fears that we are naturally prepared to develop

Anyone may fear anything at one time or another. In general, however, certain things are feared much more than others. Furthermore, fears may appear with little or no experience of certain situations which have special evolutionary significance for us as a species. Some things seem to trigger phobias much more readily than others. For example, seven-year-old Pam heard a rustling of grass in a park, thought it was a snake, and ran away down the hill, not telling anyone what she had seen. An hour later she caught her hand in the door of her parents' car and it had to be bandaged. Later Pam told her parents of the rustling grass, and she became steadily more frightened of snakes. To protect her, Pam's parents then mistakenly avoided mentioning snakes and would switch off television programmes and remove newspaper articles concerning snakes. Her phobia of snakes increased and continued until she was 20 years old.

Pam had in fact suffered far more pain from the car door on her hand than from any snake, yet she became phobic not of car doors but of snakes. This may be because as a species human brains are programmed to show fear easily towards snake-like things but not artificial objects like car doors. If we have a frightening experience with cars, bricks, grass, bicycles and animals, our fear is more likely to associate to the animals than to the other items. Certain things seem to be lightning conductors toward which our fears are directed.

Another example of how an aversion is attached more easily on to some stimuli than others comes from an adult's experience. An Israeli Arab mistakenly drove his truck into Lebanon and was immediately seized by Lebanese border guards, interrogated, tied to a chair, beaten about the head, and had his teeth knocked out. Torture continued for three days, during which time he refused food for fear of being poisoned and accepted only water to drink. After three days he was allowed to return to his family in Israel. He now couldn't eat solid food without gagging and retching, and so confined himself to a liquid diet. When false teeth were fitted, these too provoked vomiting and had to be discarded even after they had been fitted under anaesthesia. Inability to eat solids continued for a year, and he lost much weight. As with Pam, this man did not become frightened of unnatural things connected to his torture such as trucks or sitting in chairs. Rather, his painful gums and not eating for three days led to a gross exaggeration of the natural gag reflex, which we all have if we touch the back of our throats, into an intense aversion to swallowing solid food.

Ingenious experiments have shown that rhesus monkey infants are prepared to develop fear more easily of predator-like stimuli such as snakes and crocodiles than of flowers.[1] Laboratory-reared infants with no prior experience of snakes were taught to reach rapidly for food placed near objects such as wood blocks, and continued to reach for that food without fear when it was placed next to a live boa constrictor or toy snake. Those lab-reared infants, however, developed persistent fears of such snakes after watching wild-reared monkeys showing fear of the snakes and failing to reach for the food near those snakes. Lab-reared rhesus infants, however, did not develop snake fear if they saw videotapes spliced to depict artificially the wild-reared monkeys being terrified of flowers rather than of snakes. Similarly, the infants associated fear more easily towards a toy crocodile than towards a toy rabbit despite having no prior experience of either animal. In the same vein, European blackbirds showed more mobbing (aggressive fear) on hearing the alarm cries of a fellow blackbird when they saw a predator-like stuffed, noisy friarbird as opposed to a plastic bottle.

If the infant monkeys had an initially neutral experience with snakes this 'immunised' them against developing subsequent fear towards even naturally prepared stimuli like snakes. First seeing non-fearful monkeys behaving non-fearfully with snakes protected those youngsters from becoming frightened on subsequently seeing fearful monkeys showing fear of snakes.

Humans may be prepared to develop other fears that fly in the face of logic, e.g. an aversion to touching AIDS sufferers. I myself experienced something similar. In a leper colony in Brazil I was briefly introduced to and shook hands with a man whose leprosy had caused minor facial disfigurement and loss of a few fingers. Moments after exchanging a few words and walking away, I had a strong irrational sense of contamination and urge to wash my hand. This continued for hours despite my knowing there was practically no danger of infection, and it took a powerful and prolonged effort of will to stop myself from washing in the hours needed before the intense feeling of being contaminated receded.

Our readiness to fear certain things despite knowing they are not dangerous contrasts starkly with our slowness to develop fear of other clearly risky behaviour such as smoking, eating saturated fats and lots of salt, guns, driving very fast, and sexual promiscuity without using a condom. Such practices kill vastly more people than do sharks, snakes and spiders, yet the beasts give us the shivers far more than do the risky behaviours. We have been selected to have nervous systems responding to dangers that were common in the past, not to evolutionarily new threats.

Common fears in children: novelty, strangers, and movements

At birth human infants startle readily to *noise* or any other *intense, sudden,* or *novel* stimulus which is *unexpected*. At six to twelve months most infants start to fear or be wary of strangers. This appears once the child can tell the difference between strangers and familiars like its family. Being a bit wary of strangers is protective not only in chimps, gorillas, monkeys, lions and squirrels, among which infanticide by strangers is not uncommon,[2] but also in humans. Child abuse is 100 times more common with an unrelated than a related parent.[3]

Fear of strangers is an example of the fact that novel situations are apt to frighten many species. Chimpanzees were terrified of coming near a plaster death mask of one of their number who had died. Young children often fear strange masks or other unfamiliar objects slightly different from what they are already used to. The elder sister of a three-year-old girl stored a wig from her school play in the toy cupboard. When getting some toys out of the cupboard the little girl accidentally touched the wig. Frightened that it might be an animal, she screamed endlessly. A fear of wigs started which lasted for many years, although children's fears of this sort are usually short lived.

Although novelty may provoke fear, it can at other times cause pleasure and be eagerly sought out. New things can attract and repel in turn, as Konard Lorenz described well in the raven:

> A young raven, confronted with a new object, which may be a camera, an old bottle, a stuffed polecat, . . . first reacts with escape responses. He will fly up to an elevated perch and from this point of vantage stare at the object . . . maintaining all the while a maximum of caution and the expressive attitude of intense fear. He will cover the last distance from the object hopping sideways with half-raised wings, in the utmost readiness to flee. At last, he will deliver a single blow with his powerful beak at the object and forthwith fly back to his safe perch. If nothing happens he will repeat the same procedure in much quicker sequence and with more confidence. If the object is an animal that flees, the raven loses all fear in the fraction of a second and will start in pursuit instantly. If it is an animal that charges, he will either try to get behind it or, if the charge is sufficiently unimpressive, lose interest in a very short time. With an inanimate object, the raven will proceed to apply a number of further instinctive movements. He will grab it with one foot, peck at it, try to tear off pieces, insert his bill into any existing cleft and then pry apart his mandibles with considerable force. Finally, if the object is not too big the raven will carry it away, push it into a convenient hole and cover it with some inconspicuous material.[4]

The terror that unfamiliar things inspire in youngsters, especially if they writhe, appeared dramatically in my son as a toddler of two and a half. At that time he had never seen snakes nor knew the word for them. I had carried him over rocks from a car to a beach at low tide. The sand had dried, leaving thousands of skeins of seaweed up to a foot long. They looked like myriads of eels or tiny snakes lying dead still. Similar fronds of seaweed moved in shallow sea water nearby. As soon as the toddler saw the dried seaweed on the sand, he screamed in terror and clutched me tightly, trying to stop me sitting in the sand. When I touched the seaweed he shrieked and refused to do the same. His panic increased when gentle waves rolled the seaweed nearby or I held him over the water to see the moving fronds. Slowly I tried to get him used to the dried seaweed on the sand by playing with it myself and encouraging him to do the same. Only after half an hour of this would he sit on sand without seaweed. Then he started to grab the seaweed gingerly and quickly fling it away, but shunned the water. The next day he touched the seaweed a bit more readily, but still with fear. A week later he was throwing the fronds away but still unhappy about leaving them in his hand. With continued exposure to his feared situation his terror gradually subsided. This exposure principle is central to the treatment of fear (p. 138–149).

That writhing or jerky movements frighten monkeys and men is well known. This might underlie their fear of snakes which is particularly pronounced in humans from the age of two to four. The same is true of spider fears. Fears of animals tend to appear at about the same age; animals, too, frighten the child more if they move rapidly and jerkily toward or loom above it.

Toddlers may handle a live animal fearlessly until they see the creature stalking or rushing toward them, after which it is likely to frighten them immediately. Their fear disappears when the same animal adopts another position. The fear trigger thus seems to involve certain movements and postures as well as the animal itself.

Modelling of fear

The child of a parent with a phobia is more likely to develop the same phobia. In a frightening situation children tend to look at any adult who may be accompanying them. If the adult shows fear then the child may take fright easily. To illustrate, a mother was spooning supper to her 18-month-old girl sitting in her high chair when a bat flew in. Mum panicked, pulled her daughter by her ankles from the high chair and ran screaming from the room clutching her daughter upside down, leaving the chair upset and the dishes broken. After this, the little girl developed a fear of flying things that persisted into adult life as a fear of moths and butterflies. Such modelling of fear starting a phobia is not very common. Only one in six phobic adults have close relatives with a similar phobia.

The effect of observing fear in others depends on what seems to be frightening. Snakes frighten wild-reared rhesus monkeys now living in the laboratory, but do not terrify lab-reared rhesus infants until those briefly see another monkey show fear to snakes. Minimal observation starts a lasting fear of snakes. However, rhesus infants do not develop a fear of flowers after seeing another rhesus show fear of a flower.[5] Snakes have more fear-evoking potential than do flowers. This makes excellent evolutionary sense. In past generations, individuals who avoided snakes survived to have offspring more often than did those without fear of snakes, but the same was not true of individuals who shunned flowers. Selection was more in favour of individuals who feared snakes rather than flowers.

Children's fears are volatile and change as they grow

Fears arise in children for little or no obvious reason and die down as mysteriously without further contact with whatever has been frightening them. Forgotten fears may reappear when children become more babyish during illness and disappear once more when the child is well again. Common fears change as the youngster grows. Fears of animals are more common from age two to four years, but by four to six years anxieties about the dark and imaginary creatures like ghosts are more frequent. After age six, few develop new fears of animals unless, say, being bitten by a dog starts a dog phobia. Fears of animals diminish rapidly in 9 to 11-year-old children. Other widespread childhood fears are of winds, storms, thunder and lightning, cars and trains.

The constant ages at which certain fears come and go have varying explanations. Where the objects are encountered frequently by most children of any age, as with animals and birds, the waxing and waning of fear may partly reflect developing maturity in the child. Rhesus monkey infants showed most fear of another monkey's threat display from the age of two to four months.

Some fears start at a given age simply because that is when the child first experiences a particular situation. School phobias are a case in point. When children encounter a totally new situation, they generally show anxiety but adapt rapidly. Some fear of school is usual during the first term at a new school, but complete refusal to go to school because of fear is uncommon.

Most children show fears at some time or another, but really disabling phobias are uncommon. In general girls tend to have more fears than boys. Fears tend to become less common after puberty.

The fears of five children in one family

A psychologist, C. W. Valentine, carefully observed the fears of his own five young children for over 10 years. Loud sounds startled his infants from the age of two weeks to a few months, especially if the sounds were new. Fear of strange objects began after the age of one year, and between age one and three several of the children feared the sea. These fears had not been learned or suggested as he was with four of his five children the first time they saw the ocean. They were encouraged to go into the sea and their only previous experience of water had been in their baths, which had always delighted them. Similarly, after the age of one year several of the children feared animals despite previous familiarity and ease with animals, and the absence of any unpleasant experiences to account for the fear. Fear of the dark appeared in only two of the children when five years old.

The five children differed greatly in their tendencies to show fear. One was almost fearless from birth onward, whereas the others showed fear frequently. Their fear diminished greatly when with a trusted companion. None of the fears occurred every time a particular stimulus was presented. The degree of fear varied with the overall timidity of the child, the presence of a companion, the details of the stimulus, and the condition of the child at the time.[6]

Fears which are common in both children and adults

Staring and stage fright

Humans are sensitive to the gaze of others and staring frightens us easily from childhood onwards. From early infancy we attend closely to two eyes moving together. The suckling infant fixes his gaze on Mum's eyes. By the age of two months he will smile readily at a mask waved in front of him with two eyes painted on it. Children's drawings emphasise eyes from early on. Being looked at is an important trigger of social phobias and of stage fright. Stage fright is frequent in actors, public speakers, and sometimes even in experienced politicians.

Heights

Adults continue to have the same dislike of heights which appears in infants as soon as they can crawl. Most of us have felt an urge to throw ourselves off a cliff and drawn back in a protective reflex. Fears of heights commonly trouble people in high-rise buildings. Many feel uncomfortable in them, particularly if the exterior glass walls run from floor to ceiling. This is because they lack privacy, get dizzy looking down outside through windows which extend from floor to ceiling, and feel their flats are too brightly lit. These discomforts are eased a bit by curtains to darken the room and make it feel smaller. At daytime parties in flats like this, many guests retreat from the well-lit side of the room to throng the darker interior instead. A woman living in a flat 22 floors above London described the problem:

> ❝When my husband first saw the view, he was lyrical. He said at night it was like fairyland. [Guests] often spend the first half-hour looking out of the window. Some get dizzy though. We'd a fellow here, like a wrestler he is, short but muscular, and he wouldn't go near the windows at all. . . . I felt like that at first. Now I only notice it when I'm cleaning the windows. The windows run right over for cleaning, but I have to get my husband to do it. My stomach just leaves me.
>
> To begin with, we put the children's bunks in the little bedroom. It's so tiny we had to put them up against the window. My eldest daughter just refused to go to bed in the top bunk; she got in with the little one down below . . . I got up myself to see what put her off. It was terrifying! Like lying on the edge of a cliff, just the glass between you and all that space.[7]❞

Another tenant of a high flat commented: 'Something about it makes it feel unlike home. If you draw the curtains, you're cosy, but you're cut off from the world till next morning.'[8]

The view from a great height can, of course, not only frighten but also appeal to people. Think of the queues to go high up in London's Millennium Ferris wheel. If we are safely enclosed our enjoyment of the view tends to exceed our fear of the height.

Fears which are common in adults

Many situations frighten adults. *Examinations* unhinge lots of people; their tension may become so severe that they do badly and fail their test despite high ability. Fear is usual with *combat* or *parachuting*. Before *dentistry* or *surgical* procedures it is perfectly normal to feel anxious as the moment approaches. Fear tends to fall rapidly shortly after dental treatment and less quickly after surgery. Many people are so anxious about visiting the dentist that they skip appointments. They may worry so much that they fear even seeing ambulances or hospitals, avoid the sight of these like the plague, and switch off TV programmes on the subject.

Anxiety and motor vehicles

Driving motor vehicles is a common source of stress. Our heart rate can rise from 80 beats per minute at rest to 150 when overtaking another car. London bus drivers had higher blood pressure and cholesterol, and nearly twice as many heart attacks as bus conductors. Accidents increase when drivers are experiencing problems such as marital or work conflicts or worries about money. They are then also more likely to take alcohol and so become even more prone to error.

Women and elderly drivers are actually *less* often involved in serious traffic accidents than are young men. Excessive risks by daring young men are not reduced enough by fast reaction times. Stress during driving rises at night and in the early hours of the morning. Especially stressful are prolonged periods of driving, particularly for older people. Because of this, driving spells of over nine hours including rest breaks should be discouraged, particularly after the age of 45, and driving more than three hours without a reasonable break is risky.

Although traffic accidents kill hundreds and injure thousands of people year in and year out and kill more young people than any other cause, we fear cars and lorries less than is good for us. Compare such lack of fear with our frequent fears of spiders and snakes that kill hardly a handful of people in Britain. Our evolutionary heritage shows. We have been selected over thousands of generations to fear spiders and snakes compared with only four generations to respect motor vehicles.

Separation anxiety

Separation anxiety is another normal response to threat – that of loss of someone or something we love. *Grief* is a separation reaction to the actual loss (Chapter 3, p. 29). Most young mammals show separation anxiety when removed from a familiar figure. The first bond in mammals is usually between mother and young. They remain near each other, resist separation, and if parted try to get together again. A bonded pair resists separation by an intruder; the stronger partner attacks the intruder while the weaker flees or clings to the stronger one. If bonded partners are separated and cannot find one another, they show the distress of separation anxiety. Once a young creature is attached to a mother figure it is relaxed and adventurous in her presence but tense and inert in her absence. Human bonding is often accompanied by a feeling of love.

A primate toddler separated from its mother is likely to curl up on the floor and cry. The stranger the surroundings in which a separated child finds himself, the more anxious he becomes. Children admitted to hospital are comforted by having familiar toys within their strange surroundings. After returning home the child may show fear again when with people and events recalling the hospital.

As children grow older, they gradually learn to separate from their parents without much trouble. The first few times they go away with friends on holiday they might feel a bit homesick and shed a few tears, but the distress soon clears and they steadily become more independent. Leaving home for periods seems to be a necessary part of growing up, a preparation for living away from home. Absence of trial periods like this can lead to separation anxiety in adult life. An extreme form of such anxiety was shown by a married woman of twenty who had been separated from her mother for more than a day at a time only once, when the mother went abroad for two weeks, and then tried to phone her several times. She had had severe fear of separation from her mother since childhood, always insisted on remaining near mother whenever possible, and on being phoned frequently when separation was unavoidable. Even when seen in a hospital outpatient department, she wanted to know where her mother would be at the end of the hour's appointment. At age 12 she had gone on holiday with a friend a hundred miles away from home, but phoned home in distress several times daily; after a few days she could stand it no longer and returned home. She disliked being left completely alone at home and even avoided lifts. After marrying, she, her husband, and their two children lived with her mother. Fortunately, such an extreme degree of separation anxiety is rare.

normal reactions to death and disaster

Death and dying

A horror of death is present in most cultures. Our dread concerns the process of dying itself and the end of opportunities for us to achieve our goals and pursue our pleasures.

Children on the whole speak freely of death. Adolescents tend to be more circumspect, and for Western adults death is often a taboo topic. We do not speak about someone's death in his presence. Our talk about dying uses euphemisms like 'passing on', 'departing this life', 'going to heaven', or 'kicking the bucket'. Many mourning ceremonies soften the loss by emphasising continuing contact with the deceased in heaven or the spirit world, or by prayer about the greatness of God and irrelevance of life on earth. People who meditate try to transcend the pain of the 'I'.

As we age more of us become resigned to the inevitable, and fear of death is less common over age 60 than might be supposed. Among dying patients, less than a third of those over 60 were very anxious compared with two-thirds of those under 50. This is understandable, as dying in early life disrupts more hopes and expectations and is associated with more distressing symptoms such as pain, nausea, vomiting, and breathlessness than is the case with younger adults. Young parents with dependent children are more uneasy about their impending deaths.[1]

Dying can in fact feel perfectly comfortable. One renowned doctor, William Hunter, said as he lay dying, 'If I had strength enough to hold a pen, I would write how easy and pleasant a thing it is to die.'[2] Another, William Osler, commented that 'most people go out of life as they came into it, oblivious'.[3] Many are unaware of what is happening as life ebbs away. Dying often distresses the departing one less than the onlookers who are becoming bereaved.

After death, the body may trigger a new fear. Lots of cultures have strong taboos against touching a corpse. Ghosts and evil spirits are believed to hover around the corpse and later the grave. Banquo's ghost haunts his murderer Macbeth. The ghost of Hamlet's father is crucial to the start of *Hamlet*.

Some anxiety about corpses centres over their alteration at death and during decomposition. This threatens comforting beliefs in an afterlife. Since the start of civilisation elaborate steps have been, and continue to be, taken to prevent obstacles to resurrection: embalment of the body to preserve its shape; burying of food, valuables, and retainers in the Egyptian Pharaohs' pyramids and Chinese emperors' graves; provision of an easy exit; in the twenty-first century, payment for freezing preservation of one's body or DNA. All these practices try to fend off the finality of death.

Uncertainty about what is going to happen increases anxiety about death. Although religious belief can lessen our fear of dying, confidence in our creed is more important than our actual belief, whatever that is. Firm agnostics are less anxious than lukewarm churchgoers. Dying patients may fear their suspected fate until they are told the truth. Anxiety might then abate and be replaced for a while by depression that gradually passes off. This is a grief reaction in which people come to terms with the loss of their own future. Some fear dying so much, however, that they avoid learning their fate at all costs. Even when told the truth they forget it immediately, or deny it. Denial may not work for long, and they may then break down in acute distress. There can be no golden rule about concealing or telling the truth about dying. One has to decide in the light of the dying person's past reactions to other stress, stability of his personality, and whether he really wants to know or instead strives to avoid learning about his true position.

Grief

Grief is a special kind of separation anxiety. Generally it takes time to accept the death of a loved one. We yearn for the deceased, feel pangs of grief. Pining is accompanied by crying and searching for the lost one. The bereaved move restlessly about, think a lot about the departed, attend to stimuli that remind them of that person, and ignore other things. They may call for their lost beloved. After repeated failure to find the deceased, the intensity of searching slowly dies down until attachment to the lost person is finally broken.

The pain of grief partly reflects disrupted role functions between the bereaved and the deceased. A dead spouse may be particularly mourned in the evening at the time he or she used to return home from work. During early mourning the bereaved rehearse over and over in their minds what they used to do with the dead person. After a while the bereaved cease abortive attempts to interact with the deceased and develop new ties with other people instead.

A fine study of grief reactions was made by Dr Colin Parkes.[4] He interviewed 22 widows in London, all under age 65, at least five times in the 13 months after their husband died.

Numbness and disbelief

Most of the women had been unable to accept warnings of the impending demise of their husbands. When they actually died, the most frequent reaction was numbness. This might be preceded by great distress. 'I suddenly burst. I was aware of a horrible wailing and knew it was me. I was saying I loved him and all that. I knew he'd gone but I kept on talking to him.'[5] She went to the bathroom and vomited, and then 'I felt numb and solid for a week. It's a blessing . . . everything goes hard inside you like a heavy weight.'[6]

At first, 16 of the women had trouble accepting that their husband was really dead. 'I was in a dream . . . just couldn't take it all in . . . couldn't believe it.'[7] 'There must be a mistake. I wouldn't believe it until I see him [dead four days later]. I didn't register at all . . . it didn't seem real.'[8] The sense of being stunned was usually short-lived, but even a year later 13 widows occasionally still could not believe that their husband was really dead.

Early in their grief the widows often cried. Some became angry or even elated. One was calm at first. 'I looked into his eyes, and as he stared at me, something happened to us. As if something had gone into me. I felt all warm inside, I'm not interested in this world any longer. It's a sort of religious feeling. . . . I feel as big as a house. I fill the room.'[9] Later she cried several times and once tried to kill herself half-heartedly. Another widow got angry: 'Why did he do this to me?' She kept very busy for four days, then at dawn 'Something suddenly moved in on me, invaded me, a presence almost pushed me out of bed. It was my husband – terribly overwhelming. . . . [I saw] pictures like photographic plates, of faces.'[10] She was uncertain if she'd been dreaming, and felt numb for two weeks.

Panic and distress

Panic attacks were common in early bereavement and later too. Several times in the first month a widow ran out of her flat and took refuge with friends next door. She felt so fragile that 'if somebody gave me a good tap I'd shatter into a thousand pieces . . . If I let myself think Bob's dead I'll be overcome. I couldn't look at it and stay sane.' She felt desperate when events made it impossible to forget. Her panics slowly subsided as the year passed.[11] Individuals varied widely in their reactions to bereavement. Distress alternated with periods of numbness or restless 'busyness'. They tried to thrust aside the pain or sense of loss, and felt overwhelmed when it broke through. Numbness usually ended after about a week, after which distress rose.[12]

Many believe that grief cannot be postponed permanently and that keeping it in increases the distress that will eventually break through. 'Give sorrow words: the grief that does not speak whispers the o'erfraught heart, and bids it break', (Macbeth, act iv, scene 3, line 208). This tended to be true among the London widows in Parkes' study.

Pining and preoccupation

When the numbness ceased, pangs of intense pining for the dead person began. The widows became preoccupied with thoughts of their dead husband, kept on looking toward places and things around them associated with him, and attended to sights and sounds suggesting his presence. They also cried out for him and were restless. During this phase of grief 'There is a rush of speech, especially when talking about the deceased. There is restlessness, inability to sit still, moving about in aimless fashion, continually searching for something to do. There is, however, at the same time, a painful lack of capacity to initiate and maintain normal patterns of activity.'[13]

The typical widow in London constantly thought of her husband in his accustomed place at home. 'I can almost feel his skin or touch his hands.' She would go over and over in her mind past events in which he had taken part including his final illness.[14] This happened especially during the early months and again as the anniversary of the death approached. Sometimes happy memories of the past would be recalled.[15]

Nearly half the widows felt drawn toward places reminding them of their husband. They visited old haunts or the cemetery or hospital to feel near him. Most treasured their husband's possessions. Often, however, they also avoided clothes or photographs that evoked too intense a pining. As the year passed they began to avoid reminders less. Familiar things and places which had felt comforting during early mourning gradually lost their hold. A room strongly charged with memories of the husband could be redecorated and the furniture changed. Things that had been put away shortly after bereavement because they evoked such painful pangs were gradually brought out again. Photographs were hung back on the wall.

Frequently the widows 'saw', 'heard' or 'felt' their husband nearby, especially during the first month after death. They would interpret small sounds about the house as indicating his presence or momentarily misidentify people in the street and then realise their mistake. One woman 'saw' her husband coming home through the door in the fence; another 'saw' him sitting in a chair on Christmas Day. Belief in ghosts can arise easily out of such experiences.

Crying, irritability, and anger

Crying is so expected during grief that it may be taken for granted. Among the London widows, 16 cried during the first interview a month after bereavement. In later interviews they cried much less. They could find it hard to say why they were crying.

Irritability and anger are less well known features of grief. Among the widows 13 showed anger and felt that the world had become more dangerous. Anger might be directed at the dead husband ('Why did he do this to me?') or his doctor ('I still go over in my mind the way those doctors behaved.') or nurse like the one who had hurt the husband by ripping off an adhesive dressing.[16] Irrational anger subsided with time. A widow who'd been furious with hospital staff at the time of her bereavement denied this a year later, but admitted 'I wish there was something I could blame.' A few irritable women blamed themselves for how they'd behaved after their husband died.[17]

Guilt and self-reproach

Guilt and self-reproach are common during mourning. The widows typically said, 'I think, what could I have done?', 'Did I do right?'[18] Self-reproach might be about minor matters. A year after bereavement one widow felt guilty because she had never made her husband a bread pudding. More often the matter was more serious, but it was unlikely that the widow had been to blame, as with one who had supported her husband in his refusal to have palliative surgery, and another who blamed herself for not having encouraged his literary talents during his lifetime and tried to make amends by publishing his poems after his death.

Several women felt that they had failed their husbands during his final illness. 'I seemed to go away from him. He wasn't the person I'd been married to. When I tried to share his pain, it was so terrible I couldn't stop. I wish I could have done more . . . he was so helpless.'

Restlessness and overactivity

The widows felt 'strung up', 'jumpy', 'all in a turmoil inside', 'always on the go', 'at the end of my tether', 'can't pin myself down to anything', 'stupid little things upset me'. When very tense they might tremble or stammer. When restless the women might flare up or fill their lives with activities. Interviews with one irritable widow were carried out on the trot as she passed from one household chore to another: 'If I didn't work all the time I'd have a nervous breakdown.' At the end of the year she could see 'nothing to live for, it all seems so pointless'.[19]

Fluctuation of grief

Distress from grief lets up occasionally, at which times the bereaved might feel calm even after intense pangs. The pain might be lessened a bit by avoiding people and places associated with the deceased, disbelieving what has happened, and trying to distract oneself. In the first week after her husband's sudden death, Joan could hardly believe it and cried a lot. She stopped sobbing by keeping herself occupied with other things, avoiding going into his room and persuading her son to get rid of most of her husband's possessions. When interviewed a month later, she broke off several times for fear she would cry. A year later she was much calmer but still avoided reminders of her husband and disliked visiting his grave.[20]

The dead are often idealised. Jane, aged 59, had frequently quarrelled with her alcoholic husband and left him several times. In her first interview she remarked 'I shouldn't really say so but it's more peaceful now he's gone.'[21] During her first year of widowhood her two children left home, leaving her alone in her apartment. She became lonely and depressed and spoke nostalgically of the old days. By her final interview she had forgotten her marital problems and said she wished to marry again 'someone kind, like my husband'.[22]

Identification with the deceased

Quite a few bereaved people identify with the deceased more than when he was alive. A widow's watching of the soccer Cup Final and racing on television derived from her husband: 'I quite enjoy it because he liked it. It's a most queer feeling. . . . My sister said, "You're getting like Fred in all your ways." . . . I said I couldn't touch that [food], and she said, "Don't be stupid, you're getting just like Fred" . . . he's guiding me the whole time.'[23]

Bereaved people less often get symptoms like those of the deceased's last illness. Gill's husband had died after a week of chest pain and breathlessness. Afterwards she had fainting spells, palpitations, and panic attacks, gasping for breath and feeling that her heart was bursting 'just like my husband's'. Later in the year Gill got spasms and pain in her left face and leg which mimicked the stroke her husband had suffered five years earlier.

Uncommonly, widows felt that their dead husbands were inside them.

❝My husband's in me, right through and through. I've got like him. . . . I can feel him in me doing everything. He used to say, 'You'll do this when I'm gone, won't you?' He's just guiding my life. I can feel his presence within me because of his talking and doing things. It's not a sense of his presence, he's *here* inside me. That's why I'm happy all the time. As if two people were one . . . although I'm alone we're, sort of, together . . . I don't think I have the will-power to carry on on my own, so he must be.[24] 〞

The dead husband might be located within the children. 'Sometimes I feel as if [my daughter] is my husband . . . she has his hands; it used to give me the creeps.'[25]

Half the widows had vivid and realistic dreams of their dead husband. The dreamer often awoke with surprise and disappointment that her husband was not present after all. 'He was trying to comfort me and put his arms around me. I kept turning away and crying. Even in the dream I knew he was dead. . . . but I felt so happy and I cried and he couldn't do anything about it. . . . When I touched his face it was as if he was really there; quite real and vivid.'[26] Another typical dream: 'He was in the coffin with the lid off and all of a sudden he came to life and got out. . . . I looked at him and he opened his mouth. I said, "So he's alive, he's alive". I thought "Thank God, I'll have him to talk to." '[27]

Physical and other problems

Insomnia is usual during the painful period of grieving and half the widows took a sedative drug in the first month. Many couldn't get to sleep, or woke during the night, or woke early. At night they were at their most lonely. Several could not fall asleep in the marital bed and lay awake thinking of him much of the night. Often they ate poorly and lost weight in the first couple of months. Some even lost their love of their children, cut themselves off from friends, and shut themselves up at home. The widows with jobs stayed away from work for about two weeks but eventually found fresh interests and friends, sooner than the widows who had no jobs to take them out of their homes.

Recovery from grief

Most people get over their bereavement in time. Jo had been close to her husband. After his death she felt numb for several days, became anxious and depressed, was preoccupied with his memory, and felt his presence strongly. Her family supported her, and her grief began to diminish in the third and fourth months after bereavement. In the seventh month she visited her sister in America and felt wanted. She returned confident and refreshed, prepared to care for an ailing relative and to be the centre of a united family.

Grief takes a variable time to subside. It's not always gone even after a year. In some sense grief never ends. Widows of long standing may say 'you never get over it'. During anniversaries or when an old friend comes to call unexpectedly or a forgotten photograph is discovered in a drawer, the acute pining and sadness return in a mini-bereavement. As time goes on grief is aroused less often and less intensely than before, and the interests and appetite which were lost after the death gradually return.

When we mourn the loss of a loved person or a missed opportunity, we need to 'work through' feelings triggered by the loss. We should be able to talk about the meaning to us of the person we have lost and the things we used to do together, and be able to cry openly. Many cultures recognise the need to mourn departed relatives, and prescribe a ritual period of grieving which helps the bereaved to get over their loss. In some cultures the bereaved are expected to wail and express their grief unashamedly. In working through grief, however, as well as mourn the past we have to explore new ways to live in the future and how to replace the loss by new relationships and activities.

Perhaps the most anxiety-evoking event most of us have to come to terms with one day is that of our own dying. We tend to associate successful treatment with getting well, but care for the dying assumes the inevitable will happen and tries to smooth the path toward death as much as possible. Many medical centres now recognise that dying people need special care to reduce their worries. People can be helped to accept their own impending demise calmly, even when this takes a long time. An elderly lady in a ward for the terminally ill watched six of her room mates die over several months. When asked if she had found any meaning and purpose in these many days of suffering, she thought for a while and said, 'Yes, I feel I've honestly had a helpful relationship with the other patients in my room who've died.'[28] Given preparation for it, one can die in peace and dignity despite pain.

Abnormal grief

The time it takes to come to terms with loss of a loved one varies enormously. If the grief persists for longer than, say, a year, and the bereaved person avoids things connected with the deceased then we usually say the grief is becoming abnormal. The avoidance can be overcome by guided mourning therapy which encourages bereaved people to look at and handle photographs and possessions of the deceased, visit the grave and other reminders of their lost loved one, and think of that person for up to an hour a day.[29] Guided mourning resembles the exposure therapy for anxiety disorders you can read about in Chapters 11 and 12.

Alec overcame abnormal grief by guided mourning

Alec was a dentist aged 43 who had been depressed and found it increasingly difficult to work for four years, stopping work 10 months before being seen. At interview he cried twice when speaking about his father's death abroad

10 years earlier and changed the subject. He agreed he wanted help with this issue. During three weekly 50-minute sessions Alec was encouraged to talk about his father and the bereavement, and between sessions was persuaded to write and speak about this for 40 minutes a day. He said his father had also been a dentist and expected Alec to become one too. Alec had flown abroad for his father's funeral but had no time to mourn him, being then under great pressure of work. By the third session Alec became able to think and talk about his father without crying, his mood improved, and he said he had put his loved father on the shelf. Over the next few months he was helped to carefully organise graded re-entry into professional dentistry, and he was well and working at the two-year follow-up.[30]

Extreme trauma

Disaster has always been lurking round the corner. Today's TV screens proclaim victims all over the globe: earthquakes in Turkey and Taiwan and India, floods in Mozambique and Madagascar, mudslides in Venezuela, hurricanes in the Caribbean and the USA, volcanoes in the Philippines, war in Africa, 'ethnic cleansing', mass shootings, hostages, fires, crashes, rape, robbery and torture anywhere.

Reactions to extreme stress take several forms. If warned of approaching danger, people become acutely afraid and try to escape. Long after danger has passed many continue to be jittery and alert to minor threat they would ordinarily disregard. During and immediately after a trauma there is often brief stunned immobility and freezing of movement. Some people wander about for hours dazed and distracted. Shortly after the peril has passed people frequently become depressed and apathetic and lack energy, initiative, and interest, but do not usually feel suicidal. They might automatically obey anyone giving leadership. Once the most urgent rescue and relief operations are over, victims often become aggressive and irritable.

Anxiety is not the main problem in saving communities from extreme stress. A big problem is lack of co-ordination among many people each acting on their own different definitions of the situation at the time. Emotional reactions to disaster might intensify with separation from family and by intimate contact with dead or injured people.

It is surprising that panic is not a more common reaction to disaster. Panic occurs when escape still seems possible, not when one feels completely trapped. It disrupts organised group activity and during panic usual social relations are disregarded. Panic is accompanied by a sense of helplessness, impotence, and aloneness and is more likely to arise when in contact with other agitated people who feel in similar danger. During panic there is blind flight from the threat with no attempt to deal directly with the danger itself.

War

Modern conflicts tend to afflict civilians as much as soldiers. The hazards may be sudden sharp exchanges of fire for a few seconds a week or constant bombardment for days on end. It is unnatural not to feel anxious in such circumstances. Severe stress reactions occur more commonly during continuing and severe danger.

Among aircrew emotional breakdown is most likely during dangerous missions. The more that aircraft are lost, the greater the stress reactions. Chance factors play a big part in determining whether a particular trauma leads to breakdown. A pilot's position in a flying formation influences what harrowing events he can see. It matters much if the parachute of an escaped friend opens safely or catches fire or blows into another aircraft. It makes a difference whether an exploding plane and its occupants are blown beyond the field of vision, or whether the expression on a wounded or parachuting man's face can be seen. What a man looks like in danger, how well the observer knows or likes him, all influence whether surviving crew break down.

Extreme danger can induce fear in the bravest of people, who disbelieve the phobia they have developed. A trainee pilot said of his flying phobia: 'I have a yellow streak up my back a yard wide and I don't know where I got it. I never used to be yellow.'[31]

When aircrew become anxious they feel airsick and dizzy and fly over-cautiously. Flying phobias often develop when something happens to remind the pilot of the danger. This might be a trivial accident, an unexpected gust of wind, a momentary problem with the controls. Fear often begins at the start of an advanced step in training, such as the first flight at night or in a more complicated or new type of plane.

Among aircrew with post-traumatic stress reactions, after three to six weeks of rest almost all resumed non-combatant duty, though nightmares often persisted. A few returned to combat flying. One man's reaction developed on a mission during which his plane was twice damaged badly and two crewmen were killed. At a rest home he spent the first two weeks lying face down on the grass, deeply depressed, speaking to no one, preoccupied with guilt and whether he was alive. At first he could not eat, sleep, or mingle with others. He would not talk about flying or listen to others talk about it and was jittery to any noise and intensely phobic of his air base. He improved slowly at first and then rapidly. After six weeks he started ground duty.

Prolonged extreme stress

The longer that severe stress continues, the more widespread and lasting the disturbance it causes. This happens all too often with man's inhumanity to man. Even 12 to 25 years after being liberated from holocaust concentration camps, nearly half the survivors still had troublesome anxiety, nightmares and other sleep disturbances, and the rest had other problems.[32] Horrible memories would recur repeatedly and could not be discussed with closest friends or relatives. These memories would be triggered by the most harmless events: seeing someone stretch his arms would revive scenes of fellow prisoners hung up by their arms during torture; seeing an avenue of trees would be associated with rows of gallows with swinging corpses, a commonplace sight in the camps; children playing peacefully might suddenly call to mind other children who had been emaciated, tortured, and murdered.

Two-thirds of the survivors had been disturbed while in the camps – severe chronic anxiety and depression, inner restlessness, despair. Fear was particularly experienced by those who had been in death cells for long periods or taken part in illegal organisations which had been exposed, leading to execution of other members. The more serious the cause of arrest, the greater was the likelihood of anxiety. Bombing attacks terrified those locked in their cells while bombs and buildings fell around them.

The anxiety continued after release. The more severe the torture in the camp, the greater the subsequent disturbance. Symptoms of anxiety still troubled ex-inmates up to a quarter of a century later. Many could only start to talk of their terrible experiences fully 40 years later in the 1990s, when holocaust books burgeoned as survivors felt the end of their life approaching.

summary

Let us briefly review the ground we have covered so far, and then look ahead. We have seen that anxiety and fear, being normal responses to everyday worries, affect everybody. Mild anxiety can help us to be especially alert in carrying out tasks, and tension becomes troublesome only when it is extreme. Extreme tension can cause many forms of handicap, at which point it requires systematic self-help or professional aid. Just because they need help for severe fears does not mean the sufferers are insane, just that they have a particular problem. People with phobias go to great lengths to avoid whatever brings on their fear, and there may be gross disproportion between the apparently trivial trigger and the extreme panic it produces. This disparity makes it hard for laymen to understand or sympathise with sufferers. As a result, many sufferers are ashamed of and conceal their phobia, making it all the harder for them to learn how to overcome their problem.

Like other species, humans are predisposed to become afraid of certain things very easily, even without any traumatic experiences of those things. At certain ages young children usually develop fears of sudden noise, movement, strangers, and animals. Most of us dislike being stared at, or being near the edge of a cliff, or being pricked or cut by a dentist or doctor. No one likes being separated from his or her loved ones, and their death is a pain we all have to bear eventually. Many people also have to endure calamities like fires, tornadoes, or floods. Fortunately the human spirit shows considerable resilience in the face of such adversity.

Up to this point we have dealt with worries which afflict most people. In Part 2 we turn to more severe fears which bother only a minority and can be overcome systematically. People with phobias have nothing to be ashamed of. Because you are afraid of dirt or the dark does *not* mean you are guilty about dirty thoughts or dark secrets that must be uncovered before you can get well. There is no need to delve into the past to lose our worries. The most reliable way to overcome phobias successfully is to allow ourselves to approach those dreaded situations we have been avoiding, and despite the ensuing panic, to remain exposed to those situations until we get used to them. Slowly but surely our fear will then reduce. To carry out this approach may require some ingenuity. As we go along we shall see how other people did this. At the end you will see in detail how you can help yourself successfully from start to finish.

part **2**

forms of nervous tension and their treatment

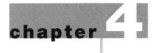

depressive and anxiety disorders

The rest of this book will outline forms of severe worry and how it is managed. Perhaps you may have one of the problems you'll read about. None needs special help unless it interferes with your life. Many people find it a relief to learn that they are not alone in their burden and that it can be lightened. You will see examples of people who eased their problem themselves or whom therapists treated successfully. The final chapter will teach you step by step how to cope with your fears.

Anxiety and depression are only considered abnormal when they exceed the usual response to stress in a given culture and handicap one in everyday life. Sufferers usually seek treatment if their problems become more marked, frequent, or persistent than is usual for them or their peers. Anxiety and depression appear in many psychiatric problems. Several such problems show distinctive patterns over time – these we call syndromes. The labels are useful, although a cynic once quipped:

> A group of symptoms unexplained you label a neurosis.
> And this is rather clever, for you've made a diagnosis.[1]

The various syndromes differ regarding their sex incidence, frequency, and age of onset. In psychiatric clinics more women than men complain of bad depression; but generalised anxiety, social phobias, and obsessive-compulsive disorder appear equally in both sexes. Depressive disorders are more likely to start as we get older, whereas anxiety disorders begin more often in young adult life. Severe depression is more often accompanied by anxiety than the reverse.

The number of sufferers is enormous. Ten per cent of people get a depressive or anxiety disorder in the course of their lives. Most of them do not seek treatment for their problem.

Causes of nervous tension

Depression has several causes which may act together in varying combinations. There is a clear genetic contribution to severe depression, especially that of manic-depressive disorder. Loss of a loved one, status, or ideal is a normal cause for gloom which eventually clears up in most people but in a few goes on to become a depressive disorder. Especially vulnerable to loss are those who lost parents when young or had emotionally deprived childhoods, single parents rearing small children unaided, and people who are isolated, poor, ill or undergoing severe life stresses.

This book focuses on anxiety disorders such as phobic, obsessive-compulsive, post-traumatic stress and sexual disorders. In several of these conditions research found that the genes play some role, but not a large one. Presumably because of biological boundaries of learning, some types of phobia tend to appear much more often at certain ages than at others, and the range of cues that are feared is rather limited. As we saw, many phobias are exaggerations of normal fears that humans seem to be programmed as a species to experience.

What causes normal mild fears to inflate into phobias is often a mystery. Depression or trauma can trigger phobias or obsessions. An overprotected childhood may increase the chance that normal fears will not disappear naturally with experience. Relatives with phobias and obsessions can, by example, pass them on to other members of the family, though this is less common than one might suppose. Certain subcultures pass on particular taboos and fears.

Overcoming anxieties needs no search for hidden origins. The problems do not point to dark secrets which have to be uncovered for treatment to succeed. The worries clear without digging and delving for dirt if the sufferer just confronts the troublesome situation for often and long enough to get used to it, without reconstructing his personality.

Let us look now at the various patterns of anxiety and depressive disorder that often trouble adults.

Depressive disorders

Anxiety commonly rises and falls with other features characteristic of depressive disorder. Depression can vary from brief spells of moodiness, which nearly everyone has at some time, to serious illness and even suicide. In the form of depressive disorder called bipolar, despair and utter dejection alternate with periods of mania and feelings of euphoria and being on top of the world and able to achieve anything. More often there are only gloomy spells of varying duration and degree. Fortunately depression tends to improve even without treatment, though it tends to recur in some people. Another positive feature is that though depression is common, it is also eminently treatable, as will be seen in Chapters 11 and 12.

When depressed, people feel down, cry often, sleep badly, no longer enjoy eating and other previously satisfying activities, and feel excessive guilt about things they may have done or not done. They may imagine that they have cancer, heart trouble, or other diseases. They might pace up and down in agitation, wringing their hands in trembling apprehension. Suicidal feelings may appear.

Generalised anxiety and panic disorders

In these disorders troublesome anxiety or panic appear without cause. If the problem is mainly continual tension it is called generalised anxiety disorder. If there are sudden peaks of panic it is called panic disorder.

The two forms of disorder commonly co-exist. Pre-existing tension may escalate into panic attacks that come out of the blue and last usually for a few minutes or less often longer. During panics, sufferers feel they are choking, a lump in the throat, being smothered, cannot breathe. They may over-breathe with sensations of pins and needles in the hands and feet. They often experience palpitations, rapid heartbeat or chest pain, nervousness, dizziness, light-headedness, weakness or faintness or sense that the ground is moving, tire easily and get irritable, and think that they have heart trouble and might fall, faint, or die, or scream out loud, or go mad. Panic can be intensely paralysing, rooting one to the same spot for minutes until the tension diminishes. Sufferers may run to different specialists for help, depending on the chief kind of complaint.

Panic attacks usually last a few minutes or, rarely, hours. They may pass, leaving the person feeling as fit as before until the next attack the same day or weeks or even months or years later. People may feel nervous throughout the day with panic as occasional punctuated increases of the constant tension. The attacks may occur only once in a few days, or come in waves every few minutes to become so troublesome that the suffer is confined to bed.

The intensity of nervousness varies from terror to mild tension. Some people are not even aware that they are anxious but simply complain of changes in their body due to anxiety, for example, that they sweat too much, that their heart flutters in their chest, or that they cannot take a deep breath. Anxiety may continue for long periods without discrete attacks of panic. It may be mixed with mild depression, desires to cry, and even occasional thoughts of suicide, but serious suicidal urges are not a feature.

Breathing difficulties are common ('I can't get enough air', 'my breath keeps catching') and the sufferer may actually show repeated catches in breathing, or the opposite problem of over-breathing. Choking and swallowing feelings may get worse in crowds, so one has to open a window in crowded places.

Chest discomfort may include pain over the region of the heart, an awareness of the heart beating, and pressure over the upper abdomen. There may be desires to pass urine or faeces with a need to be constantly in reach of a toilet. In some people tension causes nausea and vomiting with secondary fears of vomiting in public places, so that victims eventually avoid such situations. They may lose their appetite, cease eating, and then lose weight. Sometimes they might have mildly loose stools.

Faintness and dizziness may appear especially when walking or standing, so that sufferers feel they have to hold on to a nearby chair or walk close to the wall of a nearby building. One man said, 'I feel I am walking on shifting ground which is always falling or rising like the deck of a pitching and rolling ship.'[2] A woman felt that 'my legs are made of jelly and I'm walking on cotton wool'.[3]

Panic feelings may intensify in certain situations and lead to the avoidances typical of agoraphobia, as we will see in Chapter 5 on agoraphobia. People anxious like this often avoid hot, crowded rooms or stores and will stay clear of a cinema, theatre, hairdresser, or church, or if they do go to these places will sit near the end of the aisle to ensure that exit is possible with speed and dignity. Crowded streets, buses, and trains can become unendurable ordeals which bring on repeated attacks of panic, so that the sufferer may increasingly restrict his activities until he is virtually confined to his home. Strangely enough, such people often remain able to travel by car even when all other forms of transport are avoided and even when they may be unable to walk alone in the streets. The fears are often lessened by the presence of reassuring adults, so that someone may be able to do accompanied what is impossible alone. Sometimes the person may require company even at home, and husbands and wives may need to give up work and remain at home with their spouses.

When anxious people believe that they have heart disease or cancer they may entreat their doctors repeatedly for reassurance on this score. Such reassurance usually affords but transient relief. Normal results of repeated investigations do not persuade the sufferer for more than a few minutes or hours that doom is not around the corner. Generalised anxiety sufferers are commonly irritable, lose their tempers easily, snap at their spouses and children. They tire readily and find it hard to get through the day's work.

Other complaints are of feeling strange or unreal, detached or far away from one's surroundings. This feeling may come at the height of a panic, or at other times when there is no sense of anxiety. Let us look at two contrasting case histories showing that anxiety disorders can affect people who were previously calm and sociable, whilst in others they seem to be an exaggeration of a life-long nervous tendency.

An anxious mathematician

Joe, a mathematician aged 35 who had previously been well-adjusted, complained of episodic palpitations (awareness of his heartbeat) and faintness over 15 years. He had been free from these for up to five years at a time, but in the past year his symptoms had increased, to the point of stopping him working in the last few days. At any time and without warning he would suddenly feel he was about to faint and fall down, or tremble and experience palpitations, and if standing he would cringe and clutch at the nearest wall or chair. If he was driving a car at the time he would pull up to the curb and wait for the feelings to pass off before resuming his journey. If they occurred during sexual intercourse he would immediately separate from his wife. If they happened while lecturing, his thoughts became distracted, he could not concentrate, and he found it hard to continue. Joe was becoming afraid of walking alone in the street, driving his car, or travelling by public transport for fear that these would trigger episodes. Although he felt safer when accompanied, this did not abolish his complaints. Between attacks he did not feel completely well and remained a bit tremulous. The feelings would come on at any time of day or night. He lacked energy but was not depressed and he said he felt no fear, anxiety, or panic during the attacks.

Joe had had a happy unanxious childhood, led an active social life when free of his attacks, and had a contented marriage and vigorous professional life. No members of his family had had any psychiatric trouble.

During interview Joe gave a clear history of his problem but seemed unduly humble for a man of his achievements. His head and hands persistently trembled slightly and his palms were cold and sweaty. His heartbeat was fast. While his blood pressure was being measured he suddenly became very anxious, restless, and sweaty and would not lie down. He cringed when he stood up and immediately sat down, crying weakly 'help, help'. He tried to tear the blood pressure cuff off his arm, saying it was painful. After about three minutes he calmed down again but wanted to remain sitting in an easy chair.

Over the next 18 months Joe gave up driving alone or travelling by public transport and stopped working. After treatment he resumed travelling and working. Milder episodes unrelated to any particular situations persisted, but he felt better able to cope with them.[4]

A nervous administrator

Generalised anxiety or panic disorder can also manifest as an increase in anxiety which has long been present for most of a person's life. Ben was a 52-year-old civil servant who had been anxious all his life. As a child he was timid and avoided rough fights and sports. Twice he had played truant from school when a bully had threatened him. He did poorly in examinations, partly because he became very anxious in them. In oral exams he stammered to a halt.

Ben's mother had been highly-strung, and both his siblings had been treated for anxiety attacks during times of marital stress. As a young man Ben had been very shy but had fought against this by making himself do public speaking. He married at 28 and worked as an administrative assistant. Any alterations in his routine threw him into a panic, and he would worry for days in advance over minor difficulties at work. He had visited his doctor frequently over the past 25 years and found that sedatives eased increases in his anxiety. The current episode had begun three months earlier when he had been given additional responsibilities at work and as examinations grew nearer.

At interview, Ben complained of pervasive feelings of anxiety, tension in the neck, palpitations, dry mouth, and sweating. He was prescribed small doses of a sedative drug and during supportive interviews learned to take a realistic view of his capabilities and shortcomings.[5]

Cultural aspects of anxiety

Generalised and anxiety disorders may be more common in certain cultural groups. In Malaysia and Thailand psychiatrists see more Chinese than other groups with this problem.

Culture also affects how anxiety is expressed. There is a strong belief among South-East Asian Chinese that male genitals are essential for life, and semen is highly prized. The people have a folk saying that '100 grains of rice make a drop of blood, and 100 drops of blood make a drop of semen.' Excessive sexual activity is regarded as unhealthy. Anxious male Chinese commonly complain that they have lost semen, but Malay patients rarely say this.[6] (In nineteenth-century Britain and America, masturbation was regarded as a cause of insanity and countless adolescents went through agonies worrying about the consequences of masturbation.)

Worries about sexual activities help us understand a condition called *koro*, a Malay word describing a form of acute anxiety seen among South-East Asian Chinese. The Chinese call the condition by a phrase which means 'shrinking penis'. Usually only one or two people in a community complain of *koro*, but *koro* epidemics occur occasionally. The patient has acute panic with fear that his penis is shrinking into his abdomen, which might kill him. To prevent this he or his friends or relatives grasp his penis. They may tie chopsticks or string to the penis to prevent its retraction. Together with this panic, the patient is aware of his heartbeat, feels faint, breathless, and that he can't see properly, experiences pain in his body and tingling in his hands and feet, and may vomit. *Koro* is sometimes seen even in women, who complain of retraction of the nipples of their breasts or even of the vulva.

Worry is not a privilege of industrial society. Anxiety about being bewitched was common enough in medieval Europe; a famous book called *The Hammer of Witches* was published as a detailed guide to recognising witchcraft. It includes a vivid description of how witches deprive men of their genitals. An extreme mysterious fear of being under a spell has resulted in voodoo death: someone who thinks he has been 'spelled' to death by pronouncement of a medicine man; or someone else stops eating, goes into a decline, and literally lies down and dies within a few days.

Pre-industrial Australian aborigines had many physical complaints commonly found with anxiety, such as tiredness, insomnia, backache, and breathing problems. I have seen the same kind of agoraphobia, sexual, and obsessive-compulsive problems all over the world in China, Japan, Thailand, India, Israel, Saudi Arabia, Europe, North and South America, South Africa and Australia. The pictures are similar whatever the race or religion. The main differences are the languages in which the anxieties are expressed.

Epidemics of acute anxiety

From time to time brief epidemics of acute anxiety sweep through a community. They do not last very long and sufferers have no lasting effects. Usually one can find some events beforehand which have led up to the epidemic. The form of the anxiety partly depends on the culture.

In Singapore one such epidemic took the form of *koro* noted above. In July 1967 swine fever broke out in Singapore, and amid much publicity pigs were inoculated to control the outbreak. In October a few people complained of *koro* and rumours spread that *koro* could be caused by eating pork from infected or inoculated pigs. Over the next few days up to 100 cases of *koro* a day appeared at general hospitals, and many more patients consulted their doctors. They worried that their genitals were disappearing into their bodies, and even attached wooden tongs to the penis to prevent this dreaded disorder. On the seventh day, at the height of the epidemic, a panel of experts appeared on television and radio explaining that *koro* was psychological and that it was impossible for the penis to retract into the abdomen. The day after this broadcast very few people complained of *koro*, and the epidemic ended shortly thereafter. Most of the *koro* sufferers were southern Chinese and the great majority were male. Nearly all the sufferers recovered fully without any serious consequences.[7]

Epidemics of acute anxiety with over-breathing and faintness sometimes appear in young women, especially among those associated together in institutions, for example, schoolgirls, nurses and nuns. During such an epidemic in a girls' school in Britain two-thirds of 500 girls developed anxiety symptoms and one-third was admitted to hospital. Many had repeated episodes.

The way in which this epidemic began was clear. Earlier in the year the town had received widespread adverse publicity during a polio epidemic. Immediately before the anxiety epidemic the schoolgirls had been to a ceremony due to include a member of the Royal Family. The ceremony was delayed by three hours because of late arrivals, and the girls waited in parade outside the building. Twenty of them felt faint and had to break ranks to lie down. The next morning there was much chatter about fainting. At assembly in school one girl fainted, followed shortly after by three girls saying they felt dizzy. When another girl was asked to get a glass of water for the original fainters, she too said she felt faint. Over the next two periods more girls felt faint and were placed on chairs in the main corridor. A mistress thought that to prevent them falling off the chairs in a second faint they should lie on the floor. They lay thus in the corridor in full view at the mid-morning break. The phenomenon now became epidemic. The chief complaints were excitement and fear leading to over-breathing and its consequences, faintness, dizziness, pins and needles in the extremities, and eventual cramps in arm and leg muscles. Many of the girls looked alarmingly ill.

The epidemic began among the 14-year-olds and spread to younger girls. On the first day a quarter of them were affected. More cases appeared each time school assembled and twice more frequently during break than at any other time. By the twelfth day the nature of the epidemic was realised, and firm management prevented the problem from spreading further. The symptoms of anxiety slowly subsided over a few days.

summary

Mild anxiety and fear are a normal response to stress and only when they become excessive and handicapping is help generally sought. Anxiety appears as part of many patterns of disturbances that we call syndromes or disorders. Depressive and anxiety disorders affect up to one in ten of all people in the course of their lives.

Nervous tension has many causes commonly acting together in varying degrees. These include heredity, loss of loved ones, status or ideals, and severe life stresses. The pattern of disturbance partly depends on age, and biological factors influence which stimuli can easily become the targets of fears. Trauma, overprotection by parents, and cultural taboos all influence the development of anxiety.

Depression can range from mild blues to serious illness and suicide and in one form can alternate with euphoria. Depressive disorders usually improve with time, and are eminently treatable. Anxiety states can also fluctuate and might vary from mild tension to paralysing attacks. Sufferers tend to attribute these to bodily problems. Anxieties are not restricted to Western societies, being also common in pre-industrial peoples. At times short-lived epidemics of acute anxiety sweep through some communities, for example, fear that the penis is shrinking (*koro*) among South-East Asian Chinese, or episodes of over-breathing and feeling faint in Western young women. Intelligent and calm management can overcome these cultural waves of panics.

Anxieties discussed so far have no readily identifiable triggers. In the next few chapters we will look at worries cued by specific situations – phobias, obsessive-compulsive and post-traumatic stress disorders, and sexual difficulties.

phobic disorders i:
agoraphobia (panic disorder)

A *phobia* is anxiety that is triggered by a particular situation, unlike generalised (free-floating) anxiety, which has no obvious stimulus. Phobias can occur in almost any situation, but some things tend to be more feared than others. Phobias may be minor complaints or pretty handicapping problems. We saw earlier that they can appear as part of a depressive disorder. When a phobia is the main problem and is disabling, then we call it a phobic disorder. Phobic disorders can range from an isolated fear in an otherwise healthy person to diffuse extensive fears occurring together with many other problems.

Agoraphobia

Agoraphobia is probably the most common and distressing phobic syndrome for which adult patients seek help from psychiatrists. The word comes from the Greek root *agora* meaning an assembly or market-place, and was first used by the German psychiatrist Westphal in 1871 to describe the 'impossibility of walking through certain streets or squares or possibility of so doing only with resultant dread or anxiety'. Today agoraphobia still describes fears of going into public areas such as streets, shops, or vehicles in variable combinations. At one extreme some people simply have a mild travel phobia or fear of closed spaces with no other problems. At the other extreme, people may have not only agoraphobia and other phobias but also panics without obvious cause, depression, and many other difficulties. American psychiatrists call the condition panic disorder with agoraphobia.

The main features of agoraphobia are fears of leaving home to go into streets, shops, crowds, closed spaces such as lifts, theatres, cinemas, or church; of travel on underground trains, surface trains, buses or coaches, ships or aeroplanes (but not usually cars); fears of going on to bridges, into tunnels, having haircuts or hairdos, of wide open spaces, and of remaining alone at home. These fears occur in many combinations over a variable period of time and are commonly associated with other problems such as panics, depression, obsessions, and feelings of being unreal.

Agoraphobia usually begins in adults aged between 18 and 35 and is rare in childhood. Some children with severe phobias of going to school never improve in this regard and go on to show agoraphobia in adolescence. About two-thirds of agoraphobics are women, whereas generalised anxiety disorder tends to occur equally in both sexes.

Agoraphobia often starts after a major life stress such as serious illness in oneself or a relative, acute danger or discomfort, leaving home, the death of a loved one, engagement, marriage, pregnancy, miscarriage or childbirth, or after an unpleasant scene in a shop, street, or bus. Sufferers often regard some trivial event as a trigger to the disorder even though such events might previously have occurred without undue trouble. Other problems too, such as depression, schizophrenia, or coronary thrombosis can start after drastic changes in one's life. Often agoraphobia begins without any obvious alteration in one's life circumstances.

Autobiographies of agoraphobics

It is instructive to read the autobiographies of agoraphobics. One such account comes from a man in 1890 whose agoraphobia began when he married at age 22.

> ❝The first noticeable symptoms . . . were extreme nervous irritability, sleepless ness and loss of appetite. Any little excitement would throw me into a state of almost frenzy, so completely would I be overcome. Palpitation, spasmodic breathing, dilation of the eyes and nostrils, convulsive movements of the muscles, difficulty in articulation, etc., were the more prominent features. A sense of impending danger seemed to descend, spoiling every pleasure, thwarting every ambition. The dread of sudden death which was at first marked, gradually subsided, giving way more to a feeling of dread – not of dying suddenly – but of doing so under peculiar circumstances or away from home. I became morbidly sensitive about being brought into close contact with any large number of people. Finding myself in the midst of a large gathering would inspire a feeling of terror on my part. This could be relieved in but one way – by getting away from the spot as soon as possible. . . . I have left churches, theatres, even funerals, simply because of an utter inability to control myself to stay. For 10 years I have not been to church, to the theatre, to political gatherings or any form of popular meeting, except where I could remain in the background, with means of egress convenient. Even at my mother's funeral . . . I was utterly unable to bring myself to sit with the other members of the family in the front of the Church. Not only has this unfortunate trait deprived me of an immense amount of pleasure and benefit, but it has also been a matter of considerable

expense. More than once I have got off a crowded train halfway to the station for which I was bound, merely from my inability to stand the jostling and confusion incident to the occasion. Times more than I can recall I have gone into restaurants or dining rooms, ordered a meal and left it untouched, impelled by my desire to escape the crowd. Times more than I recall I have bought tickets to theatres, concerts, fairs or whatnot, merely to give them away when the critical moment arrived and I realised the impossibility of my facing the throng with composure. To illustrate: I remember once going from Chicago to Omaha with my little boy. On entering the sleeper I found it crowded. I at once became ill-at-ease. As the train moved on I became more and more desperate, and finally appealed to the Conductor to know if I could possibly procure a section by myself. There was nothing eligible but a stateroom. That I took, paying 10 dollars extra for it. Had it been 100 dollars and I had the money, I should have bought it without once counting the cost. . . .

[A fear of open spaces] has been at times very pronounced. Many a time I have slunk in alleys instead of keeping on the broad streets, and often have walked long distances – perhaps a mile – to avoid crossing some pasture or open square, even when it was a matter of moment to me to save all the time possible. The dominating impulse is to always have something within reach to steady myself by in case of giddiness. This feeling is at times so strong that even when on a steamboat or a vessel, I cannot bear to look across any wide expanse of water, feeling almost impelled to jump in out of sheer desperation. . . . This malady . . . has throttled all ambition, and killed all personal pride, spoiled every pleasure . . .

At times buoyed up by stimulants or temporary excitement, I have faced situations which would ordinarily have filled me with extreme trepidation; but as a rule I have to yield or suffer the consequences. What those consequences would be, I do not know.[1] 〞

Yet another autobiography illustrates agoraphobia gradually becoming increasingly restrictive as it spread to different circumstances. In addition to the phobia itself there was a background of panic attacks and continual anxiety.

〝I am now in middle life and I have not seen a well day since I was about 12 years of age. Before I experienced any of the symptoms of agoraphobia I recall that . . . I was taken suddenly with 'spells' which lasted about 30 minutes. . . . I was more liable to these attacks during times of excitement; for example, one of the worst attacks I ever had came over me while I was attending the funeral of a relative. . . . When my strange illness came upon me, I worried over it, fearing that I should die in one of the attacks. . . . [After a boy in the village was murdered] I almost feared to be alone, was afraid to go to the barn in the daytime, and suffered when put to bed in the dark. . . . During the months which followed . . . I experienced the first symptoms of agoraphobia. There was a high hill not far from my home in the country where we boys used to coast in the winter time. One evening, while coasting, in company with other boys in the neighborhood, I experienced an uncomfortable feeling each time we returned to the top of the hill. It was not a well defined symptom of this horrible . . . malady, but later experiences have taught me that it possessed the unmistakable earmarks. As the months went by I commenced having a dread of high hills, especially when the fields consisted of pasture land and were level with the grass cropped short like the grass on a well kept lawn. I likewise commenced to dread high things and especially to ascend anything high. I even had a fear of crowds of people, and later of wide streets and parks. I have outgrown the fear of crowds largely, but an immense building or a high rocky bluff fills me with dread. . . . Ugly architecture greatly intensifies the fear.

The malady is always present. . . . I am conscious of it during every hour that I am awake. The fear, intensified, that comes over while crossing a wide street is an outcropping of a permanent condition.[2] **"**

Agoraphobia may fluctuate a lot, often for no apparent reason. The same sufferer describes this variability, and things that helped his phobias – darkness, storms, changeable landscapes with a limited view, riding a bicycle, gripping a suitcase.

" At times my phobias are much more pronounced than at other times. Some-times, after a strenuous day, on the following morning I find myself almost dreading to walk across a room; at other times I can cross the street without any pronounced discomfort. . . .

Usually I feel better in the evening than in the morning . . . the darkness seems to have a quieting effect on me. I love a snow-storm, a regular blizzard, and feel much less discomfort going about the town or riding on the train on such days, probably because one's view is obstructed. In fact, I welcome stormy days . . . . on such days I make it a point to be out and about the town.

I dread going on water in a boat, especially if the surface is smooth; I much prefer to have the waves rolling high. The most restful place in all the world for me is in a wood, where there is much variety in the trees and plenty of underbrush, with here and there little hills and valleys, and especially along a winding brook. . . . I love quiet, restful landscapes. . . . let the landscape be bold and rugged and bleak, and it strikes terror [into me]. . . .

I ride a bicycle along the streets with comparative comfort where I should suffer agony were I to walk. In walking I feel least uncomfortable in passing along the street if I carry a suitcase or travelling bag – something to grip. . . . I have such a dread of crossing a long bridge on foot.[3] **"**

The above man never sought medical aid for his fears and led an active public life while hiding his disability. Agoraphobia sufferers may conceal their disorder for long periods if they manage to hold down a job. Another man published his account fully 48 years after his agoraphobia began. Only closest relatives and friends knew of it, and he continued as a university professor during this time, living very close to the campus.

Onset of agoraphobia

Agoraphobic symptoms may clear up after a few weeks or months without treatment. The onset can be sudden, within minutes, or gradual over weeks, or slowly over years after initial vague intermittent anxiety. Some people start with an acute sustained panic, followed by phobias confining them to their homes within a few weeks. Others begin with vague fluctuating anxiety that gradually becomes agoraphobic over many years. Many feel uneasy for decades about going out alone but dextrously manage to hide their fears until the fear increases rapidly in new situations, when they seek help because the family cannot cope any longer. All kinds of variations appear between these two extremes.

Inge aged 18 suddenly came home one day from work and screamed she was going to die. She spent the next two weeks in bed and thereafter refused to walk beyond the front gate of her home. She did not improve after four months in a psychiatric hospital and after discharge left her home only twice in the next seven years. Inge spent her time gossiping with neighbours, listening to the radio, and with a boyfriend by whom she had a child at age 27, although she continued to live with her mother. From age 32 until last seen at 36 she improved slowly and became able to go on short bus rides and shopping expeditions.[4]

Although Inge had wet and soiled her bed until the age of 12, before her phobias started she was a good mixer, had many friends, and often went dancing. She was sexually cold until age 32, after which she had normal orgasm with her boyfriend.

By way of contrast, agoraphobia developed very gradually in Marge aged 17. She slowly developed fears of leaving home at 17 which improved at 20 when she had psychiatric treatment. They became more marked after she gave birth, at 26, to a son, when she became afraid of meeting people and of getting lost in a crowd. For the next two years Marge was limited to travelling by bike or car to her mother's home a mile away, and thereafter did not go beyond her own home and stopped shopping. She improved when admitted to hospital at age 29, became pregnant after discharge, and improved a bit more after her second child was born. For the next six years, until last seen, Marge only did local shopping, fetched her child from school, and went out with her husband. She had always been a shy, dependent person dominated by her mother.[5]

The panics of agoraphobia

Typically agoraphobia starts with repeated episodes of anxiety away from home, as already described for generalised anxiety. The panic can become so intense that sufferers are glued to the spot for minutes until it diminishes, after which s/he may just want to run to a safe haven – a friend or home. As one woman said:

> ❝At the height of a panic I just wanted to run anywhere. I usually made towards reliable friends . . . from wherever I happened to be. I felt, however, that I must resist this running away, so I did not allow myself to reach safety unless I was in extremity. One of my devices to keep a hold on myself was to avoid using my last chance, for I did not dare to think what would happen if it failed me. So I would merely go nearer my [escape route] and imagine the friendly welcome I should get. This would often quiet the panic enough for me to start out again, or at least not to be a nuisance or use up any good will. Sometimes I was beaten and had to feel an acute shame and despair of asking for company. I felt the shame even when I hadn't to confess to my need.[6]❞

Once the panic is over the sufferer may be reluctant to return to the scene of the panic for several months.

The panic attack may go on for a few minutes to several hours. It can pass off leaving the person feeling as fit as before, and many months may go by before another panic strikes. Episodes of panic can be followed by periods of normal activity, and a succession of panics may occur for years. Such episodes may lead to consultation with a doctor, who will find nothing abnormal except signs of anxiety. Eventually agoraphobics will begin to avoid certain situations for fear they might precipitate further panic. Because they cannot get off an express train immediately a panic starts, they restrict themselves to slow trains; when these too become the setting for panic, they restrict themselves to buses, then to walking, then just to walking across the street from home; finally they will not venture beyond the front gate without a companion. Rarely, they may become bedridden for a while, as bed is the only place where the anxiety feels bearable. Typically agoraphobics have periods when they feel better and times when they feel worse.

Conditions which affect agoraphobia

Agoraphobia fluctuates not only over time, but also with changes in the sufferer and the environment. In Westphal's first full description of the problem a century ago, he noted that the

❝ agony was much increased at those hours when the particular streets dreaded were deserted and the shops closed. The subjects experienced great comfort from the companionship of men or even an inanimate object, such as a vehicle or a cane. The use of beer or wine also allowed the patient to pass through the feared locality with comparative comfort. One man even sought, without immoral motives, the companionship of a prostitute as far as his own door. . . . some localities are more difficult of access than others; the patient [walked] far in order not to traverse [the dreaded spaces]. . . . in one instance, the open country was less feared than sparsely housed streets in town. One case also had a dislike for crossing a certain bridge. He feared he would fall into the water. In this case, there also was apprehension of impending insanity.[7] **❞**

An agoraphobic usually feels easier in the presence of a trusted person, pet or talisman, and may rely on the relative, pet, or object for peace of mind. Less often, agoraphobics may find it easier to travel alone. Many become afraid of being left alone or in any situation in which they cannot reach 'safety' with speed and dignity. Their need for constant company can strain relatives and friends. Tricks which some find useful include the grip of walking sticks, umbrellas, suitcases, shopping baskets on wheels, prams, folded newspapers under the arm, a bicycle to push rather than to ride, or a dog on a leash. Chewing gum or sucking strong sweets in the mouth divert a few from their fears. Deserted streets and vehicles are much preferred, and rush hour is abhorred. Trains (and buses) are easier to go on if they are empty, stop frequently at stations, and have a corridor and a toilet. Some journeys are easier if they pass the home of a friend, or a doctor, or a police station, when they feel that help is at hand if they panic. In such cases if the sufferer knows the friend or doctor is not at home, the journey becomes more difficult. It is the *possibility* of aid which helps such sufferers during their journey. One patient would go on a particular bus route because it passed a police station outside which she would sit if the tension got too great. Agoraphobics usually find it easier to travel by car than any other way and may comfortably drive themselves many miles even though they cannot stay on a bus for one stop.

Agoraphobics often feel easier in the dark, and move more freely at night than in the daytime. Wearing dark glasses can give relief. Some find that their fears improve during rain or storms and worsen during hot weather. A fear of heights is common, and agoraphobics prefer to live in a ground-floor apartment. This also avoids the need for lifts.

The nearer home is to shops, friends, and helpful relatives, the easier their lives will be. They may ask for help in taking the children to and from school, or in getting to and from work. Agoraphobics may go to work if it is a short walk or bus ride away from home, but fail to manage if they have to cross a crowded main road or change buses in order to get there. They may find it easier to work at their own pace in a quiet room with few others present rather than as part of a chain of workers or busy assembly line which requires split-second efficiency.

If agoraphobics go to a cinema, theatre, or church they feel less frightened in an aisle seat near the exit so that they can make a quick getaway if seized by sudden panic. A telephone at hand to call a trusted person can afford similar relief and reduce their social isolation.

A phobic correspondence club jokingly put all these features together in a popular figure called Aggie Phobie: a woman walking at night up a dark alley in the rain while wearing dark glasses, sucking sweets vigorously, with one hand holding a dog on a leash, the other trundling a shopping basket on wheels.

Quite a few other tricks have helped various people. An agoraphobic man removed his belt during anxiety attacks; a woman had the urge to rid herself of all clothing when panicking and could wear only garments that she could close in front by zips, and had to carry a pair of scissors and a bottle of beer in her bag when she left home. An army officer who felt anxious crossing a square when in civilian clothes felt much better when he wore his uniform with his sabre at his side. A man who feared crowds was able at times to face them when he clutched a bottle of ammonia in his hands lest he felt faint. A clerk also afraid of crowds carried a bottle of sedatives in his pocket, though he had not taken them for years; the bottle was a magic talisman.

Driving a car may mask agoraphobic disability for years as even severely affected sufferers can feel safe in a car despite distress with any other form of travel. If they can do their work at home and there is help, again the problem can be concealed for years.

Minor changes in the view can also affect the intensity of agoraphobia. Usually the wider and higher the space walked in, the greater the fear. If a view can be interrupted by trees, or rain, or irregularities in a landscape, the phobia lessens. During a party on a private lawn an agoraphobic felt his anxiety would have been relieved if he could have broken down the surrounding fence. A clergyman felt dizzy as soon as he went into the open, but obtained relief by creeping around hedges and trees or, as a last resort, by putting up his umbrella.

Certain agoraphobics hate being confined in a barber's or dentist's chair or at the hairdresser's because they cannot escape immediately – someone called this 'the barber's chair syndrome'. Again, because of the difficulties in making an immediate exit, some people won't bathe in the nude. While standing in the street or on a railway platform agoraphobics may feel drawn to jump beneath an approaching bus or train and therefore have to look away from the oncoming vehicle. This fear is related to the impulse normal people often have to jump when looking down from a great height, a fear also found in some agoraphobics that is countered by withdrawing from the edge of such heights or avoiding them completely. Fears of bridges are similar, especially long narrow bridges with open sides high above a river. Let there be a waist-high parapet between the agoraphobic and the edge of the cliff or bridge and the fear recedes.

Fear of fear can be quite crippling. For weeks before a planned journey agoraphobics may die a thousand deaths anticipating it. Let the same journey be sudden and unexpected and they can do what they cannot do if forewarned. They might board a bus if they do not have to wait for it at the stop, but should there be any delay, panic rapidly builds up and prevents them from boarding the vehicle when it finally arrives.

Any stress can increase agoraphobia. Depression is common, during which time the phobias can become crippling. When the mood improves, the phobias may lessen to their previous level of disability. Tiredness and physical illness aggravate agoraphobia. So does confinement to bed, since this results in loss of practice at going out and makes it harder to resume former activities when the patient gets up again.

As with any anxiety, alcohol and sedative drugs can afford relief for a few hours. They may help sufferers break new ground temporarily, but usually the effect wears off after the drug has been excreted. Patients often keep a stock of sedatives which they take shortly before a journey or some other anticipated stress. A small minority eventually get addicted to sedatives or alcohol, but most people manage to stop the drugs or drink once their anxiety has gone.

Intense emotion sometimes arouses agoraphobics to activity for a while. They manage to go out again when they are intensely angry or during emergencies; for example, if there is a fire in the house they will jump through the window rather than be burned.

Impact on the family

Most agoraphobics live with their family. Social activities lessen or are abandoned. As restrictions increase, the spouse or a child may be asked to escort the patient to and from work and take over the shopping. Even a child may be kept from school or a spouse from work just to keep the agoraphobic company. One woman had arranged her life so that she had never been left alone more than a few minutes over 16 years of marriage, to the great inconvenience of her husband and daughter. The restrictions to daily activities can cause many arguments between partners.

The role of will-power

Anything which heightens motivation can increase the phobic's tolerance as long as the motivation continues. The limits of tolerance fluctuate in many circumstances. In an emergency such as an accident, patients can temporarily overcome their phobias and sally forth. Once the crisis subsides, the phobia reappears. A Jewish woman could walk only a few blocks from her home in Vienna. When the Nazis came she had the choice to flee or be placed in a concentration camp. She fled, and over the following two years travelled halfway around the world until she arrived in the USA. After settling in New York the same travel phobia she had had in Vienna returned.[8]

The fluctuating nature of agoraphobia makes it hard for family and friends to accept that it is a disorder and not a sign of laziness, lack of will-power, or avoidance of awkward situations. Many say that if the patient can master her phobias in an emergency, then she just needs to exert herself more when there is no emergency, and so has to be forced to go out. However, nobody can be expected to muster energy to treat every minor shopping expedition as they would a fire at home. It is not only agoraphobics who can perform unexpected feats in an acute crisis. It is hard to demand such feats constantly of everyone as a routine, and in a panicking agoraphobic, any minor sally outside the house requires great effort, trivial as it might be for the average person.

When there is much generalised anxiety and depression, agoraphobics find it particularly difficult to exercise their will-power. A woman aged 31 described this state:

> **❝**I could barely get myself to the office or stay in it until it was time to go. I was always exhausted, always cold; my hands were clammy with sweat; I cried weakly and easily. I was afraid to go to sleep; but I did sleep, to wake with a constricting headache, dizziness, and tachycardia. To these now familiar symptoms were added waves of panic fear followed by depression. The panics almost overwhelmed me. I felt very much more frightened when I was alone and but little less frightened with other people. There were only three with whom I felt at all safe and able to relax, though even with them I was behind the screen of my fears.[9]**❞**

Once an agoraphobic feels reasonably comfortable away from those places which evoke anxiety, it becomes easier to go out repeatedly to try and conquer the phobia. Sometimes she discovers by accident that she can in fact go out again. One woman had a modified leucotomy operation for severe agoraphobia and felt more relaxed thereafter, but remained confined to her home for a year out of habit. By accident one afternoon a friend who had just called left a handkerchief behind. The patient rushed into the street to return the handkerchief and to her surprise felt relaxed in the street she had previously dreaded; she proceeded systematically to do more and more, and remained relatively well four years later.

Although high motivation or will-power is not enough to cure agoraphobia, it is an asset, as with any disability. It can be of great value in helping the sufferer plan a systematic campaign to overcome various fears one by one, as will be seen in Chapter 12.

Treatment of agoraphobia

Effective behavioural treatment has been developed for the lasting relief of phobias. Unlike older psychoanalytic treatments, this approach does not explore unconscious fantasies. There is no search for hidden meanings. Instead, sufferers carefully work out all the frightening situations which bring on panic and plan and execute graded re-entry into each one repeatedly for at least an hour a day so that they can learn to develop tolerance instead of dread. They learn to enter and stay in each phobic situation until they feel easier there and to repeat this so much that they become thoroughly used to it and it ceases to holds terrors for them. The principle behind this is *exposure* to whatever frightens them until they becomes accustomed to it. As we go along we will see how this principle is applied to help each kind of problem. This will prepare you for the detailed approach to treatment given in Part 3 of this book. Let us look, then, at how two agoraphobics were treated when therapists used to accompany sufferers during their first exposure exercises (since then research has found that sufferers do at least as well in the long run if they devise and do all their exposure homework tasks unaccompanied).

Jean, aged 40, had been agoraphobic for 15 years and in the past year had not left her house without her husband. Before starting treatment she agreed with her therapist that there were two main targets she wished to achieve by the end of treatment, that is, crossing a moderately busy street alone and shopping in small shops nearby without crossing streets.

Treatment began with her therapist taking her to the road just outside the hospital and helping her across. They repeated this several times, the therapist gradually leaving her side, staying first a few yards away and then further away while she crossed on her own as he watched. By the end of the first 90-minute session Jean was very pleased and surprised with her performance and at how much calmer she felt compared with the first time she crossed the road. She was asked to practise crossing roads of similar traffic density near her home before she attended the next session. The following session she made similar trips outside the hospital, but this time more of them alone and further from the hospital. She said she still panicked in streets and held on to people, and during lunchtime at work a friend helped her cross the road. She was asked now to go to work and return by bus alone instead of relying on lifts from people. She and her therapist worked out a programme of longer walks and bus journeys to complete between sessions. By the end of session 8 Jean was shopping regularly alone on nearby streets without anxiety and had improved in crossing moderately busy streets. Jean was discharged at this stage but was asked to continue to set herself targets to accomplish. Her improvement continued at 6-month follow-up and she became able to do even more things alone.[10]

Using the method of steady exposure to the actual frightening situation, agoraphobics usually improve within 10 sessions. Sometimes treatment can take longer. John was a 58-year-old professional. For 25 years he had been agoraphobic and driven to drink by his anxiety, so his job was in jeopardy. He found it impossible to get even beyond the hospital gates alone, and in open places he carried a heavy bag to 'anchor' him to the ground. He found it very hard to travel on underground trains or buses, visit crowded places, drive in a car over an overpass, walk on the pavement with traffic passing him, or climb stairs. This hampered his professional work which required visits to clients and lectures.

John and his therapist agreed on five treatment targets to be achieved: using a stairway to the third floor in buildings, travelling by train, visiting crowded places, walking along a narrow road with cars passing by, and driving over an overpass.

At the start of treatment the therapist accompanied John beyond the gates of the hospital into a neighbouring road; he often clung to the railings or rushed into the bushes, perspiring profusely. However, he became accustomed to this task and his walking boundary extended steadily further from the hospital toward a neighbouring village. His first nine sessions concerned his walking toward and around the local village, which he gradually did without the nurse and with decreasing anxiety.

He then tackled his problem with heights by initially standing on a staircase in a hospital building. This caused great unease, but with coaxing he stayed there. As he learned to endure this height, he was persuaded on to a higher and steeper staircase in an adjoining building and gradually became more confident in high places. Session 17 involved further stairs in public buildings and then a bridge crossing a busy road near a railway station. John found this almost intolerable; once they had to stop the session when he clung to the therapist in panic, frightened that passers-by were looking at him. At the next session the therapist persisted gently in helping him get used to the bridge across the road, with increasing success. John then agreed to go across the footbridge across a river, at first getting no further than 10 yards. In the early phase of treatment, John had not completed the exposure homework tasks between sessions that he had been asked to do, but now he co-operated increasingly in doing these. He drove twice daily across an overpass, travelled by train, and visited busy streets and shopping centres alone. Although frequently tempted to return to alcohol, he refrained from it and was praised by the therapist and his family for his efforts.

After discharge he continued to treat himself. John sat alone in empty lecture theatres and then attended actual lectures, first in a seat from which he could escape easily and then in the front where it was hardest to leave. He often feared he would disgrace himself by interrupting the lecture, but these panic episodes gradually died down. He resumed attending conferences required by his work and felt almost completely at ease in them. He kept in touch with his therapist by phone. A year after discharge he was very much better, was back at productive professional work, had resumed all his former responsibilities, and had not touched alcohol. He had travelled hundreds of miles by train, had been with his wife regularly to parties, movies, theatre, concerts, and professional meetings, and had lectured at a night school. His wife was most pleased with his progress.[11]

Using such exposure therapy, which we shall see later in more detail, agoraphobics (and their families) can generally learn to lead a more normal life in four to 14 sessions. The treatment calls for considerable effort from the sufferer, but improvement is usually worthwhile and lasting, even though some anxiety may remain.

In a treatment programme it is best to start with activities which will help one resume normal work and social life. With progress, harder tasks can be undertaken. One might start in the presence of a reassuring person, then do the tasks alone when crowds of people are not expected. Phobics wishing to practise going on a bus or train can avoid rush-hour travel at the start, choosing trains or buses which stop frequently so that they feel free to get out whenever they wish. Then they can progress to more difficult tasks. In a cinema, theatre, or church at first they may be more relaxed sitting on an aisle seat near an exit; as they get used to such places they can seat themselves in a more central position from which it is harder to escape with speed and dignity.

summary

When particular situations trigger anxiety, we speak of a phobia. Some phobias are very mild, while others are socially crippling. The most common phobic syndrome seen by psychiatrists is agoraphobia, denoting fear of going into public places. It usually starts in young adult life, and two-thirds of sufferers are women. Typical agoraphobia features include fluctuating fears of going into streets, shops, crowds, public transport, and auditoria. Entering such places evokes extreme panic. Sufferers then avoid these situations and may become totally housebound, which may severely cramp family life. Agoraphobia can strike out of the blue. More often it comes on in stages. It fluctuates not only over time, but also with many other events.

It is usually less bad with a trusted companion and in places from which the sufferer can leave quickly without fuss.

We have seen examples of how agoraphobics can overcome their problem by exposing themselves to their dreaded situation and remaining there until they become accustomed to it, a process which usually takes hours. This therapeutic principle of exposure applies equally to all forms of phobia. In the next few pages you will see how exposure treatments work in cases of social phobia, after learning what it is like to have such a phobia.

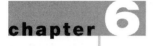

phobic disorders ii: social and illness phobias, and post-traumatic stress disorder (ptsd)

These three unrelated types of problem are grouped here for convenience.

Social phobias

Most people often get a bit anxious in social situations. This is perfectly normal and even public personalities have a slight fluttering in their chests before major appearances. A little tension can be better than none at all to help keep us alert and on our toes. Only when the fear of social occasions becomes too great does it disrupt activity. Hippocrates described someone who 'through bashfulness, suspicion, and timorousness, will not be seen abroad; loves darkness as life and cannot endure the light or to sit in lightsome places; his hat still in his eyes, he will neither see, nor be seen by his good will. He dare not come in company for fear he should be misused, disgraced, overshoot himself in gesture or speeches, or be sick; he thinks every man observes him.'[1]

Unlike most other phobias which are more frequent in women, social phobias are equally common in men and women. They usually start between the ages of 15 and 25 and develop slowly over months or years with no obvious cause. A few start suddenly after triggering events, as with a young man at a dance who felt sick at the bar and vomited before reaching the toilet, making an embarrassing mess, after which he became afraid of going to dances, bars, or parties.

Social anxiety relates to what individuals might think of one, rather than a crowd in which the people who make it up seem anonymous. Agoraphobics' fear of crowds concerns being crushed or enclosed or suffocated by the crowd rather than being seen or watched by people in it. Social phobics are sensitive about being observed and only manage to do certain things as long as nobody is watching them. A glance from someone else precipitates panic.

Social phobias are quite common.[2] Sufferers may fear eating and drinking in front of other people; their anxiety may relate to their trembling hands as they hold their fork or cup, or they may feel sick or have a lump in their throat and be unable to swallow as long as they are watched. 'When I go out to eat in strange places I can't eat, my throat feels a quarter of an inch wide, and I sweat.' The fear is usually worse in smart crowded restaurants and less at home, but a few cannot even eat with their spouse. They avoid going out to dinner or inviting friends home for fear that their hands will tremble when drinking coffee or handing a cup to a friend. Social life becomes restricted.

For fear of shaking, blushing, sweating, or looking ridiculous some people cannot face another passenger in a bus or train or walk past a queue of people. They are terrified of attracting attention by seeming awkward or by fainting. Some may leave their house only under cover of darkness or fog. They avoid talking to superiors and stage fright prevents them performing to an audience. They stop swimming to avoid strangers looking at their bodies. They shun parties and are too embarrassed to talk to others. 'I can't have normal conversation with people. I break out in a sweat, that's my whole problem even with the missus', said a man who still continued normal sex with her.[3] The fear may appear only in the presence of the opposite sex, or manifest itself equally in front of men and women.

Social phobics frequently fear writing in public and so will not visit a bank or shop because they are terrified their hand will tremble when writing a cheque or handling money in company. For fear of shaking, a secretary may cease taking dictation or typing; a teacher may no longer write on a blackboard or read aloud in front of a class; a seamstress will stop sewing in a factory; an assembly line worker will become unable to work on a production line. Knitting or buttoning a coat can induce agonising panic when done in front of others.

Generally the fear is that their hands or heads *might* shake, yet it is rare for social phobics to actually tremble or shake so much that they write with a scrawl, rattle their coffee cup against the saucer, spill soup when raising their spoon to their lips, or nod their head visibly when talking. Such phobics contrast strikingly with sufferers from brain diseases which actually cause obvious shaking. People with Parkinson's disease, for example, do not fear doing things in public despite their shaking heads and hands. Similarly social phobics' fear of blushing is irrespective of their actual facial colouration.[4]

Vomiting phobias

Some fear they might vomit in public or see others vomiting. The fear can reach such proportions that sufferers avoid anything remotely likely to make them or others vomit such as travelling on a bumpy bus or coach, going on a boat, or eating onions.

A secretary who feared vomiting

Vicky, aged 34, had feared vomiting for 13 years.

> ❝As a child my mother couldn't help the kids when they vomited and instead would ask my father to clean up the mess. I remember being upset by other children vomiting when I was only about five, but didn't develop the phobia until much later, at age 21. At that time I became afraid that other people or I myself would vomit on the train, so I began avoiding travelling to some places. This fear got worse over the last five years. I wake at 5:15 am daily to travel to my office before the rush hour. With a great effort I might rarely manage to return during rush hour. Over the last two years I've drunk a bottle of brandy a week to calm my fear of travelling, and also take sedatives at times. I worry that I drink ever larger amounts of brandy. In the last five years I've avoided eating in public places, in restaurants, or in strangers' homes. I've also stopped going to theatres with friends if I can help it because it's easier to leave the theatre if I'm alone when I get this awful fear of vomiting. The funny thing, though, is I've never vomited in a public place nor have I seen anyone else vomit for many years.[5]❞

When alone, Vicky was not anxious and worked well. After treatment she became able to eat in restaurants alone or in company without undue worry. She resumed travelling in crowded subway trains and enjoyed mixing with people more than before.

A mother's dread of vomiting

A mother had all her life feared vomiting or other people vomiting.

> ❝I can't mix with people as I constantly fear they might be sick. My life is so restricted that I often take sleeping tablets in the afternoon as the days seem so terribly long. My only daughter is pregnant and has been vomiting almost ceaselessly over the last 10 weeks. I go down and sit with her, but nobody knows the terrible fear and strain I feel. When she's vomiting I go out in the garden or turn up the radio (it's the sound of sickness I fear) and wish I'd go stone deaf. I take sleeping tablets so that for a few hours I'm released from my constant terror. Although I sleep with earplugs, a sudden cough or movement from my husband is enough to make me start sweating and trembling because I think it might be sickness.[6]❞

Intense feelings can sensitise someone to develop social phobia. Ilse's fears of trembling in public began at her wedding while walking up the church aisle with her father, wondering if her husband-to-be was really good enough for her. This fear increased shortly afterward when her husband was admitted to hospital and Ilse ate alone in a restaurant after visiting him.

Some social phobics may not only fear social situations but be anxious and depressed at other times too and may resemble severe agoraphobics. Consider Ethel.

A clerk with social phobias and depression

Ethel, aged 20, had social phobias for three years which reduced her socialising. She had not been out alone for a year except to travel to work, and since stopping work two months previously had been out nowhere alone. Ethel came to hospital with her mother. She dreaded people looking at her, that she might shake while drinking or walking out in public, or any other social situation. Even at home Ethel was on edge, shaky and restless, and unexpected panics punctuated her background anxiety. She only relaxed after alcohol or sedative drugs. For two years she had also been depressed and wanted to cry at times.

Lack of self-assertion, shyness

Lack of self-assertion is common even in otherwise well adjusted people. This may stop them accepting promotion at work and restrict their lives. Ed's shyness since childhood worsened when at 18 he was beaten up by youths after a row in a dance hall. Ed worked so well in a garage that he was offered the post of manager but declined this because he could not assert himself with juniors. Ed was nevertheless quick-tempered at home. He had a happy sex life.

Shyness amounts to a social phobia if it becomes marked. Extreme shyness can prevent people from making friends and lead to great loneliness. Lots of persons are isolated because they fear contacting others, worry they might seem foolish and look silly, and never make the first move towards companionship. They might tread a lonely path between working in a boring office where they keep to themselves and a room in lodgings where they speak to nobody and spend their time reading or watching TV and going for solitary walks. In a few a fear of others or lack of social skills leads them to become hermits, shut up, isolated, and unemployed in a dark room, living on a pittance from social security. They might draw down the blinds or dark curtains so nobody can see inside their home. People with schizophrenia, too, may hide similarly, but due to delusions of being persecuted.

Extreme shyness in adults can be a continuation of marked childhood shyness that never cleared up. Such problems are called diffuse (generalised) social phobia or avoidant personality disorder. Sufferers who seek help for this are far more often men than women.

Worries about our appearance (dysmorphophobia, body dysmorphic disorder)

Anxiety about how we look also leads to handicap like that from other social anxieties. Many of us think we are too fat or too thin, too short or too tall, or are sensitive about our ears or bottom or baldness. Women may feel too flat-chested or too bosomy. Most people adjust to the body they are born with. Famous actors and singers even make a virtue of their huge nose or fat figure, turning these proudly into an amusing and profitable trademark. An unfortunate few people do not accept their appearance and are endlessly preoccupied with minor or totally imagined defects.

Leo thought his nose was bent, a fact not evident even to the keenest observer. So sensitive was he about it that he had not used public transport for a year nor been on holiday, and dropped his friends. Leo worried so much about his nose that it was only with great difficulty that he could be persuaded to write and say 'my nose is ugly' as part of exposure therapy.

Dan feared that his hair was falling out and imagined that if he didn't look at his reflection in the mirror it wouldn't fall out. He stopped looking in mirrors or at photographs of himself or touching his scalp because he thought others scorned his appearance. Dan withdrew from company and became a loner.

Plastic surgeons have queues of patients wanting their noses made smaller or bigger or straightened or to have bat ears retracted or excess rolls of fat removed from their belly. When a very visible defect is actually present then surgery to improve the appearance might yield psychological benefit. All too often, however, the physical defect is either invisible or so tiny that most people would not worry about it, in which case surgery cannot help and the sufferer has to reconcile himself to his discomforting idea and test himself out as he is.

Anxiety about one's body might be not only about its appearance but also about its odour. Some unfortunates think they smell excessively, however much they wash and use deodorants, and so shun company and become a recluse.

Worries about one's body are related to those of illness. Concern about a little red spot on one's hand can start an idea that one has cancer, or a mark on the penis can trigger fears of sexually transmitted disease. We will examine worries about illness shortly.

A variant of social phobia involves hearing rather than seeing people. Here the fear is of going through a door if voices can be heard on the other side or of answering a knock on the door. An occasional worry concerns using the phone. 'I fear answering the phone so much that I have a code with my husband and children so that if the phone rings I know it's them. If it's anyone else, I can't answer the phone. I used to be able to when I was working because I knew then it would be about business, but I'm frightened at home.'[7] This fear has led sufferers to give up work as a secretary or in a call centre. The fear can be of stammering on the phone. The same worry may be aroused by asking for fares when travelling or ordering meals in a restaurant.

Treatment of social anxieties

Social fears can be overcome in the same way as is agoraphobia. Phobics are encouraged to actively confront what they fear until they feel better.

Emma had for seven years feared eating or drinking in company. Her problem began in a busy office when she panicked while taking tea to a group of accountants and they laughed at her. Thereafter she avoided eating and especially drinking in public, and even became uneasy drinking tea in the office with friends. At a social event like a meal with her friend she could make the anxiety bearable only by having a stiff vodka beforehand, and during the meal or a party would nip out to the ladies' room with a hidden half bottle. Cinemas and other public places where she was not expected to drink did not bother her.

Over six treatment sessions Emma was persuaded to do the things she feared. She drank coffee in a busy cafe for 30 minutes, then soft drinks in a moderately busy pub, and thereafter soft drinks in a very busy pub. At the end of that session her therapist allowed her one alcoholic drink.

Between sessions Emma was asked to attend a restaurant daily for lunch and coffee houses each afternoon, and to stay there until her anxiety had fallen. On her final (sixth) treatment session she was asked to spend two and a half hours making trays of tea and coffee in outpatients and to carry these to staff and patients all over the building. This was hard at first but became easier as time wore on. Shortly after this she made her first panic-free visit to pubs and parties with friends. Emma's self-confidence soared, her spirits rose, she stopped avoiding things, and she remained well when last seen at the six-month follow-up.

Exposure treatment and role play

Treatment can include role play, as in the case of Pat who had social fears for four years. Pat was petrified if she visited people in their home and refused to eat a meal with them. She would eat a meal in a restaurant or office cafeteria when alone but not while sharing the table with someone else. She had always been shy and reserved with a limited social life. She and her boyfriend visited each other's homes once a week, but no meal was taken in either.

Before treatment Pat agreed with her therapist that she wanted to become able to eat a meal with three other friends and at her boyfriend's home. To start treatment, Pat lunched with her therapist, feeling very anxious at the beginning but by the end an hour later felt comfortable. The next time she felt fine eating a meal with her therapist but remained unable to eat with her boy friend. He was not able to join treatment sessions, so instead Pat described to her therapist a detailed imagined scene of having a meal with her boyfriend. The therapist prompted Pat's flow of talk when she flagged.

Pat then role-played asserting herself appropriately. In 'playlets' to overcome Pat's shyness, her therapist pretended to be a shop assistant and Pat acted the part of a customer returning defective goods. This was recorded on videotape and played back to show her how she had performed. Pat was taught what to say as a disgruntled customer, and they played the same parts again. Then they switched roles with Pat as the salesperson to get the feeling of what it is like to be on the other side of the fence. They acted further situations such as asking the way in the street from a stranger or refusing to carry out an unreasonable request from a colleague. The therapist showed Pat what to do first and then asked her to do the same thing. She did well with this modelling and coaching and then lunched with a strange man.

At this stage she joined five other socially phobic patients for a day-long group session lasting nine hours. In the morning their therapist outlined the programme over coffee. They played contact party games to encourage them to mix, like having one of their number break out of a circle made by the others, and without using hands transfer an orange held under the neck to another patient. These warm-up exercises led into role play of increasingly difficult social situations. Toward evening the group split into small parties to shop for the meal they were to cook together in the therapist's flat. They chatted a lot to one another and then ate the meal together. After initial unease they enjoyed themselves and planned to meet one another after the group's conclusion.

Pat felt she had gained a lot from her day-long group session. Her other sessions were with the therapist alone. After 18 sessions she felt she had achieved as much as she wanted to. By the six-month follow-up she was eating with her fiancé and his family and in selected restaurants with him and occasionally including a larger group of friends. She still did not enjoy meeting many strangers but now coped without avoiding them.

Social skills training

Pat's group session had involved *social skills training*.[8] Inhibited people are trained gradually to do increasingly difficult social tasks, whilst over-aggressive people learn to express their feelings in a more acceptable fashion. Problems like these can be treated either alone or in a group. The social training exercises gradually become more taxing. A group of people with similar social troubles act out with one another scenes such as asking a stranger in the street what the time is or the way to another street nearby or far away. Patients first act out these roles in the group and then do the same thing outside in real life. Other exercises might be asking in a shop for something they cannot describe precisely, being a customer in a shoe shop and turning down pairs of shoes they have tried on, having dinner in a restaurant and asking the waiter for a detailed explanation of the bill, and introducing oneself to and conversing with a stranger at a party. This approach has helped many people who have difficulty in dealing with others.

Illness phobias (hypochondriasis)

Illness worries flit through most of our minds at one time or another. Who has not looked at a spot on his hand and wondered if it is malignant melanoma or another disease? Medical students typically think they harbour whichever disorder they are studying at the time, and experience a succession of illness fears as they progress through their curriculum. These are transient, not disabling, worries and need no treatment.

A few people have such insistent fears of illness that they consult doctors. Fears of multiple bodily symptoms and a variety of illnesses are called hypochondriasis. Fear focusing on a single symptom or illness in the absence of another psychiatric problem is an *illness phobia*. Hypochondriasis was well described in 1621:

> "Some are afraid that they shall have every fearful disease they see others have, hear of, or read, and dare not therefore hear or read of any such subject, not of melancholy itself, lest, by applying it to themselves that which they hear or read, they should aggravate and increase it.[9]"

A physical illness might trigger the phobia or sensitise someone to develop symptoms later, but commonly there is no history of past disease to explain it. Indeed, in a few cases development of the feared disease resolved the fear. One man was so frantic with fear of sexually transmitted disease that he was admitted to a mental hospital. After discharge he got syphilis with a visible ulcer. From that moment his fear disappeared and he attended happily for regular anti-syphilitic treatment.

Illness phobias concern something we cannot escape – our body. However, fear of illness might be triggered by particular circumstances which sufferers start to avoid, as in a woman with fear of epilepsy who would not go out alone lest she have a seizure. A man who had had so many X-rays that he thought he might get leukaemia refused to be out of contact with his wife more than a moment in order to get her constant reassurance.

The endless quest for reassurance due to hypochondriacal or obsessive-compulsive worries is rather like an addiction. Reassurance reduces the anxiety briefly, but tension soon builds up again so further reassurance is sought within weeks, days, or minutes, the interval between reassurances growing progressively smaller. Similarly, drug addicts get withdrawal symptoms when their drug is withheld but feel fine for a while after they have had their 'fix'. As their addiction deepens their need for the drug increases in frequency and dose.

Culture and family affect fear of illness

To some extent illness phobias reflect worries about disease which are fashionable in the culture at large or in one's family. Many people developed fears of tuberculosis after an early twentieth-century campaign to educate the public about that disease. Today it is unfashionable to fear tuberculosis despite its return in drug-resistant form, and fears of AIDS, cancer and heart disease are more usual.

People who grow up in very health-conscious families are more liable to develop fears of illness. Having had a disease in a particular part of the body may sensitise one to that area. We may identify with a parent or sibling who has a particular disease. AIDS fears may reflect guilt about sexual adventures. Such factors may be added to by growing up in surroundings where undue attention is paid to physical disease, or during public campaigns about a given illness. A woman who had relatives with epilepsy developed fears that she, too, would have seizures and became frightened of going out alone. Some illness fears may simply result from a failure of patient and doctor to communicate well. A patient may misinterpret the silence of a taciturn doctor as an ominous sign of frightening information being concealed.

Fears can lead to endless worry and search for reassurance

People with illness phobias are usually perfectly healthy yet persistent fear distracts them from everyday activities more than if they actually had the disease they dread: 'fear is more pain than the pain it fears'. Sufferers constantly search their body for evidence of disease. No skin lesion or body sensation is too trivial for their keen senses. They misinterpret normal tummy rumblings. Their worry itself produces fresh symptoms such as abdominal pain and discomfort due to gut contractions which reinforce their gloomy prognostications. Women may examine their breasts for cancer vigorously and so often that they bruise their breasts.

While most of us have minor worries about illness at some time or another, these do not come to rule our lives to the exclusion of all else. Contrast the billionaire Howard Hughes. His terror of infection led to extraordinary precautions and cleaning rituals that he also forced on his servants. He became a recluse, ate a strange diet, and refused to see doctors. His fear may have hastened his death. When he became really ill and emaciated a doctor could be brought to him only when he was unconscious and about to die. Elementary medical attention could have helped him earlier.

Illness phobics may make hundreds of phone calls and visits to doctors throughout their district in a vain quest for reassurance. Telling them all is well allays their worries but briefly, and reassurance-seeking soon starts again. Their distress and handicap can be so dramatic that it is hard to believe case histories like the following, yet they are about real people.

Extreme examples of illness phobia

Moira had gone to 43 hospital casualty departments over three years and had every part of her body X-rayed. At various times she was frightened she would die of stomach cancer, a brain tumour, thrombosis. Examinations never revealed any abnormality and Moira emerged each time from the hospital 'rejuvenated – it's like having been condemned to death and given a reprieve'.[10] But within a week she would seek out a new hospital 'where they won't know I'm a fraud. I'm terrified of the idea of dying, it's the end, the complete end, and the thought of rotting in the ground obsesses me – I can see the worms and maggots'.[11] Moira was petrified of sex with her husband, imagining she would rupture and burst a blood vessel, and afterwards would get up at two in the morning and stand for hours outside the hospital so she knew she was in reach of help.

Worries about illness can cause grave handicaps. Over 28 years Ian had consulted doctors hundreds of times and asked innumerable factory inspectors and water supply officials about the purity of substances he touched. He had been off work almost half his working life. Ian made his wife phone countless doctors and other authorities to get reassurance. As he had had over 100 X-rays, Ian developed fresh worries about their having caused leukaemia. His illness fears and urges for reassurance were associated with compulsive rituals.[12] This association is not rare, as will be seen in Chapter 9.

Treatment of illness phobias and worries about one's body

Someone who fears illness is helped by steadily confronting the idea that he might have his dreaded disease – AIDS, cancer, heart disease, or whatever. This exposure is achieved in various ways. Someone who fears having a brain tumour may imagine that 'your doctor has just told you that you have a brain tumour and have six months to live and should start settling your affairs to provide for your family. You are shown an X-ray of your skull and the doctor points out the tumour. At first you cannot quite take this in but as you leave the consulting room and go outside you suddenly realise what he said.' The sufferer may write out scenes like this for an hour daily until they no longer evoke anxiety and simply bore him. He might speak descriptions of such scenes into a walkman, carry that audiotaped recording of his voice round with him all day, and play it for long periods every time he imagines he has a brain tumour, until hearing the descriptions no longer upsets him.

A woman with cancer phobia might ask for a cancer specimen in a sealed bottle to keep by her side so she can look at it every day until it terrifies her no longer. She might stick up articles about cancer and pictures of tumours on the walls of her bedroom and kitchen so that she gets used to them and stops running away from the mere idea of cancer.

What to do about constant requests for reassurance

Long-suffering relatives from whom phobics have constantly sought reassurance can help in the treatment. Sufferers asking for reassurance hope to hear that they are not ill or contaminated. Their anxiety then falls briefly, only to surge up again later. What they are avoiding is the thought we all have at times that we might be ill and die soon. Unlike most of us, however, they desperately try to avoid this idea instead of facing it realistically. Using the exposure therapy principle, reassurance must be foregone so the idea of illness is not switched off immediately; the sufferer has to learn to tolerate the idea just as the rest of us do. Their repeated requests for reassurance remind one of an alcoholic who wakes up with the shakes and finds that a nip of alcohol settles him for a while, but soon the shakes start up again, more alcohol is needed, and so the vicious circle continues. Only stopping all alcohol helps the addiction in the long run. Similarly, addiction to reassurance is broken by consistently withholding reassurance.

If an illness phobic is in the habit of asking his wife 'Do I look pale, do I look ill?', she needs to learn to reply, not 'No, you seem okay to me' but instead, in a monotonous voice, 'therapy says no answer'. A therapist may several times rehearse the scene in which the phobic asks his wife for reassurance and she replies monotonously each time 'therapy says no answer'. This is repeated time and again until the couple does it just right, the wife's voice remaining dully monotonous even when her husband demands reassurance increasingly angrily. The two may have to rehearse the scene up to ten times in front of a therapist before they get it pat. At home, if the wife forgets to answer requests for reassurance monotonously with 'therapy says no answer', then they may phone the therapist on two phones on the same line to role play the scene properly again.

It is easier to advise relatives to withhold reassurance than for them actually to do this after years of being trained to answer 'you're all right, love'. Nevertheless, repeated rehearsal soon helps them to change course. The patient's doctor, too, may need to be taught to withhold further examinations and tests if he's satisfied these are unnecessary. Reassurance is withheld because an illness phobic has to learn to tolerate the discomfort of being uncertain whether he's ill or not.

When we sometimes wonder whether a spot on our hand is becoming cancerous, a single medical examination and test passing it as benign allows most of us to dismiss this idea. An illness phobic needs to develop the same facility, but will not until reassurance stops. Once reassurance is withheld hypochondriacal worries may actually increase for a few hours or days, but if the spouse consistently stops reassuring without giving in, then the worries gradually die down over a few weeks. Couples may need to contact the therapist for support in going against instinct in withholding comfort from loved ones, even if it is to help them overcome an illness phobia permanently.

Treatment of a woman who thought she smelled

Worries about our body can lead us to avoid places which trigger our fears. Treatment involves persuading phobics to stay in contact with their frightening setting that they usually avoid until they feel comfortable in it. Let us look at Jill, aged 35, who for 16 years had worried intensely that her sweat smelled terrible.[13] It began just before her marriage when sharing a bed with a close friend who said someone at work smelled bad, a remark Jill felt was directed at her. For five years, for fear people might comment on her smell, she would avoid going anywhere except when accompanied by her husband or mother, and shunned the cinema, dances, shops, cafés, and private houses. She sat away from her in-laws when visiting them. Her husband was not allowed to invite friends home nor to visit them. Jill constantly sought reassurance from him about her odour, but his replies never satisfied her. TV commercials about deodorants scared her. She would not pass people in the street. Standing in a bus queue made her sweat and feel too anxious to wait. She refused to attend the local church because it was so small and its members lived nearby. Her family had to travel an extra eight miles to a church where they sat or stood away from the other congregants, who were strangers. Her husband bought her clothes for her because she wouldn't try them on in front of shop assistants. She had not spoken to neighbours for three years because she thought she had overheard them speak about her to friends. She locked her front door all day, not answering strangers who rang the bell. On rising each morning, Jill washed completely from head to toe. She used vast quantities of deodorant and bathed and changed her clothes before going out – up to four times daily.

At assessment Jill was timid, blushed often, and averted her gaze. Treatment was designed to help her go back repeatedly for long periods into places where she felt she smelled until her worry died down. She agreed to start walking past three neighbours in their garden alone, and to sit in the living room with friends talking about smells. Before session 1 she was asked to take her son to the bus stop each morning and shop with her mother on two days. Her husband was asked to praise her when she had done these things but not to reassure her when she mentioned smell. By the start of session 1 Jill and her husband said she had done most of these tasks. She had asked him often for reassurance and he had found it difficult not to give in. In session 1 Jill and her therapist travelled by bus to a shopping area and remained there for two hours; Jill entered three shops and stayed in each one until her anxiety decreased. She watched her therapist go into the most crowded areas and stand in the longest queues, then did this herself with her therapist nearby. Over the next two hours her discomfort dropped greatly, though she sweated profusely, blushed, and often asked whether she smelled. She needed much persuasion to remain in crowds, but returning to the hospital on a crowded bus caused little anxiety and she no longer asked about her own smell.

She agreed before session 2 to shop alone at local shops, take her son for an hour's walk daily, and go to the cinema with her husband, and to come to all subsequent sessions without having used a deodorant or having washed. By session 2 a week later she had done those tasks and was pleased with her progress. Session 2 was staged in large stores in central London, again with the therapist. Slowly Jill's discomfort diminished, and she had hardly any anxiety by the time she was travelling on a crowded train or bus.

The next three sessions were at two-weekly intervals. Jill again went into crowded places in central London and her therapist gradually withdrew to leave her alone. By session 5 Jill was travelling by bus alone, remaining in large stores up to one and a half hours with only slight tension, eating in crowded restaurants, and standing in long queues. She made the two-hour journey from home to London by public transport. At home she did more shopping alone and waved to neighbours and visited friends, but still worried about shopping in her local town and travelling by bus. Her husband said she asked less often about her smell, bathed less, and used less deodorant. She did bathe before going to the hospital, and stopped for a meal at a restaurant on the way home.

At session 6 Jill went on a shopping spree in London with her husband. She tried on clothes in two stores (the first time for four years) and took her husband into many crowded shops – he had difficulty in getting her to leave.

She was asked to shop more around their own area, first accompanied and then alone.

From now onward the therapist simply monitored progress by weekly phone calls. Jill visited friends after a long shopping trip, changed her clothes only when going out in the evening, and felt more relaxed. Over the next year she improved further. She resumed going to the nearby church with ease, visited neighbours and attended a social gathering at her son's school for the first time. She and her family went on their first holiday together for years. Friends came to stay at her home for holidays and weekends, and she travelled freely despite slight unease. She looked the therapist in the eye at a year's follow-up , smiled frequently, spoke freely about her past difficulties, and was much more assertive and cheerful.

Post-traumatic stress disorder (PTSD)

Disasters are part of the human condition. The media thrive on daily reports of fires, floods, earthquakes, war, ethnic 'cleansing', concentration camps, torture, rape, hostage taking, shootings, muggings and accidents. The normal reaction to extreme stress is to feel numb, apathetic and depressed, followed later by aggressive irritability and often grief from the losses common with such events (see pp. 29–39 in Chapter 3). A more intense reaction is called post-traumatic stress disorder (PTSD). Sufferers feel tense, euphoric, startle easily, cannot sleep, have nightmares and flashbacks about the trauma, and avoid places, people, thoughts and other reminders of what happened. Depression is frequent.

Occasionally there is a delay of up to several years between the time of the trauma and the start of the distress. The more intense and prolonged the trauma the worse the PTSD. People who have had previous anxiety or depressive problems are likely to suffer more. Torture survivors who are committed to a political or other cause are less likely to break down under torture[14] and a torturer from the Spanish Inquisition observed that certain individuals seemed able to endure ghastly ordeals without complaint (see p. 151). Many people who experience repeated bombing over months and years come to regard this as part of normal living. The proportion of survivors continuing to suffer from PTSD diminishes rapidly in the first few months after a disaster and more slowly thereafter. In some PTSD continues for decades and may never clear up if the trauma was particularly horrible and drawn out.

A natural disaster may have surprisingly little effect on pre-existing anxiety symptoms. In the two weeks after a severe earthquake that was followed by hundreds of aftershocks, panic and obsessive-compulsive disorder patients said the earthquake evoked much less fear than did the usual triggers for their problem.[15]

Fortunately PTSD sufferers can be treated very successfully by exposure or cognitive therapy, as can be seen from the cases below and that on p. 156 in Chapter 11.

Nell's exposure therapy for PTSD

Nell worked for a security firm collecting money from pubs and depositing it in a bank. A year before, as she parked her car next to the bank a man came to her window, said he had a gun, got in the car, and told her to do as he said. Nell drove him for 15 minutes to park in a housing estate. He asked her for the key to the safe in the boot of her car. She fumbled in finding it and he shouted at her. She thought she was about to be killed, and found her keys. He emptied the safe, handcuffed her to the steering wheel, and said someone was watching her and would harm her if she shouted for help. For 20 minutes she sat in the car too terrified to ask help from passers-by. On seeing a couple leave a flat opposite she called to them to bring the police. They refused help until she became extremely distressed. Finally they called the police who came and called the fire brigade to free her. Nell was taken to hospital with shock and discharged a few hours later.

At assessment she had frequent intrusive, distressing and unwanted thoughts and images of the trauma, and was sleeping up to 14 hours daily to escape them. Her irritability and quarrelsomeness upset her partner and young children. Nell was depressed, tearful, could not concentrate, and no longer enjoyed former hobbies. She avoided walking, shopping, crowds, or going anywhere alone. At work she was hyper-vigilant; if a car was behind her for a few minutes she became anxious and wrote down its number. She avoided the bank where she had been abducted. The trauma also revived Nell's past bad memories. At the age of eight she had been abducted by a neighbour and held in his flat for eight hours in an estate like the one where she was later held near the bank. Nell was terrified by the experience and by later interviews with the police. Between the ages of 10 and 14, an uncle came once a week to her room at night to fondle her breast and genitals and rub his penis on her buttocks until he ejaculated. Her childhood had been unhappy due to this and to abuse by her alcoholic mother. Nell had never known her father.

With her agreement, Nell's exposure therapy sessions were audiotaped. In Session 1 she related in detail how she'd been abducted at the bank, and became very distressed. In the next week she listened to the audiotape of Session 1 for an hour a day, and her anxiety fell from 6 (8 = maximum, 0 = none) to 2. In Session 2 she said a critical point during her abduction had been when she thought she would be killed, relived this scene in detail by 'rewind and hold', and cried throughout. In week 2 she listened to the audiotape of Session 2 daily and anxiety fell to 1. In Session 3 she again relived the entire abduction and critical points and rated distress at 0. Listening daily to the audiotape of Session 3 caused no distress. In Session 4 she relived her childhood abduction; this evoked peak distress which then fell from 8 to 4. In week 4 a neighbour actually hit her during a row; she was treated in a casualty department for cuts and bruises and was pressing charges, even though this made another attack possible. She was too distressed to do exposure therapy so she was supported for 30 minutes. During week 5 she listened daily to the audiotape of Session 4 about her childhood abduction and anxiety fell to 2. By Session 5 she was less distressed and exposure was restarted, now to imagining scenes of her sexual abuse; distress fell from 6 to 2.

By the start of Session 6 Nell's mood and PTSD had improved; she had no intrusive images about the bank or childhood traumas, and was sleeping normally, but phobias remained. Live exposure now began. She devised a hierarchy of feared situations. With her therapist she went into small crowds, habituating to them. Week 6 homework was going into crowds for an hour a day, first with her partner, then alone. She remained fearful of going into a crowd alone, so Session 7 focused on this. In Sessions 8 and 9 she deposited money in the bank near where she had been abducted. In week 9 she did this with little discomfort, so in Session 10 her therapist accompanied her shopping in central London. For homework in week 10 she did such shopping alone, with minimal anxiety. After ten treatment sessions Nell was almost symptom free and avoided nothing, although she was a bit wary at work. At the 6 and 12-month follow-ups she was 98% improved and had begun a college course.

An alternative successful way of treating PTSD is by cognitive therapy, as Jeff's story below shows, and as does Tim's on p. 156 in Chapter 11.

Jeff's cognitive therapy for PTSD[16]

Jeff was at home with his girlfriend when two men broke in and hit him repeatedly across the head and arms with a hammer and tied him up. They robbed the house while continuing to assault him, fractured his ribs, arms and wrists, and badly bruised and cut his head. Thereafter he had frequent intrusive and distressing memories of the assault, and reminders (e.g. seeing groups of men in the street or violent films on TV) caused intense distress, palpitations, trembling and sweating. Jeff tried to avoid thinking about the assault by keeping himself busy decorating and making his home secure. He was fearful of being at home alone, over-alert when outside, and stopped seeing friends and going on public transport. He felt detached but irritable and angry, sad, tearful and hopeless, and slept badly. His concentration and memory were poor.

During cognitive therapy Jeff kept a Daily Thought Record to spot negative thoughts which came automatically when he was anxious. One was: 'When there's an unfamiliar knock at the door, I'm going to be attacked again.' He *challenged* this negative thought by calculating the likelihood of that happening. Jeff calculated that he had answered about 14,500 knocks at the door and only been attacked once, giving a 1 in 14,500 (less than 0.007%) chance of being assaulted by an unfamiliar caller. To challenge his negative thought, Jeff generated the rational thought 'I've had over 14,500 unfamiliar knocks on my door and it's never been an assailant.' He also *generated evidence against the thought* such as 'I've moved and the attackers don't know where I live.' Jeff *spotted the thinking error* he made in this situation as 'over-generalisation' – thinking that one bad experience means one will always have another bad experience in similar circumstances. Jeff produced such cognitive challenges whenever the negative thought recurred and his belief in it dropped from 80% to 10%.

From his Daily Thought Record Jeff spotted another negative thought: 'If I lose my temper, I'll hit someone.' He could find no evidence to support this thought but produced evidence against it such as 'I haven't been in a fight for ages.' When someone tried to pick a fight with him he kept calm. He spotted thinking errors he had made as 'jumping to conclusions' and 'catastrophising' and generated the rational response 'I can control myself, even when someone picks a fight.'

Near the end of treatment Jeff regretted his loss of earnings and of his girl friend since the assault. Negative thoughts included 'It's my fault I'm in such a mess.' He challenged this thought by generating evidence for and against it and looking for thinking errors in it, and reattributed his loss of earnings to his PTSD. He began to use spontaneous cognitive challenges to other negative automatic thoughts that occurred when he was in a bus and elsewhere and used these to enable him to tolerate anxiety-evoking situations.

By a week after treatment ended Jeff had far fewer intrusive thoughts, and those were less distressing. He slept better, was less irritable, not hopeless or depressed, no longer feared losing control, and began work again. Soon afterwards at a party someone tried to strangle him. Intrusive thoughts and irritability returned. However, he continued working and when seen two and five months later he was feeling better again.

summary

Unlike agoraphobia, social phobias occur equally in men and women. They tend to start gradually in young adult life. The phobia may be of very specific social situations, for example, of eating in formal restaurants, or at the other extreme may be diffused with excruciating shyness everywhere leading to severe isolation and loneliness. Worry about one's appearance is common and many sufferers ask for cosmetic surgery.

Social anxieties can be treated effectively by prolonged exposure to whichever social events trigger the fear. Where social anxiety reflects ignorance about how to behave with people, we talk of a social skills deficit. In such instances treatment also includes social skills training to show sufferers how to react in different social contexts. The patients then rehearse such behaviour in role play in individual or group sessions.

Phobia of illness may be no more than mild hypochondriasis or a crippling terror with an addiction to countless fruitless quests for reassurance and investigations by one doctor after another. Illness fears are fostered in families which are excessively health-conscious, and public fashion affects the choice of illnesses that are feared. Some fears reflect lack of knowledge. Triggers for the fears can be external, such as an article about AIDS in a magazine, or internal, such as a pain or lump in the body.

Illness phobics may devote their lives to seeking reassurance. As with other addictions, only brief respite comes from yielding to the addiction, which in this case is to reassurance and investigation. The tension soon builds up again. As part of the treatment, relatives need to help as co-therapists by withholding reassurance from the sufferer. This can take time to learn, since it goes against one's natural inclination. The sufferer needs to learn to live like others with some uncertainty about his health and to develop a tolerance of talk about illness.

Post-traumatic stress disorder (PTSD) is common after natural or personal disasters. Sufferers have many anxiety symptoms and intrusive thoughts and tend to avoid reminders of the traumatic situation. PTSD tends to clear up within a few months, but if it persists sufferers can improve greatly with exposure to reminders of the trauma and/or with cognitive therapy.

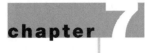

phobic disorders iii:
specific phobias

Animal phobias

Most children go through a phase of wariness of animals between ages two and four. It usually starts without them ever having come to harm or seeing anyone hurt by any creature. Human young seem to be programmed to develop this fear for a while even with little or no bad experiences with animals. The fear soon fades in the great majority and by the time they reach puberty few children are scared of animals any longer. In a tiny number the dread continues into adult life, this minority usually being women. It is most unusual for a fear of animals to start after puberty. Adults who complain of an animal phobia tend to say that it began before age six or 'as long ago as I can remember'. A few remember a brief period when they did not fear any animal before their phobia developed at about age three.

Mild aversion to spiders, mice, dogs, and other creatures is widespread in our culture, but is rarely strong enough to be called a phobia. Psychiatrists see far fewer adults with an animal phobia than with agoraphobia or social anxieties. Animal phobias appear much more in young children than in adults, most of which subside after puberty; those seen in adult life are usually the persisting remnant of childhood fears.

In adults, an animal phobia is distinct from agoraphobia. The disturbance caused is more localised and associated with few other problems. Once begun, animal phobias run a rather steady course, unlike agoraphobia, which can fluctuate a great deal.

Reasons adults ask for help

By the time adults seek help for an animal phobia they have usually had it for decades. Some change in their lives has usually prompted them to ask for help at that time. City dwellers can generally avoid most animals and insects without affecting their lives much, but may become crippled if they move to a place where the creature they fear abounds. Meri managed well in a town flat but became anxious and sought treatment after she moved to a country cottage infested with spiders; she felt better again after moving to a house free of them. Georgia began treatment when she could not take up a residential scholarship in an old spider-infested hostel, so jeopardising her career. Rose moved from a town with few pigeons to a different city where they thrived, and asked for help when she started to avoid walking to work through streets containing pigeons.

Other people seek treatment on hearing for the first time that help is possible. Yet others come for fear of passing their phobia on to their young children. Some see a doctor first for other problems such as depression, and the medic then spots their animal phobia and suggests that it be treated. During depression, pre-existing problems are often magnified and cause the sufferer to seek help with a minor disability which she could tolerate easily before. A few people ask for help with a specific phobia in the silent hope that other problems they find hard to talk about will also be dealt with. People who lead lonely lives seem more likely to present with a minor problem, social contact with health professionals providing some satisfaction in an empty life. Given the same disability, lonely people seek medical aid more than do others.

Origin of animal fears

In adults the origin of an animal phobia is usually lost in the mist of early childhood memories, but a few are dated to specific incidents.[1] A cat phobia began when a little girl watched her father drown some kittens. Occasional dog phobias begin after dog bites. A bird phobia started after a child posed for a photograph in London's Trafalgar Square which teems with thousands of pigeons. She took fright as a bird alighted on her shoulder but didn't move while she was posing – the photograph recorded the start of her phobia. A feather phobia began when an infant strapped in a pram took fright as a strange woman with a large feather in her hat bent down to look at the baby.

Sigmund Freud described the onset of animal fears in children.

> The child suddenly begins to fear a certain animal species and to protect itself against seeing or touching any individual of this species. . . . The phobia is as a rule expressed towards animals for which the child has until then shown the liveliest interest, and has nothing to do with the individual animal. In cities, the choice of animals which can become the object of phobia is not great. They are horses, dogs, cats, more seldom birds, and strikingly often very small animals like bugs and butterflies. Sometimes animals which are known to the child only from picture books

and fairy stories become objects of the senseless and inordinate anxiety which is manifest in these phobias. It is seldom possible to learn the manner in which such an unusual choice of anxiety has been brought about.[2] 』』

It is surprising how seldom animal fears appear in relatives, as one might expect such fears to be modelled on the behaviour of close family. Occasionally one does see the same fear in several family members, passing on from one generation to the next, but these are exceptional.

In most children, animal fears disappear as mysteriously as they began, or after experience of situations in which the youngster got used to the animal. Occasionally the fear can be imprinted to become a phobia if others tease the child repeatedly with the feared creature or if overprotective parents help the child always to avoid it. We usually do not know why a small fraction of animal fears continue beyond puberty. Adults seeking help generally complain of a longstanding phobia of some animal or insect and tend to be free of other problems.

What are animal phobias like?

Practically any living thing may be the focus of a phobia. Pigeons are often feared, while smaller birds like canaries are tolerated more easily. 'I would just be terrified. I put my hand up to my head – I'm frightened pigeons will fly at my face, I suppose, and it's their wings, the flapping of their wings.'[3] Phobias of spiders, bees, and wasps are quite common. 'Spiders terrify me – it's the way it moves – stealthily. They're black and hairy and evil.'[4] Some people ask for treatment of fears of dogs, cats, worms, frogs, or flying insects. The phobia may be a nuisance rather than a big problem, as in a country woman who wouldn't go near ponds where frogs were plentiful, nor look at pictures of frogs in books. Intense phobias of plentiful animals can cause marked handicap. Sarah who feared birds would not go to work through London streets that abounded in pigeons, gave up her job and remained indoors all day, venturing out only at night when pigeons no longer flew about.

Although animal phobias are specific in adults, they can be far from trivial. Striking distress results from contact with the feared creature. Sufferers experience panic, sweat, and tremble in terror. Laura screamed on finding a spider at home, ran to find a neighbour to remove it, shook fearfully, and kept a neighbour at her side for two hours before she would remain alone at home again. Ann found herself on top of her refrigerator in the kitchen with no memory of how she got there; terror at the sight of a spider had made her lose her memory for a moment.[5] Sandra with a spider phobia had jumped out of a boat, even though she couldn't swim, to avoid a spider she found in it. Once she jumped out of a speeding car and on another occasion off a galloping horse to escape spiders she had found near her.[6] 'I'm scared to go to any parks or even into my garden', said Barbara, aged 42, who feared pigeons. 'I've missed many appointments because if there are any birds near the bus stop I just have to walk away. Going shopping is torture for me – I have to cross and recross the road to avoid birds. I have nightmares about them.'[7] A middle-aged woman with the same phobia never had any windows open in her home lest a bird should fly in. The sight of one 'reduces me to a jelly. If ever a bird flew at me I'd have a heart attack from fright.'[8] She sometimes arrived late for work because it took so long to pick her way among the birds near London's Waterloo Station.

Spider phobia sufferers dread the approach of summer and autumn when spiders abound and feel really happy only in winter when arachnids are rare. Some sufferers are plagued by recurrent nightmares of the feared animal. They dream they are surrounded by large spiders or swooping birds from which they cannot escape. After improving with treatment the nightmares disappear.

Phobics search for the feared object wherever they go. The slightest evidence of its presence will disturb them where most people never notice it. A sign of improvement during treatment is diminished awareness of these creatures in the surroundings. A dog-phobic woman had in her mind a 'dog map' of her neighbourhood concerning streets she could safely go in and streets she should avoid; once she recovered with treatment she no longer thought about dogs and went freely everywhere.

Treatment of a student with a pigeon phobia

Phobias of animals are usually easy to treat, needing only a few hours of contact with the animal concerned for the fear to subside. If the contact is continuous for several hours, one or two afternoons may be all that is needed.

Jane, aged 20, had feared pigeons for over seven years. She had nightmares of pigeons attacking her and checked doors and windows at night so that they could not get in. She would not sit in her room with the window open, and her fear was beginning to affect her studies. In the street she often took a detour to avoid walking past pigeons. She disliked watching them on television or looking at photographs of birds.[9]

In treatment Jane was encouraged to get used to pigeons by gradually going closer to them, despite the terror this inspired in her. Before this, she was asked to hang pictures of birds around her room and to buy and handle stuffed and dummy birds. In session 1 she stroked and handled a pigeon held by the therapist and then managed to be alone in a room with a caged pigeon a few feet away. At session 2 she sat in a park with the therapist, fed pigeons about three feet away, and sat outside the park café while pigeons flew around and fed near her table. In session 3 she walked through the park accompanied by the therapist, looked at the pigeons, and sat three feet away from them feeding. Between sessions she became able to walk past many birds in the street and look at them without shuddering. Jane began to keep pictures and models of birds and handle these without fear. During the day she began to keep the window of her room open while she went away. In further sessions she learned to tolerate pigeons flying about her. She was discharged much improved after nine sessions. At a year's follow-up she was well with no fear of pigeons, slept with the window open during summer, and had been to parks and to London's Trafalgar Square which swarms with pigeons.

Early in treatment there had been an unexpected complication. In the park in the presence of the therapist, whenever a pigeon came near Jane she screamed loudly, disturbing other people nearby so much that the park attendant approached the therapist and threatened to 'make him unconscious' if he did not stop frightening the young lady! Further treatment sessions were held at 7 am to avoid the park keeper and the general public.

Other specific phobias

Almost anything can trigger a phobia in some people, and there is really an endless list of phobias one could describe. Starting with some rarities: a young woman was phobic of round arches and tunnels, not square ones.[10] She shut her eyes in round tunnels, which became a problem when she learned to drive. During driving lessons she closed her eyes when approaching a tunnel and went rigid if her eyes were open. She had nightmares about tunnels. Other rare phobias for which treatment was sought included wearing clean white shirts, hearing running water, being grasped from behind, reading books or letters, dolls, firemen's helmets, or even leaves: 'I'm terrified of leaves, especially rhubarb. I can't go near them. If I come close my heart thumps and I go all shaky. I've always been frightened and have memories of this since I was two. My husband can't stand it and I'm too embarrassed to go to a doctor for help.'[11]

Much more common than such curiosities are phobias of *natural phenomena* such as heights, darkness, and storms.

Heights

A mild fear of heights is natural enough, but severe incapacitating height phobia is not. Severe height phobics may avoid going down a flight of stairs if they can see the open stairwell, yet manage if it is closed. They may shun looking out of a high window which stretches from floor to ceiling but not if the window is obscured to waist level or higher. They have difficulty crossing bridges on foot because the edge is near, but may be able to do so in a car.

Anxiety about heights can also be evoked by looking at high structures. 'Looking up at tall buildings, you feel as though they're leaning toward you – you get a dizzy feeling, a panicky feeling – always a feeling that you want to jump off, and feeling that the ground is coming up to you.'[12]

Fear of falling: space phobias

Occasionally fear of heights is linked to an acute fear of falling if there's no support within a few feet and the phobic is afraid of being drawn over the edge of a height. This is like the feeling many individuals get when standing on the edge of a railway platform that they will be drawn down on to the rails under a train.

A fear of falling can become extreme. At age 49, Jenny was running for a bus when she suddenly felt dizzy and had to hold on to a lamp post for support.[13] This recurred, and gradually she became unable to walk anywhere without holding on to a wall or furniture to support her – she was 'furniture bound'. Jenny could stand only if she could see a support a foot or less away from her. If this support was removed, she would become terrified and cry, although actual physical contact with the supporting object was not essential. She was perfectly calm when sitting or lying down. Jenny had no trouble with her inner ears of the kind which sometimes produces an abnormal sensation of falling.

People with this falling fear seem to have disturbed perception of space. Celia felt she might fall down if unsupported and had to clutch on to something for support. For six months she had to crawl on her knees around the house. Despite this she could dance vigorously unsupported on a crowded dance floor, but had to be supported if the crowd went away. She felt no discomfort when swung around while dancing. Celia had difficulty getting on a bus because she would not let go of the railing, but could board it if accompanied. She needed only light support when holding someone's arm but felt momentarily that she might fall and then clutched tightly. Twice during 18 months she had fallen forward and hurt herself. Rosemary had a similar fear if, when driving, she encountered a wide open road or hollows; on seeing either of these she had to hand over the driving to her husband; she felt similarly anxious on seeing very steep slopes or stairs, heights or bridges.

Real physical handicap can be greatly aggravated by fears of falling. A vigorous elderly lady became quite incapacitated shortly after recovering from a stroke which had left one leg weak. She had progressed very well and was quite independent until one day she tripped and fell over the edge of a carpet; after that she became terrified of venturing anywhere alone and had to have someone holding her wherever she went. Although she had good power in her legs, the collapse in her confidence prevented her from using them.

Darkness, thunderstorms, and lightning

Phobias of darkness are perfectly normal in childhood but rarely handicap adults. Some people have a phobia of wind or storms rather than thunder. Others specifically fear thunderstorms and lightning. A 20-year-old female bus conductor said 'I'd give anything to be helped with my phobia because I'm afraid of losing my job if there's a storm while I'm on the bus. I scream and feel sick and have an upset stomach afterwards. People think I'm crazy. I can't stop by myself when a storm is on, but I'm just as frightened and hysterical when I'm with people [during a storm].'[14]

People with thunderstorm phobia dread the approach of summer and long for winter when thunderstorms are rare. They listen to weather forecasts frequently or besiege meteorological services with a constant stream of anxious inquiries about the weather. If thunder is forecast that day their terror may stop them venturing out of doors and make them wear rubber boots indoors, and switch off the lights and television to reduce the 'risk' of attracting lightning. In a storm they may keep away from windows and hide in a cupboard or under the sheets or the bed.

Noise

Dislike of intense noise is common enough but rarely goes on to become a phobia. Some people, however, are so terrified of balloons popping that they avoid parties where this may happen. Abi complained of a terrible phobia about balloons being blown up and felt it was silly at her age of 42. Candida had an unusual phobia of whistling at a particular frequency. She could hold a bird without fear and easily tolerated the sound of a cuckoo or parrot, but a high soprano voice made her tense and a human whistle sent her into a frenzy of terror. She was greatly incapacitated in her film-making work, because if anyone whistled there this caused such fear and anger that she could not face going back to the same studio for the next few days.

Travel

Phobias sometimes develop of driving a car, especially after a car accident, or of other forms of travel. The most common fear of travel is usually part of the agoraphobic syndrome. Many people who lead otherwise unrestricted lives are afraid of travelling by aeroplane or underground train.

Enclosed spaces (claustrophobia)

The same applies to *claustrophobia* which is common with agoraphobia but also often occurs as an isolated phobia. Claustrophobics fear being shut in enclosed spaces like tunnels or lifts. 'If the lift were to stop, I would just panic very rapidly. I would start banging the sides of the lift.' One such sufferer had worked as a roof expert and had to complete a job on the roof of London's 600-foot-high Post Office Tower. He walked to the top twice a day rather than go up in the lift.

Flying

Flying is important in modern living, but many travellers find it unnerving. Lots of people have to fly because of their jobs and a flying phobia can prevent promotion and limit travel to see family or friends or a holiday destination. One woman wrote: 'I'm planning to move to California at the beginning of the New Year, but as I suffer from claustrophobia, I can't trust myself to think I can stay on a plane for five hours without getting panicky . . . surprisingly enough, if I know there is a doctor around, I don't panic . . . I'm ashamed to ask for reservations on a flight when a doctor would be on the plane, but I'm sure I'd travel much better if I knew there was one around.'[15] Another woman said 'I've flown, but at great intervals, under great duress, and always suffer a thousand deaths.'[16] A man was afraid 'to be closed in, high and away from earth'.[17] The mood was expressed by a transatlantic passenger who, breathing a sigh of relief on landing in London, said, 'Well, we cheated death once more.'[18]

So common are flying fears that an organisation was formed in New York for air 'cowards' to help them learn to fly without fear. It chartered special aircraft to fly passengers under soothing conditions designed to help them overcome their worry. Some airlines have treatment programmes for flying phobics. Subjects first get used to being in an aeroplane simulator while pilots explain the meaning of different aeroplane noises and movements, and then go on special group flights. Flying phobics can also help themselves by first *imagining* themselves buying an aeroplane ticket, going to the airport, boarding a plane and flying, and when they are used to that, doing these things in real life.

Unexpected events can impede the smooth path to recovery. Rachel, a travel agent, got used to the idea of going on a plane by imagining it repeatedly in treatment. Finally she went to London airport and boarded a flight to Athens to begin her holiday. While Rachel was waiting in the plane ready for take-off, the pilot announced an hour's delay due to mechanical failure – not the most therapeutic of events, and Rachel felt all her worst fears had been confirmed. She ran out of the plane back into the terminal lounge. An air hostess eventually persuaded her back into the plane, Rachel flew off, and her fears improved. Many years ago, as part of her flying-phobia treatment programme, another lady boarded the famous flight from Tel Aviv to Paris that happened to be hijacked to Entebbe! Such events are fortunately rare.

What about pilots?

Even pilots can get phobias of flying, especially in wartime. The phobias of World War II aircrew made little practical sense in that they often developed for safe manoeuvres but not for dangerous ones. An outstanding fighter pilot took part in combat with delight yet was unwilling to fly over water. Several men refused to fly higher than 8,000 feet, although they risked with ease danger below that level. Some pilots feared parachuting so strongly that they rode severely damaged planes into a crash landing and were decorated for choosing the more hazardous course.[19] A navigator who was terrified of flying was shot down and soon afterward came upon a few dispirited infantrymen hemmed in by a large number of the enemy: his joy at being on the ground enabled him to lead the men out of their very dangerous position. Flying phobias increased a man's own danger, for they led to uncertainty and inefficiency in the air. Seized with a nameless fear before landing, a few men smashed their planes as a result; not a few bailed out unnecessarily or made serious navigational errors.

Swallowing, hypersensitive choking, food fads

A few people have a phobia of swallowing solid food which will force them to resort to a liquid diet. They feel that they have a lump in their throat and find it hard to swallow when they are intensely anxious. As Hilary, aged 49, said: 'Since I've been a child I've had this stupid phobia of swallowing. Whenever I drink or eat, the muscles of my throat go into spasm and I make this crowing noise, my eyes water, and I get a terrible panic.' This happened whether Hilary was eating alone or with other people, and so embarrassed her that she often would not eat out, which hampered her job in public relations. Hilary thought she had acquired the problem after watching her mother, whose stridulant noises while eating in front of other people caused embarrassing memories.[20]

A variant of swallowing fear is *hypersensitivity of the choke reflex*. We all choke when we stick a finger down the back of our throat. The stimuli that trigger hypersensitive choking can widen to include very minor pressure on the neck. Paul, aged 20, had had this trouble since the age of six. He stopped wearing high-necked sweaters or a tie, thus restricting his job opportunities. Sometimes he would choke while dictating letters on the phone, especially to strangers. When choking he could not open his mouth or speak.[21] Sucking sweets helped, but he had sucked so many that his teeth had rotted. Paul would not open his mouth for a dentist as this made him choke, so he was on the waiting list for dental treatment under an anaesthetic. He could not say 'aaahh' during a medical examination, would choke if he had injections in the upper arm but not elsewhere, and might suddenly clam up when ordering a meal or tickets in a cinema. He had dreams of being choked and could not stand being under the bedclothes.

When interviewed Paul seemed relaxed but took a sweet to suck before speaking. He could not stick his tongue out beyond his teeth nor open his mouth widely. He wore an open-necked shirt and when he tried to close his collar at my request, he had to stop speaking. If he or I touched his neck, his eyes watered and he choked intensely.

Food fads are frequent. Only rarely do they increase to amount to a *food phobia*. People become anxious or disgusted by special foods, especially meat. Something similar is produced by religious taboos about eating certain foods. Many Hindus are vegetarian; Muslims and Jews are forbidden to eat pork. If religious people eat their taboo food by mistake or coercion, they may feel sick or vomit for days, as Mahatma Gandhi, a vegetarian, described in his autobiography after eating meat.

Medical procedures, blood, injury

Many people are terrified of *dental treatment* or *injections*. Severe dental decay may appear due to their avoidance of dentists. Medical treatment, too, may be delayed for fear of seeing doctors. A young woman was so petrified of ambulances and hospitals that she stayed at home for nearly two years lest an ambulance should appear. Asked what would happen if she should need an ambulance herself, she answered 'without a doubt I'd rather die than go in one of those'.[22] Fears of needles and injections are not uncommon and can be so severe that sufferers refuse major surgery or life-saving injections.

A related frequent phobia concerns *blood* and *injury*. Although it is natural to feel faint on seeing blood or severe wounds, most people can get over this squeamishness. In a few, however, a blood phobia becomes so intense that women refuse to become pregnant because they cannot bear the blood associated with childbirth. One woman feared becoming pregnant because it usually involves medical examination, and this terrified her although she had normal sex with her husband.[23]

Fears of blood and injury have one interesting difference from other phobias. With most phobias our heart rate speeds up when we see what we fear and it is rare to actually faint as opposed to feel faint. However, people who dread blood and injury commonly keel over on seeing blood or a gruesome sight; this fainting results from a marked slowing rather than an increase of the heart rate. The reason for this is unclear – we might speculate that it is related to feigning death or playing possum seen in some species of animals.

Treatment of blood phobia

Mary, aged 29, had fainted since the age of four at the sight of blood or injury or even when hearing the subject discussed.[24] She was unable to fulfil her longstanding ambition to become a teacher lest she might faint in dealing with children's cuts, which would be part of such work. She avoided films and plays that might include bloody scenes. She became ashamed of this problem and was determined to overcome it after she fainted in a hospital emergency room with her son sitting on her lap while his scalded foot was being dressed.

Mary and her therapist agreed on four treatment targets: watch blood being taken from someone else and herself, learn to cope with her children receiving first aid, and get her varicose veins treated. Treatment was by exposure therapy. In the first few sessions she looked at scenes of blood and injury while lying down to prevent fainting by allowing the blood supply to continue to her brain even if her heart rate slowed down greatly. In Mary's first session she lay down and watched blood being taken from her therapist. She was delighted that for the first time she could remember she did not actually faint or feel faint on seeing blood. She then had blood taken from herself while lying down and again remained conscious, but felt very faint when she tried to stand afterward. She took home an ampoule of her blood to keep in her bedroom.

In session 2, because of the inconvenience of arranging to see many real situations involving injury, Mary instead imagined these and watched them on films. She described out loud scenes in which she had a car accident with severe injuries to her legs, and later that her fingertips were cut off in another accident. Then she watched films of operations, accidents, blood donors, blood transfusions, traffic accidents, and open-heart surgery; she fainted once while watching these films, but persisted in watching them to the point of boredom. Finally she visited a nearby hospital and had her blood taken there.

Between sessions, at home Mary dealt successfully with small emergencies concerning her children and had her varicose veins injected. At eight-month follow-up she remained free of her blood–injury phobia, enrolled in a first-aid class, began to attend a teacher-training college, and went freely to films and plays depicting blood and injury.

Urination and defecation

Some people avoid being far from public toilets for fear that they might wet or soil their pants. Despite this they might be unselfconscious about being in the nude or having sex. In some sufferers the problem is like a phobia even though they don't actually experience fear and just have the physical feelings and signs associated with fear. They might have an urge to urinate or defecate in social situations and so run to the lavatory dozens of times, or avoid social gatherings instead, or choose only those parties where they can reach a lavatory easily. Occasionally men may be unable to urinate in front of anyone else, and waste much time at work and other places waiting for the urinal room to empty.

Treatment of a phobia of urinating away from home

Joan asked for help at age 50 because for 30 years she had been unable to pass urine outside her own home. She therefore avoided going away to visit friends at weekends. Joan could retain her urine for up to 48 hours if necessary. Surprisingly she could defecate in a public toilet and have normal sexual relations.[25]

In treatment Joan had to get used to sitting on the seat of a public lavatory for long enough for tension to fall to the point where she could pass urine. She was asked to come to session 1 at 3 pm without having urinated that day and having drunk five cups of coffee beforehand. On arrival she was asked to sit in a nearby lavatory and remain there until she urinated, however little, and no matter how long it took. In sessions 1–3 her therapist waited far from the lavatory, in sessions 4–8 outside close by, in sessions 9–12 he spoke to somebody just outside, and in sessions 13–15 waited there silently with another person (this stressed Joan more than having the doctor wait and talk outside). The first time Joan took fully two hours to pass a few dribbles of urine. Within a few sessions she urinated in the outpatient lavatory within 10 minutes. By session 12 she passed fully two litres almost immediately on demand – her bladder had developed a tremendous storage capacity over the years.

Before treatment began, Joan had no desire to pass water outside her home even when her bladder was mightily distended. At treatment session 10 she rushed to the hospital half an hour early with an urge to urinate, voiding eight minutes after arrival. Several days later she voided successfully at a friend's, who said it was the first time in their 10-year acquaintance that she had asked to use the loo. She then told her story, this being her first confession to anyone other than a doctor, and felt great relief. She voided again without delay at the home of another friend, who also expressed surprise at her asking to use the toilet. She confided her story again, feeling pleased.

At one-year follow-up Joan continued to urinate in public lavatories without difficulty, though she still had not performed at the loo near her office at work, which had not been involved in treatment.

Asthma, sweating, nausea

Phobia-like avoidance can appear to be due to discomfort other than fear. Some asthma sufferers avoid attack-triggering circumstances such as a row with the boss or spouse. People who *really* sweat or blush excessively (not just fear that they might) may avoid certain social situations because of the embarrassment. Other persons avoid parties because heavy alcoholic drinking makes them feel sick.

Competitions, tests, gambling

Athletes may get wound up before an important race, and at work employees might be ratty with their juniors until they get the promotion they want. Life may be impossible in the family of a concert pianist the day before a major performance. Examination anxiety besets many students, some of whom fail to take exams because those feel such an ordeal. 'Test' anxiety is the bread-and-butter practice of student counsellors.

Compulsive gambling is another worry which has ruined the lives of many. As the losses grow the gambling becomes a persistent concern making it more likely the gambler will bet yet again to relieve tension in a vicious spiral. Gary aged 33 came for help because he had been betting almost daily for six years, had lost all his family's money, and was now in debt. Money shortages caused frequent quarrels with his wife. He never bet by phone, only in betting shops in cash, eventually with borrowed money. Over weekends Gary would not leave home for fear of betting more and his wife discovering him. He usually bet on horses, but had bet up to £500 on dogs. He was tense at work because of continual urges to bet and preoccupations about the possibility of winning notwithstanding his losses. On his way to hospital he stopped in a betting shop to place a further bet, eventually losing £700. This made him an hour late for interview, and when I saw him he was wringing his hands in agitation at his loss. Despite this, Gary had intense urges to go out and gamble again immediately to try to undo the damage.

Anger avoidance

Certain problems resemble phobias in being triggered by particular events that sufferers go to great lengths to avoid because they so dislike unpleasant feelings aroused, not of fear but rather other emotions such as anger. June, aged 25, wrote about her 'noise phobia' dating back to the age of nine when her father greatly upset her by the noise from his dentures while eating.

❝Over the years the aversion has got worse and has extended to the noise of breathing, snoring, sniffing etc, from almost anyone in my company. I really find these noises quite unbearable and have had to find more and more excuses for leaving the room. I can remember all through my teens eating on my own and sitting watching television with my fingers in my ears to blot out the noise of my brother chewing his fingernails. My husband . . . urged me many times to seek help, but I found it too embarrassing and I didn't really see what could be done to alleviate it. Towards the end of our marriage I would be constantly nagging my husband to breathe through his mouth, make less noise eating, stop snoring etc, and although I don't pretend it was this that broke our marriage up, I'm quite sure it contributed very much to the decline of our relationship. At present I'm constantly having to find excuses for not eating with the family with whom I live and usually have to go to bed early to escape the noise of the light snorer in the house who dozes off in the evening.[26]❞

She had married at 17; when her husband left her she took an overdose. At interview June was lonely and tearful.

Treatment of anger phobia

Anger phobia can be relieved by exposure therapy like that for typical phobias where the emotion experienced is anxiety. This helped Peggy, aged 27, who felt revolted by pregnant women and infants.[27] Her baby had died when she was four months pregnant and she carried the dead foetus for two months before aborting, during which period she visited her obstetrician's office weekly where she saw pregnant women who, ignorant of her problem, asked Peggy about her own pregnancy. Her revulsion for pregnant women developed over this time. After finally aborting she became mildly depressed, was hostile and abusive to pregnant friends, refused to attend socials for fear of losing her temper with pregnant women, and tore up invitations to baby 'showers'. This curtailed her social life and she avoided baby shops. Peggy had marital counselling with her husband. This improved her attitude towards him but not her revulsion to pregnancy.

During two 90-minute treatment sessions Peggy imagined intense discussions with known and unknown pregnant women and infants, and learned to accept resultant feelings. By session 3 she could no longer feel any anger. Improvement continued during two months follow-up, by which time with her husband she had resumed attending social activities at which pregnant women were present and could approach them again.

A slightly different approach helped Susan's unmanageable temper outbursts with her family. During nine treatment sessions she was asked to imagine anger-inducing scenes; the therapist would then suggest ludicrous elaborations of the scenes, which made Susan laugh, and she improved.

summary

Fears of animals are normal in young children and rarely start after puberty. Adults with an animal phobia usually say it began before the age of seven. Sufferers are usually women. Their phobias tend to involve just one or two animal species. They usually seek help when a life change leads to handicap from the phobia, or when treatment becomes available for the first time. Two or more sessions of prolonged exposure to the real animal can lastingly abolish phobias which have lasted for decades.

Other specific phobias are of heights, darkness, noise, storms, lightning or being in enclosed spaces (claustrophobia). Claustrophobia often coexists with agoraphobia. Fears of flying are common and appear even in experienced passengers and aircrew. A few people fear swallowing solid food. Blood, injections and other medical procedures terrify many persons. Unlike those who fear other situations, blood phobics frequently faint on seeing blood – their heart rates usually slow down rather than rise in the phobic situation. Exposure therapy aims at allowing blood phobics to get used to the sight of blood and injury without their heart rate slowing so that fainting no longer occurs.

Some sufferers have repetitive difficulties resembling phobias in that they avoid identifiable triggers which arouse unpleasant feelings such as anger. These problems can be overcome like phobias; the sufferer learns to control his feelings while being brought steadily closer to the source of his discomfort.

So far we have dealt mainly with phobias in adults. Let us look now at phobias in children.

phobias in children

Fears are more common in children than in adults, and often start and then die down for no obvious reason. Like most of their feelings, children's fears are generally more fluctuating and intense. This intensity can make children's normal fears difficult to separate from abnormal phobias.

Fear is an inborn response to certain things that becomes differentiated from other feelings in the first year of life. The startle reaction of newborn infants precedes later normal fear. Any intense, sudden, or unexpected stimulus causes infants to throw up both hands and feet and perhaps cry. After about the age of six months, fear becomes recognisably different from startle and appears in response to strangers. Fear of animals begins a bit later.

Children's fears change as they grow. Between the ages of two and four, fear of animals is the most frequent, and thereafter children are more likely to fear the dark or imaginary creatures. Fear of animals diminish rapidly in boys and girls from ages nine to eleven, and after puberty phobias of animals are uncommon.

Between age six and ten most children have normal little rituals that are harmless and do not develop into obsessive-compulsive disorder. These rather resemble the counting and rhyming games and songs that children play endlessly all over the world, for example, 'One, two, buckle my shoe; three, four, knock at the door; five, six, pick up sticks . . .' The rituals may involve touching every pale in a fence passed on the way to school, or avoidance of stepping on the lines formed by the edges of pavement stones; the children often feel that the ritual averts some awful danger. This superstition was charmingly caught in A. A. Milne's poem 'Lines and Squares':

Whenever I walk in a London street,
I'm ever so careful to watch my feet;
And I keep in the squares,
And the masses of bears,

Who wait at the corners all ready to eat,
The sillies who tread on the lines of the street,
Go back to their lairs,
And I say to them, 'Bears,
Just look how I'm walking in all the squares!';
And the little bears growl to each other, 'He's mine,
As soon as he's silly and steps on a line.';
And some of the bigger bears try to pretend
That they came round the corner to look for a friend;
And they try to pretend that nobody cares
Whether you walk on the lines or squares.
But only the sillies believe their talk;
It's ever so 'portant how you walk.
And it's ever so jolly to call out, 'Bears,
Just watch me walking in all the squares!'[1]

Keeping to self-made rules staves off all kinds of imaginary terrors and gives the child self-confidence.

Certain fears do not decline with age. Shyness and worries about meeting new people continue to be common in adolescence, being present in just over half of 6,000 children studied in London, though they had few fears of darkness or animals. Parents tend to underestimate the number of fears that children have. Among over 1,000 children in California, 90 per cent had at least one specific fear at some stage between ages 2 and 14. The frequency of their fears peaked at age three and diminished thereafter. Out of 142 children aged two to seven in Leicester, about a third had specific fears, most of these subsiding over the next 18 months.

Although fears are very common in children, handicapping phobias are quite rare. Among over 2,000 children surveyed on the Isle of Wight, only 16 had troublesome phobias of one or more objects – five of these concerned spiders and six the dark. Out of 239 children referred to a psychiatric department, only ten had specific phobias.

Phobias in children can cause the same incapacity as in adults. A seven-year-old boy had had an intense fear of bees for two years. 'I'm very frightened of the bees and am scared they will sting and hurt me.' If he saw a bee, his mother said 'He used to go white, sweaty, cold, and trembly and his legs were like jelly.'[2] He would flee blindly from any bee, would not play out of doors in summer, and was driven to and from school during spring and summer. At least twice he had run across busy streets after seeing a bee.

Girls generally have more fears than boys. We do not know if this is because boys are expected to be brave and to suppress their fears, or because of biological gender differences, or both.

Where children live affects what they fear. Country children seem to fear animals more than do city children. However, youngsters often fear things they have never met and which do not exist in the region. Sometimes fears are acquired by imitation of family members who have the same problem. About one in six adults with fears have a close relative with a similar phobia. During World War II, English pre-school children were more afraid of air raids if their mothers showed fear. Conversely, children are less likely to develop fears if a trusted, reassuring adult is with them during a threatening experience.

Children with mental retardation or autism tend to develop many fears. Autistic children become withdrawn, avoid contact with people, and have weird repetitive habits. Their fears seem to die down less easily than in other children. A sturdy lad of 17 with brain damage caused by measles when he was four became terrified of dogs from that time on. If he saw a dog in the street he would grunt in fear, so causing the dog to snarl at him and jump, thus increasing his fear. His phobia made him unable to go anywhere alone, not even into the garden at home.[3] A 17-year-old autistic girl's terror of certain noises endangered her life. If a dog barked suddenly or a child screamed or laughed loudly, she would escape immediately without thinking and even run across the road in front of cars, so her parents could not let her go out alone.[4]

School phobia

Most children are reluctant to go to school at some time or other. Their distress is generally short-lived and clears up without treatment. Occasionally reluctance to go to school culminates in outright refusal. This can become a serious problem and is sometimes called school phobia.

Refusing school differs from truancy. Children playing truant do not refuse to go to school but use wily tricks to stay away and wander alone or in the company of other truants, their whereabouts unknown to their parents, who first learn of the truancy from the school authorities. Schoolwork suffers. Truancy tends to be associated with other delinquent behaviour, frequent changes of school, a history of parental absence in childhood, and inconsistent discipline at home.

Unlike truants, school phobic children bluntly refuse to go to school, do not show other delinquent behaviour, have no history of their parents being away from home, and have a fair standard of work and behaviour at school. They also have more physical symptoms of anxiety than truants, such as difficulties in eating and sleeping, abdominal pain, nausea, and vomiting.

The child will usually just refuse to go to school. Children may give no reason for this. They may say they worry about being bullied – the frequency of bullying is only now beginning to be recognised. The children may be scared of being teased, or fear a teacher, or be self-conscious about their appearance. They may avoid undressing in front of other children or taking a public bath or shower after games, or be anxious about doing badly at games or schoolwork. A few children fear that harm may befall their mother while they are at school. Older girls might be anxious about menstruating. Both boys and girls might worry about puberty or masturbation. Other reasons given for not going to school include fears of fainting during school assembly or vomiting.

School phobic children express their fears not only directly but also in physical symptoms, especially in the morning when encouraged to leave home for school. They may complain of nausea, vomiting, headache, diarrhoea, pain in the tummy, throat, or leg, eating difficulties, sleep disturbance, and various fears. The complaints may make the parents nervous and lead to open or tacit agreement that the child should stay home. The complaints then usually subside, only to recur the next morning when it is time to return to school. Typically a child complains of nausea at breakfast and may vomit and resist all attempts at reassurance by his worried mother until she gives in and allows him to remain home. Then he feels better unless pressure to go to school is resumed.

School refusal is usually preceded by a gradually growing reluctance to attend. The child might be irritable, weep a lot, be restless and sleep badly, feel sick, and complain of tummy pain when it is time to go to school. Insistence that school be attended will produce fear, and the child may go pale, tremble, and sweat. The fear may begin suddenly on a Monday morning following a weekend, on the first day of a new term, or on the day of return to school following illness. A common trigger is a change to a new school. Less often, school refusal can begin after the death, departure, or illness of a parent.

The peak number of school phobias is usually at those ages when children change school. In Britain and America this is about age 11 to 12, when most children move from a primary to a higher school.

Parents' attitudes can be important in cases of school phobia. Commonly the mother and father are overindulgent. Some mothers of school phobics become unusually dependent on their children as a compensation for their unsatisfactory marriage or other relationships. When both mother and child are excessively interdependent, both of them may require treatment, for treating the child alone may raise the mother's anxiety to the point where she may stop her child's treatment.

It is often said that school phobia is a misnomer for *school refusal*, on the grounds that the fear is not of school but rather of leaving mother. This is too one-sided a view. Many children are more afraid of school than of leaving mother. Some fear both school and separation from their parents.

Whatever the cause of school phobia, prolonged absence can lead to serious consequences that may be lifelong. The child loses touch with friends, social skills wither, and education suffers. The habit of avoiding unpleasantness may grow, so that in later years that person will cope more poorly with the slings and arrows of outrageous fortune with which we all must learn to contend.

Treatment of phobias in children

The treatment of children's phobias follows the lines of dealing with phobias in adults. Games are played to bring the child steadily nearer whatever frightens him and keep him there until he no longer feels impelled to escape. One jokes with him meanwhile and praises him for progress. It is helpful for fearful children to see other children doing the same thing; for example, a dog-phobic child is encouraged by seeing another child of similar age and sex patting a dog. A useful way of helping children over a fear of animals is for them to acquire a pet puppy or kitten so that they can get used to playing with it. By the time the animal is grown up, the child has desensitised to the animal and others like it. I treated my own daughter's fear of cats at age three and a half by bringing a little kitten home and teaching her to play with it; she rapidly lost her fear and became deeply attached to it as it grew into an adult cat.

When treating school phobia one must first check that the conditions at school are tolerable, that the child is not being bullied, and that unreasonable educational demands are not being made. Problems like those will need to be tackled directly. If the situation at school seems satisfactory and the main problem is that Johnny is scared of normal circumstances, the most important point in treatment is firm insistence that he return to school and stay there, however much he dislikes the idea. Interest in what he does at school and praise for work he accomplishes can also help a lot.

Returning the child to school may require the co-operation of teachers, who need to understand the problem. When the child is sent protesting back to school, crying and yelling, the parent may feel heartless. Usually crying stops quickly when the child is brought into the classroom. Until then the parent can earn angry looks from others accusing him or her of outrageous cruelty. This happened to me when my young son developed a mild fear of school after he had been away ill for a while with tonsillitis. Following the treatment principle that early return to the feared situation is the quickest way to reduce fear, I took my son by car to the school gates, his loud cries attracting malevolent glares from all around. On entering the classroom he quietened down and was soon enjoying activities in the class. Within three days he was trotting off happily to school in the mornings without a murmur of protest.

For a couple of years, each time he had to return to school after a long holiday he would protest a bit, but this disappeared increasingly rapidly after he was firmly taken to school.

Children can be taught to deal with anxiety

Children need to learn that anxiety is to be expected and that we have to be ready to face difficulties and overcome frightening situations. A courageous attitude is easier to nurture in a child who is naturally brave than one who is born timid, and we have to accept that some children are inevitably bolder than others. Youngsters also follow their parents' example. If they see parents consistently mastering frightening situations, the children will be more likely to do so themselves, and should be praised liberally for trying to master things. However, one should not ask children to do something far beyond their abilities. Nor will it help if seeing someone else courageous merely strengthens the child's conviction that he himself is a coward. When a child is sufficiently confident, gentle encouragement should be given to face mildly frightening situations until he has lost all his fear. While he faces his fear, he will need support until he has overcome it completely. Children and adults are more likely to be afraid when weakened by illness, severe fatigue, or depression. At such times they should not be made to face fear, as this may increase rather than relieve fear then. Little Johnny is best encouraged when he is feeling well.

At all ages we cope better if we are prepared in advance for potentially stressful situations, taught what to expect, and learn what to do about them. Before having dental work children can have preliminary visits to the dentist as a game to sit in the dental chair and have their mouths examined without other procedures, and be given a treat afterward. The dentist can become a friend rather than a bogey man. The same applies to visits to a doctor. If children have to go into hospital, they might visit it beforehand, meet nurses, and make friends with them before going in.

Intense separation anxiety can be prevented by having children go on holiday away from home with relatives and friends, first for a couple of days at a time, later for longer. They should be encouraged to go on trips and to camp with their friends. Although children have to learn sensible hygiene, tidiness, and study habits, these should not be taken to extremes. Their sexual maturation can be anticipated by matter-of-fact sex instruction at an early age, with their inevitable questions being answered without embarrassment. Some schools now show films of sexual intercourse to children at or before puberty. Early sex education might help to reduce sexual problems in later life. In Queensland, Australia, early intervention and prevention of anxiety at school while enlisting the help of parents succeeded in reducing children's existing anxieties and preventing the onset of new ones.[5]

Changing nightmares into dreams of mastery

A fascinating way in which children were taught to face fear was reported by K. Stewart, an anthropologist. He described how a group in Malaysia called Senoi handled a child who told them about an anxiety dream such as a dream about falling. Senoi adults would answer with enthusiasm: 'That's a wonderful dream, one of the best dreams a man can have. Where did you fall to, and what did you discover?'[6] The same comment was made when the child reported a climbing, travelling, flying, or soaring dream. The child at first answered, as he would in our society, that it did not seem so wonderful, that he was so frightened that he awoke before he had fallen anywhere.

'That was a mistake' answered the adult,

> everything you do in a dream has a purpose beyond your understanding while you're asleep. You must relax and enjoy yourself when you fall in a dream. Falling is the quickest way to get in contact with the powers of the spirit world; the powers are laid open to you in your dream. Soon when you have a falling dream, you'll remember what I'm saying, and as you do you'll feel you're travelling to the source of the power which has caused you to fall. The falling spirits love you, they're attracting you to the land and you have but to relax and remain asleep in order to come to grips with that. When you meet them you may be frightened of their terrific power, but go on. When you think you're dying in a dream, you're only seeing the powers of the other world, your own spiritual power which has been turned against you which now wishes to become one with you if you'll accept it.[7]

Over time the dream that began with a fear of falling changed into the joy of flying. The Senoi also believed and taught that the dreamer should always advance and attack in the teeth of danger, calling on the dream images of his fellows if necessary, but fighting by himself until they arrived. Dream characters were bad only as long as one was afraid and retreated from them, and they would continue to seem bad and frightening as long as one refused to come to grips with them.

summary

Most normal children have intense fears at some stage that start and then die down with no apparent cause. Newborn infants startle readily to noise, and by age one are usually wary of strangers. Between the ages of two and four, fears of animals are the rule, and in adolescence shyness and sexual fears appear. Unlike fear, disabling phobias are rare in children.

Youngsters are usually nervous when they first go to school, though they adapt readily within a few hours. School phobia or refusal is uncommon, but can become a serious problem. Unlike truancy, it is not associated with other delinquent behaviour, absence of parents, or inconsistent discipline at home. It occurs especially at times when children change schools, for example, between the ages of 11 and 12 in the UK and the USA.

Children's phobias are dealt with rather like adults' phobias, but with the use of games and other suitable rewards to persuade the child to enter and remain in the feared situation. With school refusal it is essential to firmly return the child to school, while ensuring there is no obvious bullying or other traumatic cause at the root of the nervousness. Return of the child to school may require the co-operation of understanding teachers.

Children can be educated to deal with threats courageously, but not to be foolhardy. They can be prepared in advance for potential stresses by being taught what to expect and what to do about them, for example, by playing games in the dentist's chair before formal dentistry is undertaken. Separation anxiety can be minimised by arranging increasingly long periods away from home with relatives and friends.

In the next chapter we shall look at problems associated with anxiety that occur in both children and adults and have some features distinct from phobias. These are the obsessive-compulsive problems.

obsessive-compulsive problems

Obsessive-compulsive problems can take the form of *obsessive thoughts* which intrude repeatedly into our mind against our will, despite all attempts to banish them. The ideas may concern contaminating oneself or other people, harming people, or violating another taboo. *Compulsive rituals* are repetitive actions carried out time and again although we know they are silly and try to resist them. A classic literary example is Lady Macbeth's actions after the murder of Duncan (*Macbeth*, act v, scene 1):

Doctor: . . . Look, how she rubs her hands.

Gentlewoman: It is an accustomed action with her, to seem thus washing her hands: I have known her continue in this a quarter of an hour.

Lady Macbeth: Yet here's a spot. . . . Out, damned spot! out, I say! . . . Yet who would have thought the old man to have had so much blood in him? . . . What, will these hands ne'er be clean? . . . Here's the smell of the blood still: all the perfumes of Arabia will not sweeten this little hand.

In real life, compulsive rituals do *not* usually depict an actual event. Unlike most phobias, which are rarer in men than in women, obsessive-compulsive problems occur with equal frequency in both sexes, with some exceptions. Repetitive washing is a bit more common among women, and checking among men, and an onset of obsessive-compulsive problems in childhood tends to be more common among boys than girls. Most obsessive-compulsive problems start between ages 16 and 40.

Perfectionist personality and its opposite

Obsessive thoughts and compulsive rituals tend to occur more in people who have always been perfectionist, though such problems can occur in the most slipshod persons. Meticulous habits can take many forms. You might be uneasy unless you use up that last tiny sliver of soap. Another person might be a compulsive latecomer, while others cannot bear to see a picture on the wall hang slightly askew. These harmless quirks are hardly abnormal, and people's habits differ greatly. Some of us always like to be clean and tidy while others couldn't give a damn if the house is sloppy or there is a stain on their clothing. Husbands and wives often squabble because one likes to be more tidy or untidy than the other. People differ widely in this respect. Dr Elizabeth Fenwick, a medical journalist, caught the spirit of this beautifully:

> **❝**I once met a woman who ironed nappies. When I asked her why she did it she said it was because it made them square. Aesthetically, I can appreciate square nappies as well as anyone, but there are some things I'm not prepared to make a good many sacrifices for. On a 0 to 5 Ironing Rating Scale, I would probably score around 2, in front of the people who don't iron sheets and only do the bits of their husband's shirts which are going to show, but way behind the pyjama and towel and vest and nappy ironers. . . .
>
> I suspect [my mother's] like me, but better at hiding it. She woke up once, clinging to my father. 'I've had a terrible dream,' she said, 'I was in the kitchen, trying to make myself a drink, and I couldn't. There was rice in the tin marked coffee and sugar in the tin marked tea.' . . .
>
> [My grandmother] used to make ginger biscuits. Each biscuit was three inches in diameter and weighed half an ounce. It weighed half an ounce because she cut off a piece of dough and trimmed it and weighed it on her scales until that was what it weighed, and there was no cheating by weighing a two ounce lump and cutting it into four, either. All this sort of thing takes time, of course, which is one reason why I'm not as obsessional as I might be. My grandmother never cut a piece of string in her life, no matter how enticing the contents of the parcel. She undid every knot and wound it into a neat little ball, and put it away in a Terry's Gold chocolate box labelled String (Oddments), and in the left hand front corner of the drawer next to the one marked Candles, which contained candles. Whenever there was a fuse or power cut at home it was always quicker to nip round to grandmother's and borrow a candle rather than hunt around in the dark for our own.
>
> If I was obsessional I'd be like that. I wouldn't sling the leftover garlic butter into an empty dish and bung it into the refrigerator. I'd put it into an old yoghurt pot with the lid on, and I'd label it Garlic Butter and I'd put it in the back right hand corner on the top shelf in the refrigerator, where the left over garlic butter always goes. Then I wouldn't make it into coffee butter icing when I came across it three weeks later.[1] **❞**

Distress from obsessive-compulsive problems

Neatness and cleanliness in moderation are virtues that facilitate work and other activities, but can mount to a point where they become a disability. Then it's called an obsessive-compulsive disorder, a cause of much suffering. A woman of 25 portrayed this vividly:

&& The biggest thing I've got is this obsession which spoils everything I do. If I had the courage I'd kill myself and get rid of the whole lot – it goes on and on, day after day. The obsession governs everything I do from the minute I open my eyes in the morning until I close them at night. It governs what I can touch and what I can't touch, where I can walk and where I can't walk. It governs whatever I do. I can touch the ground but I can't touch shoes, can't touch hems of coats, can't use the toilet without washing my hands and arms half a dozen times – and they must be washed right up the arms. If anybody touches their shoes I can't let them touch me – because then I would feel unclean and have to wash. Basically it all started from the toilet – first human dirt, then dog's dirt – now it's especially dog's dirt. I can't bear dogs – when I go out on the street I must be careful where I walk. It's always in my mind that I might have stepped in some dirt – the fear that I might have done so.

[And if you actually get contaminated?] That's the funny thing about it – it's not all that bad. My first feeling is panic, and my first thought is that I want to die – that's what first comes into my head, but I know you can't die just by wishing it, so then I've got to wash with a special procedure which is so long drawn out it never seems to come to an end – have to wash the tap and round the tap before washing my hands. I know it's all in the mind, I know it's ridiculous, but I can't accept it. I don't know why I'm so afraid of dirt all the time, but I am.

[Do you fight the feeling?] Yes, I do all the time, and usually succeed in the end after an hour or two, but the fear is still there. It frightens me because I don't know how to handle it, or what to think. Nothing in life interests me, I don't care what I look like, or what I eat. Mind you, I do get flashes where I care very much, but it lasts just a minute and it then disappears. I used to spend an hour washing every bit of me in the bath – washing all the time, but I only take half an hour, and now I can go and use a public toilet if it's clean. But the fear is more outside now – watching where I can walk. Things seem to change, and the fear slides over on to something else. What the fear started off with is still there, but it enlarges, and spreads to things I could have touched all right before. Once a long time ago I tried stopping washing for a week – but it was terrible, I got awful nightmares, and was ready to scream all the time, especially if anybody looked at me. After that I never tried stopping it again. But I can't go on like this, I want to care, I don't want to go on feeling life's useless.[2] &&

Obsessive fears of contamination are usually accompanied by compulsive washing and rituals of avoidance.[3] Sufferers may feel contaminated each time they go to the loo, or after being near dogs, and may have to wash for hours after every such occasion. Beth felt her son was contaminated and began complicated rituals of washing his clothes, his room, and everything connected with him. Arthur felt that dogs were dirty and spent much of his life avoiding any chance of contact with dogs, dog hair, or even buildings where dogs may have been. He gave up his job after hearing that a dog may have been on another floor of his office building. Intense washing of his hands and clothes followed the remotest possibility that he might have been 'contaminated'. Unlike a dog phobic, Arthur feared the hair plucked from a dog as much as the dog itself. An obsessive fear is less a fear of a given object or situation than of the results thought to arise from it. Arthur would rather touch a dog with his hands than let it touch his clothes, because hands are easier to wash than clothes. Similarly, Carla, obsessed with the idea of injury from glass splinters, was more afraid about fragments she suspected but could not find at home than of the glass splinters she actually found and removed with her bare hands.

Worry about harmful actions: are they dangerous?

Obsessive fears of harming, killing, stabbing, strangling, beating or maiming other people or themselves may lead sufferers to avoid potential weapons and carry out protective rituals. They may hide sharp knives in the kitchen out of reach to remove temptation. Mothers may need constant company for fear of strangling their baby if left alone. People may go to ridiculous extremes to guard against the remotest possibility of swallowing pins, broken glass or other sharp objects.

The risk of translating obsessive ideas into terrible actions is tiny. It is rare for sufferers to actually perform the terrible deeds they dread. Out of the thousands of patients with OCD whom I have seen, only three yielded in any way to their impulse to harm someone. Agnes felt compelled to pick scabs off her young son's skin when they formed after he'd scratched himself. It was hard to restrain her physically from lunging at a scab on her son's skin when she saw it. After treatment this problem disappeared. Sally had a less happy outcome. She struggled against impulses to kill her two-year-old daughter, but did not improve with treatment and Sally had to be separated from her child.

Impact on the family

Quite often OCD sufferers drag their families into their rituals.[4] Helen, aged 36, would not sweep most of her house and left dust to accumulate on the floors because she thought that dust harboured germs. She could not feed her son Luke, aged 2, for fear of giving him the tuberculosis she'd had decades earlier, so her husband had to feed Luke. She shut Luke in a playpen all day, never allowing him to crawl or walk around the house. He grew up a stranger to mum in her own home. Grandmother was never allowed to play with or even see Luke for fear she would bring germs in. Visitors were barred from entry lest they were infective. Helen spent much of her day washing her hands dozens of times until they were raw and bleeding.

Sonia was so distressed by 'contamination' of her home that she forced her family to move five times in three years and totally avoided a town nearby which seemed particularly 'dirty'. Other sufferers are so worried by 'dirt' their families might bring home that they force family members to strip naked in the entrance hall on coming home and to don fresh clothes there before entering the house. Many compulsives ban the family from bringing visitors home lest they disturb the oppressively neat, clean order inside.

Let us hear first-hand from one family how a mother's OCD affected them.

Family life before and after Delia improved with exposure therapy

Before exposure treatment

Husband: 'I was on night work at the time Delia started to check doors and taps, and had to go home for half an hour at 10 pm to see she went to bed or she'd stay up all night. I couldn't sleep because she'd wake me and say she couldn't cope. When she had a bath she'd cry, cry, and scream even when I'd pull the plug out. I'd go out just for some peace and hate going back. When we moved to another town Delia felt better for a while but her fear crept back. She'd go shopping with Hazel (our daughter) and if she'd seen something she didn't like she'd walk away and leave Hazel. I'd hate to go home after work. Delia would tell me to take off my work clothes and stand in the living room while she cleaned where I'd been. If I didn't do as she asked she'd nag me for days.'

Daughter Hazel: 'We couldn't go to where mum worked at the fish shop nor use one of the living room chairs because mum put her wages there – she gave it to grandpa to put in the bank. I couldn't go to town since we went to the carnival one year and saw some meat on the ground. I couldn't go to the beach or the village. I couldn't have my friends round and would have to go round (instead) to my friend's or nan's and grandad's house. I couldn't have any pets that went outside like a dog, cat or rabbit. I could have a hamster and fish. I have two guinea pigs at my nan's house.

I couldn't go near mum and dad's dressing table because she had something she didn't like on and inside it. I couldn't have French fruit or food. When I came home from school I had to change my clothes and wash my hands and when I came in from anywhere I had to take off my shoes as soon as I went into the hall and when we did mum always hoovered.'

After exposure treatment

Husband: 'There's been a big change. When I come home from work I go into the house without having to change my clothes. We're a lot happier and able to talk to each other more and about a lot more subjects. I look forward to going home from work and although I'm sometimes a little nervous I don't mind asking if she'd like to go out. It's nice to go out the back door to the garage or the yard without having to go out the front door and round the houses. I can go to bed before Delia without being shouted at and sleep a lot better. Work is much better. I can work things out quicker. It's good to be able to fix the car or things at home without worrying about Delia shouting at me. When we visit other people's houses they're surprised to see her with me. She's like a different person.'

Daughter Hazel: 'Now I can go to the village and the butcher and we can use the chair. We can go to town and the shops. I can have my friends round to tea and have them round unexpectedly. I've got a dog now that goes into the garden and I can feed the bird and put a nesting box up and a seed box. I use the dressing table and put my talc on it. Mum uses the cupboard for food and the bread bin. Now we have French apples. I don't change my clothes or take my shoes off when I come in, she doesn't hoover the hall any time we come in. We sometimes go to the beach. Now she likes dad's music, things she didn't like before because she didn't know where they'd been. Now she touches my aunt's cat and has it on her lap when we go there.'

Obsessions about hair and excreta

Some compulsive rituals centre around hair.[5] Nigel aged 29 spent up to five hours a day washing and combing his hair, checking for hairs in his bed and on the floor around it. He felt uncomfortable if he found hairs on his clothes and was compelled to remove them. One of Simon's many rituals was spending four hours a morning vacuuming and polishing his room at home, searching for hair, and worrying it might have penetrated electrical equipment. His worry was about hair from the head, not pubic hair or animal hair.

Lin complained of an unusual compulsion.[6] She had intense urges to watch her lover's bowel action, though this did not excite her sexually. When he went to the loo she could not bear to be shut out and shouted at him if she could not watch him. When allowed to watch she would stare at his turds for several minutes. Lin's compulsive habit rather dampened the ardour of her boyfriends.

The dislocation of sufferers' lives from obsessive-compulsive troubles can become extreme. An eminent judge avoided urinating or defecating at home for fear of contamination and excreted elsewhere including in fields.[7] He shunned sexual relations because they seemed dirty. When he saw me he had given up his job and was dressed in a shabby, stained suit, his jacket bulging from hundreds of paper tissues in his breast pocket. To open my office door he used a tissue to grasp the 'dirty' handle. He would not shake hands for fear of contamination.

An obsessive paradox

Like many other sufferers from OCD, Debbie demonstrated the irrationality of her obsession well. She washed her hands up to 100 times a day until they were raw and bleeding. She spent endless hours at the tap washing up to her elbows but wouldn't take a bath or wash her body for weeks on end. Her body smell became unbearable to people nearby but this did not bother her at all. Debbie used so many bottles of disinfectant and bars of soap that she could not afford to buy these out of her meagre salary, so she shoplifted soap and disinfectants. When she was caught shoplifting and taken to the police station, the police were unable to record her fingerprints as she had none; she had washed them completely away, and the skin on her fingertips was perfectly smooth.

Compulsive slowness

Obsessions and rituals of OCD can take up much of the day, slowing sufferers greatly in doing things most of us do without thinking. Malcolm had been out of work for three years because it took him so long to do everything. He would take several hours to dress and have breakfast in the morning. To be in time for his afternoon appointment with me, he shaved the previous day. When I asked him how long he took to have a bath he replied, 'Do you mean from the time I actually get into the bath, or from the time I start 'thinking' of having a bath?'[8] Bathing took five hours. Crossing a road took further hours, because Malcolm checked not only that no cars were coming but also that every car parked along the road nearby was not about to move off. By the time he had finished looking inside the parked cars he would have to start looking up the street several times more, by which time he felt he had to look inside the parked cars again, etc. To switch off a light, he first checked that his shoes were insulated and would look repeatedly at his soles before daring to risk electrocution by putting his hand on the light switch. This slowness affected most of Malcolm's actions, but he rationalised it by saying he couldn't take risks about being run over or electrocuted.

Compulsive hoarding

Hoarding is another obsessive-compulsive behaviour. Sufferers can't bear to throw rubbish away. For fear of throwing good food away they may spend hours sorting kitchen scraps before discarding them. They store valueless papers for decades until there's no room to move at home. Vast quantities of food, cans, and other things might be bought needlessly when no shortages are pending. If anyone removes a tiny bit of the accumulation of ages this evokes howls of protest, so rooms and passages become cluttered with old furniture, papers, tins and clothes. One man would not part with his old car which had no wheels, and kept it rusting on blocks in his garage while his new car was left exposed to the elements outside.[9]

Number rituals

Number rituals are common. Dr Leonard Cammer cited two examples. The chief of a prestigious detective agency had extensive number rituals.

> ❝I count the number of letters in the words spoken to me in any conversation, and I can tell you instantaneously the exact total of letters up to 350 or so. When you say 'Good morning, John' I make an immediate mental note that this has 15 letters. When you asked me 'Does your counting obsession interfere with your conversation with people?' I answered 'not really' but before I answered I noticed that your question contained 63 letters. I also must count the number of letters on every street sign. That does interfere sometimes, especially when I'm in a hurry to get somewhere in the car and there are lots of signs in the streets. If there are three numbers in a house or shop window I must multiply them. For example, I see 275 on a building. I multiply 2 times 7 times 5. Of course, I do it very rapidly. It equals 70.[10]❞

The second example was in a woman: 'I have to touch the venetian blinds four times, then all the *objects d'art* in the vestibule five times. That prevents harm to my older brother. He comes home safely, and proves that my ritual works. Maybe some people think it stupid, but if I don't go through with it, I start to stutter.'[11]

Treatment of obsessive-compulsive disorder

Treatment for OCD is along lines similar to those for helping phobias, but it generally takes longer and requires self-imposed prevention of rituals, and involvement of relatives as exposure co-therapists is often necessary. Let us look at this in Ann, a 23-year-old bank employee.[12] For five years she had worried that she might become pregnant during petting despite being a virgin. For 18 months she feared that a small wart on her finger was cancerous and eventually she sought treatment. Ann avoided anything that might contaminate her with 'cancer germs' and dreaded passing these from her wart to her family. She began to wash too much. Six weeks before treatment began, when her parents went on holiday leaving her alone at home with her teenage brother, her boyfriend moved into the house to ease her anxiety. It worsened instead. She became afraid to visit the loo after he had been there lest she should 'catch pregnancy'.

Ann checked 'dangerous' electrical switches repeatedly and frequently looked back over her shoulder to check for some nameless threat. She felt tortured lest she ever were to be the last to leave the bank at night when security checks would be her responsibility. She washed her hands 125 times a day, used three bars of soap a day, took three hours to shower, and washed her hair repeatedly for fear of contamination with cancer-causing germs. She said cancer took so long to come on that she could never feel completely safe.

Ann agreed that her treatment targets would include preparing and cooking meals for her parents without safeguarding rituals, washing her hair without rituals, pricking her finger at the site of the former wart and eating food with her bleeding finger. She watched a nurse 'contaminate' herself and then followed suit. Between treatment sessions she did homework to get used to 'contamination' and eliminate her checking rituals one by one. She first limited herself to using one bar of soap per day, and stopped washing under a running tap and used a plug in a sink instead. Ann decreased her number of washes and the time they took. Ann went home most weekends with a programme to 'contaminate' herself, her home, and her parents and to restrict her rituals. She looked at a nurse's scar where a breast had been removed for cancer years before and touched the scar and then herself and surrounding objects. Thereafter, without washing, she prepared meals and ate them with the nurse.

Ann dealt with her fear of pregnancy from the slightest contact with her boyfriend by having his pyjamas, underwear and towel brought into the hospital and put near her. She touched, handled and then wore his garments and used his towel. She and her boyfriend evolved a programme to resume petting, increasing from week to week until Ann became able to touch his penis first through his trousers and then under them and became able to tolerate his masturbating her.

Eventually Ann returned to work, limited herself to only one bar of soap every two weeks, and continued improved to a one-year follow-up. She went on holiday abroad for the first time in years, was promoted at work, and took charge of the normal security routine in her bank involving 13 locks! She allowed her parents to go away and leave her in charge of the house, which formerly she could not have contemplated. She now shopped regularly without mother having to be present to drag her away from checking rituals. At home she prepared meals that contamination fears had used to stop her from doing. Sexual foreplay with her boyfriend was normal.

You can see from this how closely the family may need to co-operate in treatment of some OCD problems. Page 117 shows the chart of a sample weekend that Ann spent at home. Her chart (opposite) shows the tasks that Ann, her parents and her boyfriend carried out separately at home, and the reports the parents and boyfriend wrote to the therapist after Ann returned to hospital after the weekend. Note the meticulous detailed attention paid to having Ann expose herself to her many different but connected problem areas.

Bill's exposure therapy

Bill had numerous bothersome rituals mainly to ensure he was not responsible for harming others. He had been a lorry driver for six years but now feared driving in case he caused an accident. He stopped his worries by checking his route and on one occasion with the police. He checked that taps were turned off, razor blades were put away, and rugs weren't ruffled, and had numerous other checking rituals which made normal life impossible and interfered with his previously happy marriage.

During his first two days of treatment, Bill was encouraged to do things he had avoided for over four years: driving a car, bumping into people in a crowded supermarket, putting pins, matches, and stones on the floor of the hospital lounge, turning on water taps, leaving them to drip. After each 40-minute session, Bill was asked to resist the urge to check and not to seek reassurance about whether he'd harmed anyone. Bill felt briefly sick after each of the first two days of treatment but recovered quickly and was free of symptoms at the end of treatment, remaining well when last seen two years later.

Family involvement in treatment

Obsessive-compulsive problems often impact widely on the lives of sufferers and their family and then need to be dealt with in treatment. We saw this earlier with Ann. Let us look also at Helen, whom we met earlier; her many rituals prevented her caring for her young son Luke.[13] She confined him to a playpen all day lest he got tuberculosis from dust on the floor; his food was ritually prepared by Dad; grandmother and aunt were never allowed to see Luke. Most of the house was never swept for fear of spreading germs. Helen lived far from London. Toward the end of her admission her husband lodged near the hospital and took part in treatment sessions so that Helen learned to feed Luke herself, without rituals. A nurse escorted the family home on the train and ensured that Helen touched door handles and window sashes which she seemed to want to avoid. The nurse spent two whole days with the family at home ensuring that Helen swept the whole house without fear of germs and

Weekend of 18 August

Ann's tasks:

1 Prepare a meal or help mother prepare a meal without washing hands.

2 Touch all the dishes before eating the meal.

3 Touch father's pencils and pens, wallet and razor.

4 Touch mother's rollers, handbag and purse without washing hands before or after.

5 Use own soap for washing, and wash only before a meal or after the toilet.

6 Put the plug in the sink when washing.

7 Eat yoghourt or jelly using my ring finger.

Parents' tasks:

1 Praise Ann when she does her tasks. Never say it was easy.

2 Do not give reassurance.

3 Show her fearless behaviour when she fears 'contamination', bring things she fears to the ward when she returns from leave.

4 Leave a report, however brief, for the therapist, on progress during the weekend.

Parents' report on the weekend to the therapist

Ann's day at home presented no great problems. She still finds it difficult to wash with water in the basin, and exaggerated her rinsing of hands and wrists. She was a bit rebellious once but it was short-lived. She had little difficulty on a shopping expedition regarding turning round, checking and worrying over electrical points in shops. She drove us all home in her own car. She largely prepared the vegetables and dessert for Sunday lunch without showing apprehension. Visits to the toilet create anxiety. Generally she was very much improved compared to before treatment started. We're pleased with her progress. She's keen to overcome her problem and shows disappointment when she fails to fulfil her tasks.

Weekend of 24 August

Boyfriend's tasks:

1 Go to toilet, don't wash hands, and contaminate Ann's underwear, knees and tampon.

2 Report to therapist about this.

Boyfriend's report on the weekend to the therapist:

Ann's underwear and tampon were 'contaminated' twice, on Saturday and Monday, and her knees and thighs several times (without tights). No anxiety was apparent. Close proximity on the beach, which used to worry her, was no problem. A very successful weekend.

Ann's report

Anxiety score (8 = panic, 0 = completely calm):
Contamination of leg 1, of underclothes 2, of tampon 2.

that she fed her son properly and did not ritualise. Helen's husband was asked to stop the many rituals she had taught him to perform. Once Helen had learned not to involve the family in her rituals and the husband was taught how to cope with her remaining rituals, no further treatment was needed and she had no rituals when seen two years later.

Relatives need to learn to withhold reassurance and not participate in rituals

Some sufferers ask relatives for repeated reassurance in an endless ritual: 'Darling, did I touch the dirt on the wall?', 'Are you sure I haven't put poison in the food?' Long-suffering relatives are usually badgered into settling for a quiet life by answering 'No, you didn't touch the dirt,' 'Yes, dear, I'm sure there's no poison in the food', and so on.

As we saw with illness phobias, reassurance damps down anxiety just for a moment and prevents the sufferer from learning to tolerate lastingly the discomfort caused by uncertainty about illness, dirt, or whatever. The sufferer only acquires the necessary enduring tolerance and stops seeking reassurance if relatives withhold reassurance completely. The family must therefore learn *not* to reassure, to stop the quick but temporary fix of fear-reduction given by reassurance.

The sufferer and spouse and perhaps child or parent may need to role-play a scene many times to learn what to do. For example, a sufferer might rehearse asking their spouse 'Is baby all right?' to which the spouse rehearses replying in a monotonous voice 'Hospital says no answer'. This same four-word monotonous reply given time after time to every single request for reassurance means 'it's the hospital, not me, doing this; argue with the hospital'. Sufferer and relative/s rehearse this scene several times to get it right until relatives automatically replace 'It's okay dear, he's fine, he's all right . . .' by a monotonous 'Hospital says no answer' no matter how urgently and angrily the sufferer asks for reassurance.

If sufferers and their family meet in self-help groups they are often relieved to share their experiences with others who have similar problems and can suggest solutions for one another's difficulties. They also learn what are real norms for behaviour. Many are surprised to learn that most people take less than five minutes to brush their teeth, that it is not usual to spring-clean the house every day or to boil babies' bottles for three hours before every feed.

Even young children can be taught to help parents overcome rituals. Children in one family on their own initiative pinned a notice 'Touch me' on a laundry basket their mother used to avoid, and in another family persuaded their mother to come swimming in a public pool, an activity she dreaded for fear of contamination.[14] Relatives are encouraged to praise sufferers for doing difficult exposure tasks. This does not always come naturally. Bob consistently withheld approval from his wife's diligent homework to overcome her worries about fire; for example, she left candles alight in secure holders in every room at home. Bob refused to praise her, saying, 'I can't – nobody in my family ever praised anyone.'[15] However, he devised his own solution. Into a tape recorder he said, 'That's very good dear, I'm pleased you managed it', and played the tape-recorded message to her. After a few trials of this Bob managed to say it himself without the tape recorder – he became able to praise his wife directly.

Eighteen-year-old Jo drove her family mad by lining up mum, dad, and sister every night at home so she could be sure she'd kissed them all good-night the 'right' number of times.[16] Jo also insisted on mum holding a glass of water to dip her toothbrush into repeatedly for up to an hour. With her family, Jo rehearsed asking them to start these rituals, and mum and dad rehearsed refusing firmly by replying 'Hospital says no answer'. At home they stopped joining in Jo's rituals, which then diminished greatly.

Compulsive hoarders can be encouraged to overcome fear of throwing things away by chucking items out bit by bit on an agreed schedule. A sufferer can learn to throw away 10-year-old newspapers to get used to the idea that even if information has been lost it doesn't matter. It's amazing how resistant a hoarder might be to throwing away old potato peelings or a broken chair beyond hope of repair. With encouragement, however, hoarders can learn to part with loads of things and clear living space at home so that visitors can be entertained once more.

Improvement resulting from exposure and ritual prevention therapy is usually worthwhile and enduring, provided patients do it properly. George, who had been unemployed for years because he spent most of the day washing himself endlessly, in treatment touched articles his therapist had first touched, ending up touching spots of urine and dried excrement that were the focus of his worries. He improved dramatically, and two years after treatment his mother wrote in thanks: 'He was married last September and has bought a house. He and his wife have settled in well, and it's a pleasure to call on them and see him gardening and doing various odd jobs around the house. This is a thing we'd have thought impossible a few years ago.'[17]

Overcoming obsessions (ruminations, repetitive intrusive thoughts)

You can get used to frightening, intrusive thoughts by facing them repeatedly for a long time just as you can overcome fear of externally frightening things by confronting them again and again. You can speak your frightening thoughts into a tape recorder and make a loop tape containing those thoughts that you can play over and over for an hour. Put the tape into a walkman and carry that walkman with you wherever you go. Whenever the obsessions pop into your mind, instead of trying to dismiss them, switch on the walkman and listen to them again and again and again until they are boring rather than distressing. This might well take an hour, and needs to be repeated day after day until the thoughts have lost their power to trouble you.

One caution when you record your obsessions on an audiotape – ensure that you only record frightening thoughts, not other thoughts that you might deliberately bring on to dispel the distressing ones. For example, you might be troubled by the thought 'I'll kill my baby' and try to banish that thought by the comforting idea instead 'God is good and won't let me hurt my baby'. On the audiotape you need to record the frightening thought 'I'll kill my baby', but *not* record the consoling thought 'God is good and won't let me hurt my baby'. Listening to the consoling thought will prevent you getting used to the bothersome obsession, so you need to listen to an audiotape which only contains your distressing thoughts. That is hard, but it usually works well.

A final point about overcoming obsessions. If you have several kinds of distressing thoughts, then you need to prepare a separate audiotape for each particular obsession, and get used to each one in turn. As it might take several days to get used to a particular obsession, if you have several intrusive thoughts it might take weeks or even months to overcome your fear of every one of them.

summary

Obsessive thoughts are those which intrude repeatedly into our mind against our will, whereas compulsive rituals are repetitive actions we feel compelled to carry out even if they seem silly. Obsessive-compulsive problems usually start in young adults, and are equally common in both sexes. These problems often occur in people who have always been meticulous perfectionists, but this is not always so. Worries about potentially harmful actions are almost always groundless. It is very rare for obsessive thoughts to be carried out in acts.

Relatives are frequently dragged into helping sufferers with their rituals, which tends to increase them, and the family's lives and child-rearing can be gravely disrupted. Common rituals are repeated washing, checking for contamination or harm, and doing things by number. Less common are worries about hair, serious slowness, and hoarding of all kinds of useless things.

Obsessive-compulsive problems are helped in a similar way to phobias, but can take longer because their ramifications in the sufferer's and family life are often more extensive. Exposure therapy involves deliberately facing situations which bring on the rituals and obsessions and then not ritualising for as long as possible while learning to tolerate the ensuing discomfort. Careful attention is needed to relevant details, and relatives can be valuable co-therapists by monitoring and praising progress while withholding reassurance and refusing to participate in any rituals. Families can help sort things out by meeting together in a self-help group.

We proceed now to a very different but frequent source of worry – sexual anxiety.

sexual anxieties

Worries about sex are among the most pervasive problems of adolescents and young adults. They are all the more troublesome because shame often stops people seeking advice from anyone, doctors included. Many never get the help they need.

In past times normal sexual activities like masturbation were regarded as sinful, the cause of lots of dread diseases. Even though masturbation is normal after puberty, needless guilt about it is frequent. Guilt about other sexual behaviour, too, tortures those who grew up with restrictive attitudes at home and at school. Adolescents even now may get depressed and worried by perfectly normal sexual experiments. They often die a thousand deaths from embarrassment when they meet the opposite sex socially.

Somehow most of us eventually get over any sexual hang-ups through a process of trial and error, and settle down in stable relationships with satisfying sex lives. There is a wide range in norms. A love-nip for one person is a sadistic hurt for another. One couple might veto oral intercourse as perverted while another might feel deprived if it's not on their sexual menu. Certain women might climax rapidly after penetration with minimal previous stimulation, whereas others need much longer foreplay and thrusting to get there.

Sexual information and attitudes

Today we are awash with media portrayals of sex and videos and magazines and books about it. Sex is the commonest subject of internet searches. It is hard, however, for people with problems to sort out good-quality advice from self-serving advertisements peddling untested nostrums. It is best to choose materials designed to instruct rather than titillate and that have helpful pictures and diagrams. Mere pornography can mislead and become boring after the initial novelty wears off.

Although attitudes about sex are more relaxed now than in the past, sexual behaviour may have changed less than one might expect. A study of young students showed little difference in sexual patterns over the years except that they began having actual intercourse a year or two earlier than their predecessors did and were a bit more tolerant of their partner having affairs. More oral genital sex may be practised than used to be the case. The dominant sexual pattern, however, remains a partnership between one man and woman who plan to stay together. If they eventually separate they'll try to form a stable partnership with someone else. This is serial monogamy. Free partner-swapping is for just a tiny minority. In today's permissive atmosphere the sexual norm remains fairly conventional coitus between stable partners, even though fewer actually marry. Having children without getting married is widely accepted.

Sexual jealousy

Sexual jealousy can ruin people's lives and appears more in men than in women. It is often associated with alcoholism or impotence. Extreme jealousy can lead to murder, Othello's killing of Desdemona being the classic example. This danger is recognised in certain countries' legal systems which do not severely punish crimes of passion in which a partner is discovered *in flagrante delicto*.

Murderous jealousy is hardly the norm, of course. The norm is to feel jealous only if our partner shows sexual attraction to someone else or is courted by them. Jealousy is a normal response to threat that our partner might fall in love with someone else and leave us. Mild jealousy may actually be adaptive, a sign of attachment that can bind couples together. No longer feeling jealous may signal that we have lost interest in our partner.

Marked jealousy can cause much trouble. A couple I saw had been on the brink of divorce because the husband had repeated 'funny imaginations' that his wife was unfaithful. This led to frequent rows, although both denied they had ever had sex with anyone else. Despite all this, they had regular intercourse together.[1]

Types of sexual problems

Sexual problems secondary to other causes

Loss of sexual interest or performance can occur with severe depression or diabetes or other diseases, antihypertensive and antidepressant drugs, alcohol and heroin. A sign of such disorder in men is a loss of early morning erections. Inability to perform with one's heterosexual partner may reflect homosexuality, paedophilia, transvestism, sadomasochism or some other sexual preference; in such people a same-sex partner or child or women's clothes or cruelty is associated with strong sexual desire and performance.

A common source of sexual difficulties is marital discord. If you're at war about a thousand and one things then the battleground may spread to bed. There is little point dealing just with the sexual arena if at the same time you are quarrelling endlessly with your spouse about the housekeeping money, the children's education, which colour curtains to buy, and which show to see. Until your relationship can reach a level of mutual toleration, it may be hard to improve things in bed.

It can be difficult to tell whether a couple's sexual problem is sexual in origin or the result of getting on each other's nerves in other ways. Nora had stopped sexual relations with her husband and flounced into my consulting room to announce 'You're the phobia king. Well, I've got a phobia of wearing tight clothes in the presence of my husband.'[2] Nora launched into a story disclosing that the main problem was marital discord about matters having nothing to do with her phobia or with sex, but then spilling over into sexual issues.

Unconsummated marriage

Over 99% of marriages have been consummated by intercourse within the first year. Occasionally, however, a couple may have never had sex together even years after marriage. This can be because of problems in either partner.

In one couple I saw, the problem was that the husband preferred young boys to women. Another couple had petted together to climax frequently before marriage and afterward masturbated each other to orgasm three times a week over ten years of marriage. The man had strong erections, but whenever he tried to have intercourse his wife thrust him away. She didn't mind his touching her breasts or genitals but wouldn't touch his penis or walk nude in front of him, although he could watch her having a bath.

Equally striking was another young couple who had never had intercourse over three years of marriage.[3] As a child the wife had had an excruciatingly painful abscess of her genitals and at age 19 was virtually raped by a man who then blackmailed her into repeated intercourse. When she married, these painful memories prevented normal coitus with her husband, and restricted their sexual activities to mutual genital caressing to climax. Although she didn't mind her husband's penis touching the outside of her vulva and even had orgasm that way, if he tried to insert his penis into her she'd have painful contractions of her vagina that stopped him achieving penetration.

Sexual problems in women

Painful intercourse

A common complaint from women is that intercourse hurts them. They find themselves squeezing their pelvic muscles into spasm while hating every minute of sex. This is *vaginismus*, meaning spasm of the muscles around the vagina which when very strong can stop penile penetration. Pain on intercourse occasionally indicates physical disease such as infection, hormone disturbance, or benign tumours; these should be excluded by medical examination.

Anorgasmia

A frequent problem is some form of anorgasmia. A woman may fail to reach orgasm even though she might enjoy insertion of the penis and be relaxed about it. There can be anorgasmia plus vaginismus. Some women have never experienced orgasm, neither with masturbation nor during coitus. Others may readily climax through masturbation but not during intercourse. A few have multiple climax with coitus but not with masturbation. Anorgasmia is more likely where the man is inexperienced, clumsy, or can't sustain his erection. It can also result from the woman being too timid to guide her mate to do what turns her on, for example, 'A little more to the left. Press harder. Yes, do that again. Lovely!'

Sexual problems in men

Lack of social skills

A man who lacks certain social skills may fail to win a sexual partner. Although women approach men more now than in the past, men are still usually expected to take the sexual initiative and have to learn how to relate to women before sex becomes a realistic possibility. They have to learn how to talk to a woman, the rules for socialising, and how to make sexual approaches that are acceptable. Having done all that, a man still has to get an erection before intercourse can be achieved, and excessive fear can prevent this. Nineteen-year-old Mike complained that he was still a virgin and became nervous when with women, especially if they seemed to be rejecting him.[4] Quite a few young women found Mike attractive and approached him, but their approaches made him tense and he would break off the relationship. Petting with women gave him strong erections, and Mike often masturbated while thinking about women.

Failure of erection (impotence)

Inability to get enough of an erection for intercourse is *impotence*. Failure the first time in a relationship is not rare, but practice makes perfect. Impotence is common when men are tired or anxious or on medications to lower high blood pressure or improve mood. That ubiquitous drug, alcohol, can also hinder performance, as Shakespeare recognised when he wrote in *Macbeth* that alcohol provokes desire but takes away from performance – brewer's droop. Impotence can be caused by diabetes and diseases of the brain or spinal cord or lack of the right sort of hormones, or preference for a different sort of sexual partner or stimulation. Homosexual men and women tend to be turned off by the opposite sex, although some also have normal heterosexual relations.

Premature ejaculation

Early ejaculation, coming too soon, is a frequent problem. The man's inability to delay ejaculating until his partner is satisfied frustrates her. The problem is often combined with a failure to get a full erection, or the man may have just a brief erection and then ejaculate suddenly before he wants to.

Whether ejaculation is called premature depends a bit on how long the woman takes to reach orgasm. If she climaxes within a minute or at the same time as her partner, he is less likely to seek help for quick ejaculation. However, if she doesn't come despite his sustaining an erection and delaying ejaculation until 25 minutes of coitus, it would be misleading to call that a premature ejaculation problem; the problem is then one of her anorgasmia.

Both failure of erection and premature ejaculation happen more often if the woman is irritable or dislikes sex. Her mate might be put off by attitudes such as 'Get it over with fast' or 'All right, if you really have to. I'll still love you, dear, despite it.' Equally, a sexually demanding woman might want him to perform more than usual and his penis may then hang limp.

Failure of ejaculation

Failure to ejaculate is the opposite and rarer difficulty. The man can sustain a strong erection for hours on end but cannot ejaculate semen. His partner may reach climax after climax during this time.

Isn't good sex simply doing what comes naturally? In fact it is a complicated set of skills to learn, so it is not surprising that things often go wrong, especially at the start until the couple learns good co-ordination. An experienced partner can be a great therapist. Twenty-year-old Ralph asked for help because he couldn't get good erections with women he knew or with prostitutes, though he masturbated regularly. While on the waiting list to see a psychiatrist he met a sexually experienced woman five years older than him. She was very patient. She knew about his problem and let him try to approach intercourse slowly and repeatedly without hurrying or laughing at him. With her support within a few weeks Ralph was leading a vigorous, normal sex life.

Treatment of sexual anxieties

Before sexual problems are treated it is necessary to exclude causes such as marital discord, severe depression, alcohol, prescribed or other drugs, diabetes or other physical disease, or lack of social rather than sexual skills. For treatment to succeed, a willing partner is necessary, and shy people may have to develop social skills to this end. If you worry that someone will laugh at you or refuse an invitation out because you feel gawky, the solution lies in summoning up courage to ask someone out or accept an offer to go out, and learning to handle the situation. If you are shy, you can practise chatting to others in the canteen at work, having tea or coffee together, going out walking with them in order to make progress. As each new step becomes easier you will grow more comfortable and be able to proceed to the next stage. The role of drugs such as sildenafil (*Viagra*) is discussed in Chapter 11.

Principles of treatment

In the West sexual worries are dealt with better and more openly now than in the past. Sexual fears can be overcome in the same way as other anxieties, but in addition to overcoming fear one needs to learn how to have enjoyable sex, which skill takes time to develop. Sexual skills programmes are effective, given a co-operative couple willing to work at overcoming the problem.

Help comes from a programme of graded exposure to and learning of sexual behaviour. Sexual fears slowly subside through steadily increasing contact of partners with each other's body. Gradually increasing intimacy allows them to become comfortable together, learn what turns each other on and off, and acquire fluent sexual skills. Couples are first encouraged to talk about their sexual difficulties in detail and to learn a sexual language that enables them to tell each other clearly about their sexual activities and feelings. They need to know what words to use to describe the genitalia and various aspects of intercourse.

A good idea for self-help is to read a reputable book about sex which includes pictures of the genitals and people having intercourse in different positions. Read this together and discuss your problems in the light of what you have learned. Then explore your bodies and examine your genitals, first your own, then each other's. For women, unless you're especially agile, you may need a hand mirror to see your vulva properly. If you wish, thereafter you might stimulate your own genitals with your hands, a vibrator, or both, eventually masturbating alone to climax. After doing this enjoyably a few times, you can proceed to the next stage of mutual caressing. If you already enjoy touching each other's bodies and have no anxiety about this, but only have one of the specific problems described earlier, you can skip the next stage on sensate focus and go straight to the special techniques described for them below.

Sensate focus

The first stage of self-help works by gradual exposure. Couples start by getting used to touching each other's bodies while agreeing not to have coitus. This is called *sensate focus*. To do it the couple sets aside time (say 15 minutes) several times a week to caress one another's bodies without clothes on, learning to give each other pleasure without touching the genitals or breasts, on the understanding that neither party will move toward intercourse. To aid the caressing, some couples like to apply lotion or oil to their skin. You can inspect one another's bodies and genitals in order to overcome your squeamishness and get accurate information.

Simply lying together in the nude can cause great anxiety. After I suggested that one couple do this no matter what they felt, my secretary had a message the next morning from the wife: 'Tell the doctor that I did what he asked and I could kill him for it, but I did it.' The task in question was to sleep in the nude all night next to her husband. After doing this for a week, this woman had no qualms at all about doing so or about engaging in mutual caressing in the nude. Within six weeks she and her husband were having intercourse regularly for the first time in their three years of marriage.

Only when a couple are happy about caressing each other's bodies freely without fear is it advisable to start on steps that lead to sexual intercourse. Specific problems call for specific ways of overcoming them. In the descriptions below, you will notice that when the time comes for intercourse it's assumed that the woman is on top of the man. This is said to give the woman greater control. Some couples I have treated disliked this and preferred to start coitus with the man on top. The answer is 'Try whatever position you find most comfortable'.

Problems in men

Failure of erection

If the problem is that the man cannot get an erection, the woman is taught to caress his penis gently until it slowly stiffens up. At this point she lowers herself gently to insert his penis into her vagina. If he loses his erection, she raises herself up again, resumes caressing him until he has an erection once more, and then again lowers herself on to him. This is repeated time and again until he can tolerate being erect in her for, say, 15 minutes, after which time they can continue normal thrusting movements to orgasm.

The man has to learn that losing one's erection is not a disaster; it will return if the couple just continues love play and he does not feel flustered. The man and the woman are learning a complicated skill together and how to read each other's feelings and communicate freely about them.

Premature ejaculation

If the difficulty is ejaculating too early, then the technique is slightly different. The man has to learn to inhibit ejaculation while his penis is being caressed. There are two similar ways to do this, either 'stimulate, pause, stimulate' or 'stimulate, squeeze, stimulate.'

The wife caresses her husband's penis until it erects fully and continues caressing until he feels close to ejaculation. He tells her this, whereupon she stops caressing him. Now they can just pause for a few minutes or if they wish can also add the squeeze technique. Here she stops caressing his penis and instead firmly squeezes the glans (the bulbous tip of the penis) between her thumb and second finger. Pausing or squeezing stops the desire to ejaculate. When the man feels there's no longer a risk of ejaculating, he tells his wife, who then resumes caressing his penis.

This stimulation is continued until the man can sustain an erection for 15 minutes without danger of coming. At that stage the wife lowers herself on to his body to insert his penis into her vagina. If he feels ejaculation is close, he tells her immediately. All movement must now stop, to reduce excitement. If this isn't enough to dampen his desire to ejaculate, she withdraws for a minute or two until his urge has passed, after which they join together again. The rule is thrust, stop, separate if need be, thrust again, and so on, until good control is achieved. The couple work steadily together toward the desired target behaviour at a speed that they find comfortable, feeling free to experiment as they achieve control of their sexual behaviour.

One variant is worth considering. Instead of penile stimulation being carried out by the wife at the start, there is no harm in the man masturbating himself, pausing when close to climax, and resuming masturbation when the urge has subsided. When he has acquired control by himself, the same exercise is repeated, but with his wife doing the stimulation.

I was surprised by one couple I was advising about the husband's premature ejaculation.[5] They had listened carefully to my outline of a self-help programme at the first session. At the next session the wife complained that she found it a bit difficult to stimulate her husband's penis for as long as 15 minutes. It turned out that instead of using her hand she was in fact stimulating his penis with her mouth – they'd regularly practised oral sex in the past despite his problem. After a few sessions the husband became able to keep his erection for 15 minutes outside and inside his wife. At that point she began to tire of treatment, and ways had to be found to keep up her flagging interest. If boredom occurs, once you reach targets you've set you can reward yourselves with enjoyable activities – a weekend holiday, a night out, or a present you have wanted to buy for years.

Failure of ejaculation

Ejaculatory failure is uncommon. The man can maintain an erection for hours at a time if necessary but is quite unable to climax despite his partner's having many orgasms. For this problem, start your programme with mutual caressing of each other's bodies without intercourse. Then the woman starts stimulating the man's penis vigorously *outside* her body until he's achieved ejaculation through this masturbation. Once that's happened, during the next erection, when he reports that ejaculation is imminent, she lowers herself on to him quickly, inserting his penis into her so that he can ejaculate inside her vagina. The couple then moves the time of coming together (insertion) earlier and earlier in their sexual stimulation. This helps to make it easier for him to subsequently ejaculate inside her through intercourse alone.

Don't be discouraged by early failure

Some men think they're impotent simply because they fail a few times, or because they have unusual preferences. A clergyman and his wife came to me because they had not had successful intercourse during their four years of marriage.[6] It turned out that the clergyman had long loved little boys and had masturbated them regularly while living in another country but not since he and his wife returned to England a year earlier, although he remained attracted to young lads. During his honeymoon four years earlier, on trying intercourse he had failed to obtain an erection three times in a row. He and his wife never tried again thereafter, giving up in despair.

I told this couple that many couples fail at their first few tries at making love and that as they hadn't tried for four years it might be worth trying again. First, at home they had to sleep nude next to but not touching each other. This they achieved, and before session two they had to start caressing each other daily at home, but without intercourse, no matter how much they wanted that.

By session three they had permission to have intercourse if they so desired. By session four a few weeks after starting to see me they were having regular normal coitus with much mutual pleasure. His desire for boys disappeared entirely. The wife soon became pregnant and a few months later another impotent clergyman was referred to me on the advice of this couple.

Problems in women

Vaginal spasm (vaginismus)

If a woman gets vaginal spasm each time penetration is tried, several approaches can be helpful. Once you are used to sensate focus with your mate, that is, mutual caressing in the nude, you can start experimenting by first putting the tip of your little finger inside your own vulva and vagina, and as you get used to this, the whole finger, and then two fingers. When you can accommodate two of your own fingers comfortably, allow your partner to insert his finger into your vagina slowly, gently, and repeatedly, until you are used to it. An alternative at this stage is to pass little rounded dilators of pro-gressively increasing size into your vagina until you can move them about freely and easily tolerate a dilator a bit longer and broader than an erect penis. Your partner can then do the same to you, after which you can proceed gradually toward intercourse, with you allowing him to move more vigorously as time goes on.

Anorgasmia

If you are a woman who does not reach orgasm, you need to learn to move more vigorously during intercourse to stimulate yourself, and to teach your mate to move in ways that satisfy you. Before trying coitus it might be useful to start by masturbating yourself manually to climax in a systematic programme.[7] You can use a vibrator, too, if you enjoy the sensation.

A virgin couple ten years after marriage

It is quite common for both partners in a clinic to have some sexual difficulties. This was the case with Jean and her husband Jack. Jean is the lady aged 40 whose treatment for agoraphobia we glimpsed on p. 62. Her husband was six years older, and they had never had intercourse during ten years of marriage. Part of the problem was Jean's vaginismus, complicated by Jack's occasional premature ejaculation. At marriage both had been virgin with no sexual experience. After marriage they frequently tried coitus unsuccessfully, and five years later had their marriage annulled on the grounds of non-consummation. Later they remarried, knowing their sexual problem would continue. They came eventually for treatment because they wanted to have a child.

Jean and Jack were interviewed twice together about their detailed sexual behaviour, and this brought them closer together. They masturbated each other on five nights to the point where Jack ejaculated but Jean did not reach orgasm. Homework before session 2 was to caress each other's bodies, including their genitals, for 15 minutes daily but under no circumstances to attempt sexual intercourse. By session 3 two weeks later both reported increased sexual arousal and less anxiety during sensate focus. They had a very enjoyable week, and Jack felt very relaxed and pleased. Jean enjoyed the sensate focus and was also much more relaxed. She had exceeded instructions in allowing Jack to insert one finger into her vagina, which caused her slight discomfort but great pleasure. They now planned to prolong their sensate focus from 15 to 30 minutes, buy a vaginal lubricant, and with its aid increase vaginal exploration first by Jean and then by Jack. They used different finger widths as dilators to gradually increase the stretching. Actual intercourse was still banned, but mutual masturbation was allowed. There was no need to hurry.

By session 4 a week later, progress had been a bit less satisfactory, and they had practised finger-insertion into the vagina on only one night. I encouraged them to continue, saying 'There's no haste; you'll have bad as well as good weeks, but with persistence you'll overcome these troubles and succeed.' Two weeks later they reported further advances. The lubricant made everything easier and more exciting. Jack had managed to insert his penis for an inch into Jean's vagina and to ejaculate inside her. They'd continued their sensate focus and finger insertions to stretch her vagina. More homework was planned with further mutual caressing and finger exercises to dilate the vagina together with the help of plastic dilators. Jack was to try deeper and more prolonged penile penetration, but not to move during intercourse.

Gradually Jack became able to penetrate Jean more deeply and to stay inside for longer, though he still tended to ejaculate a bit too soon. Both partners enjoyed sex more and felt very content. Neither showed high sex drive, and intercourse was usually only about once a week. After the seventh session both said they were satisfied with the partial progress they had achieved and did not want further treatment. At follow-up six months later, they were continuing to have intercourse about once a week with pleasure to both of them, and no vaginal spasm.

You can see how a skills programme requires the couple to become well informed about sexual matters, learn to discuss them freely with each other, be able to handle each other's bodies without shame or fear, and experiment gradually as they get used to different things until they reach a satisfying compromise that enables them both to reach climax. A lot of homework is needed before this happy state is attained, and it is often easier to do this under guidance of a therapist to whom one reports progress. It is also helpful to read suitable books on the subject and, when these are available, to see films as well. The idea is to overcome traditional taboos and the veil of silence that surrounds the subject of sex. It's surprising how highly intelligent people often lack basic knowledge about sex, and of course it is difficult to succeed at anything one knows little about.

Anxiety about menstruation and the menopause

Nowadays the onset of menstruation in girls at puberty usually leads to no problems. However, when they have been kept ignorant about their bodies and sexuality, the sudden appearance of menstrual bleeding can be worrying. One reassures the young woman that monthly periods are perfectly normal, to explain what they mean, and to advise her on how to use sanitary napkins and tampons.

Premenstrual tension

Irritability and a bit of depression are common in the premenstrual week and the first few days of menstrual discharge. (We are not talking here about pain during menstrual bleeding.) In some studies women had more accidents, suicide, and other mishaps during the premenstrual week than at other times during their cycle. A few days before menstruation there is also often tenderness and swelling of the breasts and perhaps swelling of the hands and feet. With this fluid retention weight may increase by a couple of pounds. Little is known about the cause or treatment of premenstrual tension.

Menopause

The menstrual cycle ceases in women in middle life. This is the menopause, and it has been unfairly blamed for a multitude of ills in middle age. People are beginning to realise that the menopause need cause no special anxiety. Hot flushes may be inconvenient. The vagina may become dry, causing pain during intercourse, which is remedied by use of lubricants. In recent years the danger of post-menopausal osteoporosis (thinning of the bones due to loss of calcium) has become recognised; this is reduced by hormone replacement therapy and other measures under careful medical guidance.

summary

Sexual worries are common in adolescents and young adults, but are usually overcome by discussion and normal experimentation. Sexual problems can be secondary to physical or psychological disorders, and to marital disharmony.

Dysfunction in the sexual arena takes several forms. Unconsummated marriage is rare. Frequent problems in women are painful intercourse, vaginal spasm, and failure to reach orgasm. In men, common difficulties are lack of social skills preventing any form of relationship with women, failure to have an erection, and premature ejaculation. Rarely, men cannot ejaculate despite adequate erection.

Management of sexual problems involves learning about normal sexual behaviour and reducing sexual anxiety by gradually engaging in increasingly intimate sexual relations. Both partners need to be treated together and to learn to tell one another what turns them on and off. Reading sexual books and seeing sexual films together can be very useful. They can explore one another's genitals and learn to caress one another at leisure. In addition they can learn specific ways of overcoming particular problems such as failure of erection, premature ejaculation, vaginal spasm, and anorgasmia. Some setbacks should be expected in the course of treatment, but patient persistence by both partners will lead to success.

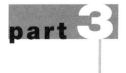

part 3

the treatment
of anxiety

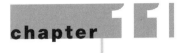

treatment by professionals

Almost every treatment under the sun has been used to treat anxiety disorders. Broadly speaking there are three main approaches used by doctors, psychologists and related professionals: (1) psychological methods which are now often self-administered too, (2) drugs, and (3) in a tiny number of cases, other physical methods such as electro-shock therapy and psychosurgery. Psychological treatments offer the most hope for lasting improvement, except where there is marked depression, in which case an antidepressant drug is useful.

Psychological management

Remember anxiety is normal and can be helpful

A bit of anxiety is perfectly OK for all of us to feel from time to time and indeed can be constructive. It can spur us on to deal with the problems producing our tensions. We all feel unhappy if we are threatened by serious illness, loss of a job, failure in important examinations, arguments with our partner or tiffs with our children. We may face financial demands we find hard to meet, or our car might break down on the way to an important engagement. Our difficulties cease only with death.

The aim is not to abolish anxiety. That cannot be done. Instead, try to put it in perspective. Cease regarding it as an enemy and instead recruit it as a spur to necessary action. Learn to roll with every stress. If you can't beat it, join it and transform it from foe to friend. We all live in the real world of difficulties which crop up every day and have to learn to cope with stress and deal with problems as they arise. There is a grain of truth in the saying, 'What happens to you matters less than how you take it.'

A little story from World War I makes the point that fear as such is less crucial than how we act. A Jewish military doctor in the Austrian army was next to a colonel when heavy shooting began. The colonel said teasingly 'Just another proof that the Aryan race is superior to the Semitic one! You're afraid, aren't you?' 'Sure I'm afraid' replied the doctor, 'but who's superior? If you, my dear Colonel, were as afraid as I am, you'd have run away long ago.'[1]

Discussion with other people can help

'Troubles shared are troubles halved.' An important part of dealing with stress is talking about it and seeking help when necessary from relatives and friends. Talking about our fears to someone we can trust is often very valuable. Chatting about our problems to a friend who can listen to us will frequently put them in a new light and suggest ways of dealing with what is bothering us. It may also ease our burden to talk to a professionally trained helper: doctor, psychologist, nurse, social worker, probation officer, clergyman. Complicated difficulties may require particularly skilled advice from specialists in the necessary treatments and recently-developed computer-guided self-help systems.

Try to distinguish between those problems we can eventually master and those which won't go away whatever we do. Sometimes we are reduced to making the best of a bad job. If a drunken husband beats his wife and children every day she might have to find a secret refuge where she and her children can live safely, find a job to bring in the money her husband refuses her, and perhaps divorce him.

Support may be all that is needed for many anxiety sufferers while others will need to adopt an exposure approach to overcome tension. Whatever way we deal with anxiety, it is important to know that we ourselves have to learn how to live with it. Therapists cannot wave a magic wand to abolish it, but can guide us to learn how to cope with distress. We should not expect a sudden miracle cure – expecting that will lead to disappointment. Benefit from exposure treatment comes gradually, and only by looking back over several days or weeks may we realise that we have actually made progress. Exposure treatment is a form of behavioural psychotherapy. Let us see what it is.

Exposure therapy

Until recently the most common psychological treatment of persistent fears and obsessions used Freudian or related models of psychoanalysis and psychotherapy. These assumed that phobias and rituals symbolised other hidden problems which had to be discovered and that when these were revealed through free association and worked through, the anxieties would disappear. Such digging and delving is time-consuming, can go on for years, and is ineffective for anxiety disorders. In the year 2000 I was told of a sufferer from obsessive-compulsive disorder (OCD) who has been having psychoanalysis for fully 15 years without benefit. Although a psychoanalytic approach does not usually relieve phobias, panic, rituals and the like, sufferers with such problems usually benefit lastingly from exposure therapy within a few days, weeks or months.

The behavioural treatment of exposure does not assume that phobias are symbolic transformations of hidden difficulties. It does not try to uncover unconscious dirt or meanings. Rather, it regards the phobia, panic or obsession itself as the main problem that is to be overcome directly by the sufferer learning how to face those situations which trigger the panic until it can be tolerated.

A wealth of research found that the exposure approach works in most cases. Even phobias which have been present for 20 years have been overcome after a few hours of guidance from a therapist or from a suitable computer self-help system, of which more anon. From 3 to 20 hours of guidance are necessary, spaced over one to two hour-long sessions over a few weeks or months. These 3 to 20 hours are in sessions spent with a therapist face-to-face or by phone,[2] or with a self-help system, apart from the daily hour or so which the sufferer has to spend between sessions doing self-exposure homework to clear the problem up properly.

The principle of exposing ourselves to whatever frightens us

Not all behavioural methods are equally effective. Relaxation is often called a behavioural treatment but does not decrease obsessions or phobias. More effective behavioural techniques which are known under many names with which I won't bore you have in common the principle of *exposure* to whatever frightens us until we get used to it. Exposure is also called confrontation. Once we confront our fear determinedly for long enough it will diminish bit by bit.

How long is long enough?

There is no quick answer beyond *longer is better*. In a lucky minority of sufferers just a few minutes of exposure to the things that terrify them reduce the fear, usually in those who have had their problem only for a few weeks or months and are really determined to get the better of it. More commonly, the fear starts to diminish within half an hour after the start of the exposure, even in people with very long-standing phobias. Rarely, several hours may be needed for the fear to start abating. The important point is to persevere in facing the panic until it starts to lessen and to be prepared to go on day after day thereafter until permanent relief occurs, which may take weeks or months.

How rapidly should I tackle my worst fears?

'Should I go little by little, slowly from my easiest to my worst fears, or should I grab the bull by the horns?' In general *the quicker you tackle your worst fears the quicker you recover*. The faster and longer we embrace the monster of our panic, the more rapidly will it fade in our arms to become a shadow of itself, an old familiar friend of mild tension rather than the monster of terror.

Can anxiety during exposure be harmful?

'No' is the answer nearly always, contrary to popular belief. The great majority of people who allow themselves to experience extreme panic eventually become unable to experience more than mild fear. If we deliberately try to panic, then paradoxically the odds are we will not be able to, or that we will bring on only a pale reflection of the real thing. Even if severe panic does strike, if we continue to face it the panic will gradually evaporate and become less likely to return in future.

Early exposure prevents phobias from growing

A golden rule to nip phobias in the bud is *Avoid escape! Encourage the facing of fear*. After a sudden accident, there is often an interim lag phase before a phobia develops. If during this phase you are immediately re-exposed to the original situation, this protects you from getting frightened of it. It has long been said that people should re-enter a traumatic situation immediately after the original trauma. Aeroplane pilots are encouraged to fly again as soon as possible after a flying accident. Car drivers are recommended to resume driving quickly after a car crash. If you fall off a horse, it's best to mount it again right away.

   With mild fear, people can be helped to overcome it by reassurance that it is fine to go back to the frightening situation and experience fear there until it dies down. Numerous tricks of suggestion have been used successfully to encourage people to face their fears. One man was bet £1,000 by his doctor that he would not die of a heart attack should he venture forth from home, and promptly found himself going out alone for the first time in months. Professional actors who were suddenly struck with stage fright overcame this on stage by constantly looking at and repeating to themselves messages of encouragement written by their doctors.

   Once we avoid a frightening situation, we are more likely to steer clear of it again the next time we meet it, and gradually a phobia builds up. It is better to risk facing a slightly unnerving situation rather than have the opposite risk of developing a phobia because you avoid the unpleasantness. While people with heart disease must not be extended beyond the physical limits set by their heart disease, one would not wish to make them invalids. The fewer the restrictions that people are hedged in by, the less likely they are to develop hypochondriacal anxieties. The general attitude needed is summarised in a short verse:

'Which epitaph shall be mine?'

She couldn't try		She couldn't try
For fear she'd die	or	For fear she'd die;
She never tried		But when she tried
And so she died		Her fears – they died[3]

Established phobias need structured exposure

Once someone is persistently avoiding the frightening situation, simple exhortations to bravery and will-power alone may not be terribly helpful. Your anxiety disorder can be aggravated if you enter situations you cannot cope with and from which you then escape. Before severe sufferers confront the source of their terrors, it is vital that they first understand the panic that will ensue and structure their exposure so that they can deal properly with that panic. They must be determined to get the better of their fear and not run away from it. The fear will not disappear by magic. *It usually takes time to lessen – even up to several hours* if the phobia is very severe, and this must be allowed for. Rather than briefly poke her nose into a dreaded crowded store, feel the surge of panic, and rush out again, it is better for an agoraphobic to reserve a full afternoon for the adventure. She should take with her a book or walkman or materials to write a letter, and when panic strikes, sit in a corner of the store and ride out the panic by reading, listening, or writing during the 30–60 minutes which may elapse before the panic passes. When she feels a bit better, she can resume her shopping.

Overcoming fear takes time

This is clear from the example you have just seen and should be taken into account in planning treatment of any anxiety. Arrange enough time for anxiety to subside in the situation you are trying to get used to. It may take an hour a day over a few days if the fear is of animals or aeroplanes. Longer and more delicate negotiations may be needed for sexual anxieties. If you are impotent, there is little point propositioning a sexy woman you have just met at a party and jumping into bed with her without more ado. Your vital part will be limp and your partner irritated that you cannot perform as promised. Shame at your poor performance will make you anticipate failure next time around, and so the problem will go on. Overcoming sexual anxiety needs patience even with an understanding partner, and careful preparation is necessary. Your partner needs to know about the problem and to agree to co-operate in the stages to be gone through before regular success is attained.

Determination and patience

These are two qualities essential to conquer rather than be ruled by fear. This is as true for helping others as for helping yourself. Parents who want to help a child overcome its school phobia must be prepared to tolerate its almost inevitable crying the first few times the child is returned to school. You will need to steel yourself to ignore the complaints of headache or pain in the stomach with which the child will greet you in the morning just before the time to go to school. Obviously if the child looks ill it might be wise to check its temperature, but if this is normal for the fourth consecutive morning the chances are that you need not carry on with this precaution. Firm but loving and consistent pressure toward school should help the child overcome the fear within a couple of weeks.

A patient's view of qualities needed for success

Here is what Lisa, aged 50, said of her experiences in overcoming her height and train phobia. Determination was crucial in following guidance from a therapist.

> ❝Your willingness to trust your therapist through thick and thin is essential, as well as your willingness to follow his instructions, however weird some seem at times. The early part of treatment is the hardest. You'll experience some real shocks and they won't be softened by tranquillisers. It'll take everything you've got to hang on when you feel like giving up. Very soon you'll find yourself going over the edge between the safe and the panic-making. I'll never forget being asked to look over the edge of the banister on the first floor landing, and nearly chickening out with fright. The therapist firmly encouraged me to stay in my panic, fight against my urge to draw back from my fears. We made it. I then went into even more anxious-making situations, after which leaning over the banister became child's play. These experiences were hell, but I learned that my will to win was stronger than my fears; that it worked at the severest point of my panic with the help of techniques I'd been taught; that I had it in me to conquer my fears. After each such experience I was left with the memory that I'd made a breakthrough, that I'd achieved the impossible and with confidence that I could do it again and more.
>
> Each further step in treatment was carefully prepared for, working towards targets agreed at the start. Between sessions I did set tasks entirely by myself.

These were a very important part of the whole thing, as they proved I could cope on my own. At times between sessions I felt anxious, at times rebellious, at times despondent. It was often a running battle between the part of me that said 'I can't' and 'I won't' and the part that replied 'I've done it before; I'll do it again in spite of my anxiety.' There were the memories of the agonies already suffered as well as of the victories already won, plus the prospect of more to come; and anyone who's had panics and avoided them knows what it feels like knowingly to expose oneself to more. But the good memories together with the will to win and the knowledge that the therapist knew what he was doing, helped to keep me going.

The treatment taught me how to cope positively with my anxieties, which haven't completely disappeared but are now manageable. More, it's really changed my attitude to life in a more positive direction. Instead of saying 'No' to my hang-ups and some of the ups and downs of life I can now say 'Yes' with much more confidence, having learned during treatment that I could cope with terrifying things. When the therapist's part was done it was over to me. The 'impossible' can be done if you're prepared to stick it out during the treatment come what may. You'll then find yourself the winner even if it's not a knockout victory.[4] 〞

Lisa then offered her services as co-therapist for other phobics. It is heartening how generous many ex-sufferers are in spending time helping others learn to overcome anxiety problems in the same way.

Failure is likely if you feel treatment is unnecessary

For treatment to be successful we may need to give up some cherished ideas, and this can be very difficult, as one obsessive hand-washer complained when told that it was all right to put her infant's dirty nappies into the washing machine without bothering whether they touched the edge of the door hatch. She put her doubts in verse:

'Coming to Terms with the Germs: An Inmate's Complaint'
(to be sung in melancholy tones to the tune of 'Oh My Darling Clementine')

To be clean was once a virtue
Next to godliness sublime
But when they put you in a nuthouse
You are told that it's a crime.
I wish the doctors and head shrinkers
Would get together and agree
Whether urine is really harmful
Or as pure as cups of tea.[5]

Sad to say, this lady never accepted that washing 60 times daily was abnormal, did little in treatment, and improved very little.

Contrast this with the positive attitude of another woman who improved dramatically, losing all her obsessions and rituals in a few weeks. 'I'm trying always to follow the golden rule "never avoid" and working hard at things until the fear goes. I'm so very grateful to be able to go about my daily life, without having to do extraordinary things.'[6]

What forms of exposure treatment are there?

In its simplest form, exposure treatment consists merely of advice to sufferers to expose themselves every day to a situation they find rather difficult and to record their daily actions in a diary which the therapist reviews at the next visit. As they gain confidence, they can set themselves fresh targets to achieve from one week to the next. They have to define weekly targets which will be useful for them to attain. An agoraphobic man who is unable to go to work because he cannot travel on a tube train might first practise standing outside the tube station every day for a few days and record his reactions, lengthening the time he spends at the station each day. Then he could go and buy a ticket several times and finally go down to the underground platform. Thereafter he could jump on and off the train before it departs, get on the train for one stop, and then for ever-increasing distances. Relatives can help the sufferer work out details of his programme, monitoring it, and praising him for any progress being made.

We know now from research that for improvement to persist sufferers must do the exposure alone rather than in the presence of a therapist. The approach to the frightening situation can be very slow and gradual, when it's called *desensitisation*. If the sufferer tackles his fears quickly this is called *flooding*. Exposure to the phobic situation can be purely in one's mind's eye (*fantasy* or *imaginal* exposure), or by viewing slides or films or videos or computer-screen or virtual reality depictions of the phobic situation, or to the actual situation itself (*real* or *live* exposure).

In general, the quicker that you allow yourself to approach your frightening situation and stay there until you feel better, the more speedy your recovery. The quicker you deal with the real situation, as opposed to merely thinking about it, the more rapid the improvement. During rapid exposure to live situations sufferers usually experience more fear than during slow imagined approach, but this price may be well worth paying for the time it saves in getting better quicker. Phobics who did rapid exposure to their really frightening situations later said this was no worse an experience than going to the dentist.

As an example of desensitisation in fantasy, a patient with a bird phobia might relax and then imagine herself first looking at a small pigeon 100 yards away in a cage. She holds this scene in her mind for a few seconds and then drops it and relaxes. If this caused her no anxiety she then imagines the same pigeon 90 yards away in a closed cage; and in subsequent scenes allows the pigeon to draw gradually nearer until after many hours she handles the pigeon in her mind's eye without fear. This approach is easy to learn, but takes so long to help sufferers overcome their fear that more efficient forms of exposure are now usually recommended. Relaxation turns out to be unnecessary – though sufferers like doing it, relaxation does not speed recovery and the time is better spent just doing exposure if possible.

Flooding

Exposure by desensitisation is like wading slowly into a swimming pool from the shallow end, and exposure by flooding is like jumping in the deep end. *Imaginal flooding* is also called *implosion*. Here sufferers imagine themselves in their most frightening situations continously for one to two hours, and may give a running description of what they are imagining. They can record this description in a walkman and play this audiotaped recording back to themselves repeatedly until it is utterly and completely boring, or write this down and read it time after time after time. For example, an agoraphobic may imagine herself leaving the house alone, tremulously walking down a busy road to a crowded high street, entering a crowded supermarket, and waiting for ages as part of a slow-moving line while she feels faint and fearful.

A young student with examination panic 48 hours before an exam was helped by deliberately feeling his fear fully without trying to escape from it.[7] He had already failed a previous examination because of a similar panic. He was asked to sit up in bed and try to feel his fear by imagining all the consequences that would follow failure – derision from his colleagues, disappointment from his family, and financial loss. As he did this at first his sobbings increased but soon his tremblings ceased. The effort needed to maintain a vivid imagination increased and the emotion he could summon began to ebb. Within half an hour he was calm. He was asked to repeatedly experience his fears. Every time he felt a little wave of spontaneous alarm he was not to push it aside but was to enhance it and try to experience it more vividly. The student practised his exposure exercises assiduously until he became almost unable to feel frightened. He passed his examinations without difficulty.

A variant of flooding is *paradoxical intention*. For example, a man who feared that he might die of a heart attack was asked to try as hard as possible to make his heart beat faster and die of a heart attack right on the spot. He laughed and replied 'Doc, I'm trying hard but I can't do it.'[8] He was told to go ahead and try to die from a heart attack each time he became worried. As he started laughing about it, humour helped him distance himself from his anxiety. He was asked to die at least three times a day of a heart attack, and instead of trying hard to go to sleep, try hard to remain awake. He improved the moment he started laughing at his symptoms and became willing to produce them intentionally.

Paradoxical intention has helped insomnia. When one man complained that he just never could get any sleep, his doctor advised him instead to 'try lying awake in bed all night. Don't get up. No sleeping pills. Just lie there with your eyes open as long as you can.'[9] The next day he apologised to his doctor for being unable to follow instructions as he fell asleep so quickly!

Rapid prolonged exposure to the actual frightening situation

An approach proven to be lastingly helpful in much careful research is rapid prolonged exposure to the actual frightening situation. An agoraphobic might enter a crowded shopping area, remain there for several hours until her desire to escape disappears, and then report back to her therapist. Prolonged exposure to the real frightening situation can be supplemented or preceded by imaginal exposure. Sessions lasting two continuous hours are more effective than several shorter periods adding up to the same total exposure time. Specific phobics can virtually lose their phobias in a couple of long sessions, while agoraphobics require longer. Patients usually become very anxious early in exposure, but this dies down as the session continues.

Before exposure begins, the sufferer must fully understand what is required and agree to do it without avoidance; otherwise he may escape during exposure, which might make him worse. Full co-operation is essential. Slower exposure is used where physical disease may make excessive anxiety undesirable, as in people with asthma or heart disease or ulcerative colitis.

Exposure to the phobic situation in imagination or on film or virtual reality

While exposure to the real situation yields the most dividends, it is sometimes hard to access that, e.g. with thunderstorm phobia, so imagining the situation, or seeing it on film or virtual reality, can be done instead. Watching well-prepared films of coitus can help people with sexual problems not only acquire much-needed information but also lose their discomfort about sex. Some sufferers prefer to experience their fears in fantasy or on film before exposing themselves to them in real life, as in the next example.

Rapid improvement in Zoe's cat phobia

Zoe had been terrified of cats since childhood. She avoided them at all costs and asked a companion to help her through streets where cats might be present.[10] After two sessions each of two hours imagining cats close to her and scratching her, she felt able to face real felines. A black cat was then held on a table about six feet away from her; looking at it made Zoe very anxious but this died down after about five minutes. Over the next few minutes the therapist gradually brought the cat nearer to her. Each change in the cat's position led to a short spurt of anxiety during which she was encouraged to keep looking at the cat. After 15 minutes she touched the cat and as the session proceeded started to stroke it and hold it on her lap. She was praised liberally for each step forward she took. If she hesitated, the therapist showed her how to touch the cat by doing it first himself. This is called *modelling of exposure*. Zoe spent the last 15 minutes of the two-hour session cuddling the cat on her lap without anxiety. After treatment lasting six hours in all Zoe was able to handle cats normally and her life was no longer restricted by fear.

Phobics of this kind can overcome their fears so quickly that it takes them a while to realise that they are no longer phobic. When Olga watched spiders running up her arms for the first time in her life without feeling scared she said she just couldn't believe this and took some weeks to get used to the idea that she could now handle spiders with equanimity.

Nora lost her dog phobia after two treatment sessions

Nora was a painter aged 20 who had feared dogs at least since the age of four.[11] She crossed roads to avoid dogs, would not visit friends who owned dogs, and avoided going out to paint landscapes because of her phobia. She had two exposure sessions, each two hours long. In the first, a gentle little dog was gradually brought nearer to her; the therapist patted and stroked it and encouraged Nora to follow suit. At first she was terrified, cried, and backed away, but slowly as exposure continued she acquired confidence. Within a few minutes she touched the dog's rump for the first time exclaiming 'It's so horrible and ugly, the whole dog seems like a head to me.' As the minutes ticked past, however, Nora's fear gradually died down and she stopped crying, began cuddling the beastie, and said she did not know why she had thought dogs were ugly before. In session 2 she allowed exposure to a larger dog in the same way. After four hours of exposure in all she no longer feared dogs. By follow-up she had visited friends who owned dogs, played with those, and no longer avoided dogs in the street, though she remained wary of big Alsatians. Nora's confidence rose so much that it spilled over into overcoming slight difficulties with her parents by becoming more assertive and getting on better with them.

An unusual twist: 'Imagine eating a dog and you'll feel better'

At the 6-month follow-up Nora had an unusual complication after hearing a story of a couple touring Hong Kong taking their pet dog into a Chinese restaurant. The waiter's English wasn't great, but they signed to him that they wanted him to feed their pet too. He disappeared into the kitchen with their dog under his arm. Dinner took an unconscionably long time to appear. Eventually the waiter appeared with a large platter which he uncovered with a flourish to display their pet poodle cooked expertly. The couple's horror can be imagined. On hearing this story Nora became upset and preoccupied with visions of cooked dogs which haunted her wherever she went. After these persisted for a few days, she asked to see me again. To help her, I asked Nora to 'imagine yourself eating a cooked dog. Try just a little bit of the leg first, please.' She hesitated and said 'I feel sick', but I persisted. 'Just take a knife and fork in your hand and cut a tiny sliver of meat off the haunch, just chew it properly.' She followed my instructions, made chewing movements and nearly vomited. With persistence she swallowed the meat in fantasy, accompanying that scene with swallowing movements, and within 20 minutes had polished off the dog and smiled with relief at her accomplishment, in contrast to her earlier tears. Her visions of cooked dogs disappeared. A year later Nora wrote saying she was fine and had married and given birth to a son.

Treatment in groups

Phobics may join groups to learn how to do exposure therapy. The groups may be led by a professional therapist, or by an ex-sufferer as in the TOP (Triumph Over Phobia) groups in Britain and in Australia (see p. 199). Sufferers can meet together to discuss useful ways of reducing their fear and then go into their frightening situations and report back to one another on their progress. The group encourages them to master their fear in phobic situations, and allows shy people to learn new social behaviour and get used to other people. Those who began by being ashamed of their handicap, not talking about it, feeling ridiculous, and avoiding eating in restaurants, looking at other people in buses or tubes or asking strangers for directions in the street, learned to cope with these situations in exposure exercises and so overcame their phobias.

Social gains become especially clear when phobics do exposure exercises on their own. They get used to speaking to strangers despite feeling anxious. Sybil was phobic of lifts and on her third exposure going up and down the lift the operator asked her why she was doing this. Feeling ashamed she told him her problem. He sympathised and immediately told her about his flying phobia! This gave Sybil heart to talk to other people when she became frightened again thereafter.[12]

Marion was phobic of underground trains and panicked when one stopped in a tunnel. She admitted this to a neighbour, who responded kindly and started talking about her own problems. Marion calmed down and thereafter whenever she went by train looked for people whom she thought she could talk to in case of a panic and chose to sit beside them.

Polly who had a social phobia panicked in a shop and started to chat to the saleswoman who was giving her change. The saleswoman politely told her to see a psychiatrist.[13] Polly left the shop shaking, ashamed, and angry. The group persuaded her to return there immediately and tell the same clerk that she had just seen a psychiatrist, who had told her to go back. When Polly did so she had a long talk with the saleswoman, who then admitted she disliked customers trying to make small talk as she felt so inhibited. The saleswoman invited Polly to come as often as possible in order to practise with Polly how to chat with customers.

Nightmares can be treated like phobias

Nightmares can express waking fears and be reduced by exposure to the frightening stimuli. On page 105 we saw how children were taught to transform bad dreams into experiences of mastery by deliberately confronting the unpleasant content and rehearsing changing it into more positive material. I used a similar approach to help 40-year-old Dale who had had a very difficult relationship with her mother who had died 14 years earlier. Dale's story is not for the squeamish. For 12 years she had been plagued by recurrent nightmares in which she pushed her mother off the roof of a house, went downstairs to check that her mother had been killed, and found the head severed from the body. She put on jackboots and then jumped on the head to make sure her mother was really dead. As Dale did so, however, something streamed out of the head's eyes toward her own eyes, pursuing her as she retreated, and just as this thing pierced her eyes she woke up trembling and thinking, 'My bloody mother, she always wins!' For the whole morning after these nightmares she would feel so depressed she avoided going to work.

I asked Dale to retell her nightmares three times in 20 minutes. At first she cried and was very agitated, but then she calmed down and retold the bad dreams more easily the second time and even more so the third time. I suggested she write them down afterwards at home and read them repeatedly. Her second visit to me lasted 40 minutes. I persuaded her to retell her nightmare with a triumphant ending, which she decided was smashing her mother's skull and squeezing the brains to a pulp in her hands and flushing them down a toilet. At my suggestion she wrote the dream down three times more, but now with triumphant endings over her mother. With difficulty she was also persuaded to swear aloud repeatedly against her mother and me and other people – something she couldn't bring herself to do previously, much as she wished to. When I saw her for the third time two weeks later, she managed this, felt far less depressed, and spoke about the nightmare with equanimity. Over the next year she remained well and free of nightmares.

A more gentle kind of exposure can also help people over nightmares. Enid aged 19 had had nightmares for four years about falling from a bridge.[14] She had had a phobia of bridges for as long as she could remember and also feared heights. She lost her fear of bridges after seven sessions of desensitisation in imagination, and her nightmares ceased. Towards the end of treatment Enid instead had two pleasant dreams about bridges and she remained well when seen six months later.

Nightmare sufferers improved by following self-exposure instructions which were posted to them in the form of a manual.[15] They improved more than sufferers who followed self-relaxation instructions in a relaxation manual that was posted to them, and more than others who were just on a waiting list for treatment. When sufferers came off the waiting list and followed self-exposure instructions from an exposure manual posted to them, they too improved. Relatives confirmed that improved sufferers slept better after treatment. This nightmare study is another example of anxiety-disorder sufferers improving by self-help.

Stress immunisation

Learning to cope

Inoculations produce immunity to an infection by exposing us to a related but less harmful bug, which stimulates our body's immune defences without overwhelming them. A related idea has been suggested to help people resist stress. Research suggests that stress inoculation is a real possibility, that people can be protected against emotional stress by experiencing similar but less extreme versions of their stress. The principle is a 'hair of the dog that might bite you tomorrow'. For example, after children had been allowed to play in a dentist's chair and with dental equipment, and to undergo mock examinations of their teeth, when they had real dentistry later they showed less fear than other children who had not played these dental games before.[16] Preparing adults, too, for distressing situations can help them reduce their suffering when the trauma comes. After having pre-surgery explanations about the problems to be expected after surgery and descriptions of the kind and duration of pain they would have, patients recovered more quickly and with less pain and discomfort than similar patients who had not been prepared in the same way.

In another study, subjects saw a gruesome film showing Australian aborigines being circumcised during a puberty initiation rite.[17] While watching the film, some subjects heard a sound track giving a detached description of the operation or saying it was not painful or harmful and the boys wanted it in order to become adults. Subjects hearing this sound track were less disturbed by the film than others who saw the film in a silent version, or with a sound track emphasising how painful the procedure was. Our mental set thus influences whether we will perceive something as threatening. Surgery patients were helped by being told that some anxiety is natural preoperatively but that it can be controlled if they rehearse realistic positive aspects of the surgical experience.

An extreme example of mastery

Some people learn coping methods so well that they endure even the most gruesome torture without undue distress. Few, however, reach the degree of control described by a Spanish Inquisitor in 1629. He was less than pleased at the indifference certain victims showed to his torture.

> ❝Some rascals trusted so strongly in the secrets they possessed to make themselves insensible to pain, that they voluntarily gave themselves up as prisoners, to cleanse themselves of certain sins. Some use certain words pronounced in a low voice, and others writings which they hide on some part of their body. The first one I recognised as using some sort of charm, surprised us by his more than natural firmness, because after the first stretching of the rack he seemed to sleep as quietly as if he'd been in a good bed, without lamenting, complaining or crying, and when the stretching was repeated two or three times, he still remained motionless as a statue. This made us suspect that he was provided with some charm, and to resolve the doubt he was stripped as naked as his hand. Yet, after a careful search, nothing was found on him but a little piece of paper on which were the figures of the three kings, with these words on the other side: 'Beautiful star which delivered the Magi from Herod's persecution, deliver me from all torment.' This paper was stuffed in his left ear. Now although the paper had been taken away from him he still appeared insensible to the torture, because when it was applied he muttered words between his teeth which we couldn't hear, and as he persevered in his denials, it was necessary to send him back to prison.[18]❞

Programmes for stress immunisation

Fortunately most of us have to contend with less trying ordeals than those of the Inquisition. Don Meichenbaum devised stress immunisation programmes for students[19] similar to what is now called cognitive therapy. Subjects are taught to recognise signs of their fear such as rapid throbbing heartbeat, sweaty palms, and tense muscles, and to become aware of anxious things they say or think when in a difficult situation, with a view to changing such self-statements.

All of us silently say worrying things to ourselves when in trouble, though we may be unaware of this until we think about it. If we are anxious, say, while talking to an audience and some people walk out of the room, we might think 'I must be boring. No one's interested in what I'm saying. I knew I never could give a speech. I'd better dry up quickly.' This further increases our anxiety until fear paralyses us. If we are self-confident, however, then members of the audience leaving might make us think 'I suppose they've another appointment to keep; pity they have to miss my good talk', or 'What a rude bunch.'

Another example: when taking a driving test, a worrier might glance at the examiner and think 'Why is he frowning like that? I'm making a fool of myself. I know I'm a bad driver.' Someone more confident might say to himself: 'Perhaps he's frowning because he argued with his wife earlier today. I'll have to be careful to show him I can manage this car. I may not be an expert driver, but I'm good enough to pass and I have to convince him that I can do it.'[20]

In each of these examples, anxious and confident people see the same event differently, and what they say or think reflects this. Part of stress immunisation is learning how to 'speak' differently to ourselves. When an agoraphobic leaves her home on an exposure exercise she could say 'One step at a time, relax, good, I can get myself to do it if I try hard enough. This giddiness in my head and fluttering in my chest is exactly what I knew I'd feel. Let me label my fear from 0 to 8 and watch it change. That's it, I'm breathing heavily, a signal to start my coping techniques. Let's see. Try slow deep breathing; one, two, in, out . . . that's the way old girl, you'll pull through yet.'

Worrying thinking may become so habitual that we're not even aware of it. We have to learn to recognise that we might be saying 'Heavens, I'm going to have a heart attack' or 'I'm sure I'm losing control, going mad.' This makes matters worse, so we have to change that. A teacher of stress inoculation might say: 'We're going to work on ways to control how we feel, to manage our anxiety and tension. We'll do this by learning how to control thinking and attention, and what we say to ourselves. This comes about by first becoming aware of the negative things we say, of our prophecies of doom, of how we don't attend to the task in hand. Recognising this is the first step toward change. When we realise what we're saying, this reminds us, rings a bell for us to think different thoughts and self-instructions to challenge and dispute our worrying thoughts. This way we learn to do things more confidently and attend to what has to be done.'

Most of us develop ways of coping with stress such as exams or visits to the dentist. We can learn to use these coping mechanisms more systematically. After learning self-instruction, a phobic woman reported 'It makes me able to be in the [phobic] situation, not to be comfortable but to tolerate it. . . . I don't talk myself out of being afraid, just out of appearing afraid. . . . you immediately react to the thing you're afraid of and then start to reason with yourself. I talk myself out of panic.'[21]

While trying to master her snake phobia by approaching a snake, another young woman started speaking to it, saying 'I'll make a deal with you. If you don't scare or hurt me, I won't scare or hurt you.' She went on to touch the snake. Other people who got thoughts they didn't want dealt with them by saying 'Screw it! I'm perfectly normal.'[22]

Each of us prefers methods tailored to our own needs. From a list of coping self-statements we can choose some to rehearse during stress inoculation training. In the first phase of *preparing* for a stressor, we could pick things to say to ourselves such as: 'What do I have to do? Make a plan to deal with it. Just think about what I can do about it. That's better than getting anxious. No negative self-statements; just think rationally. Don't worry; worry won't help anything. Maybe what I think is anxiety is eagerness to deal with the stressor.'[23]

When *confronting* and *handling* a stressor, statements might include 'Psych yourself up. Meet this challenge. Convince yourself to do it. Reason your fear away. By taking one step at a time you can handle the situation. Don't think about fear but about what you have to do. Stay relevant. This fear is what you knew you'd feel. It's a reminder to use your coping exercises. This tension can be an ally; a cue to cope. Relax; you're in control. Take a slow deep breath. Ah, good.'

To cope with feeling *overwhelmed* when frightened we might say 'When fear comes just pause. Focus on the present; what do you have to do? Label your fear from 0 to 8 and watch it change. Expect your fear to rise. Don't try to eliminate fear totally; just keep it manageable.'

Finally, once we have made small advances in dealing with fear we deserve to *pat ourselves on the back* by saying things like 'It worked; I did it. Wait until I tell . . . (relative or friend) about this. It wasn't as bad as I expected. I made more out of my fear than it was worth. My damn ideas, that's the problem. When I control them I control my fears. It's getting better each time I use the procedures. I'm pleased with my progress. I did it!'

Dr Claire Weekes wrote about handling anxiety like this. To an agoraphobic going down the road she said:

❝We're off. But, oh my goodness! Here comes Mrs X from down the street! What are you going to do about it? You advance towards her with your heart in your mouth. You can feel your heart pumping in your throat, banging in your chest. Your sensitised nerves are recording and amplifying each beat. Does it really matter if you feel your heart beating? It doesn't matter in the least. It certainly doesn't harm your heart, so don't be afraid to feel your heart pounding while you talk to Mrs X.

But she's settling in for a good old gossip. What if she were to continue for another 10 minutes, *half an hour*? You tremble at the thought and think 'I can't stand it. I'll make a fool of myself. She'll notice! . . .'

Take your hand off those screws. Let your body slacken. Loosen. Loosen. Take a deep breath; let it out slowly and surrender completely to listening to Mrs X, she'll eventually stop.

Now we're off down the street again. You feel a bit better. You made it! But now you must cross the main road, and just when you need your legs most they suddenly turn to jelly. Those old jelly legs; you stand rooted to the pavement sure your legs will never carry you across.

But here again I whisper 'Jelly legs will get you there if you'll let them. It's only a feeling; not a true muscular weakness. Don't be bluffed by jelly legs . . . let them wobble. They can carry you across the street whether they wobble or not. And don't think you must hold tensely on to yourself from collapsing. *It's the holding on that exhausts, not the letting go.* So let your legs wobble. It's only a feeling, not muscular weakness. . . .'[24]

The essence of dealing with fear is learning to ride it until the storm passes. In stress immunisation how to do this is taught as a deliberate skill. It's like learning how to drive a car.

To cope with stress we don't just mutter good things to ourselves. We become aware of the worrying things we say or do that cramp our style and upset us. Then we develop positive rules and strategies to adopt when in trouble. Finally we learn to use these repeatedly in all sorts of different problem situations. We practise these again and again until we automatically bring them into play whenever we feel frightened.

Meichenbaum's students learned coping skills in three hours of training. They imagined having unpredictable shocks, keeping their hands for long periods in cold water, seeing stressful films, feeling embarrassed, etc. The students rehearsed ways of dealing with such stressors. For pain they imagined a scene along the lines:

In your mind's eye you're volunteering for a pain experiment. You watch apprehensively as a blood pressure cuff is inflated around your upper left arm. You're asked to tolerate as long as possible the pain you're about to experience. Soon the tourniquet will induce a dull, aching, slowly mounting pain. How long will you tolerate it: 5 minutes, 20 minutes, 40 minutes? What coping techniques will you use to endure it? How would you train someone to cope better with exactly this sort of pain?

You can try and reduce the pain by relaxing your muscles and attending to your breathing while you breathe slowly and deeply. Start this breathing now. See that you don't go over 14 breaths a minute; that's it. Just let your muscles go loose while you're doing this.

You don't need to focus on the pain. Just focus on other things. Why not do mental arithmetic? How about subtracting 7s from 100 in order? Thereafter you can count the number of tiles on the ceiling. That took quite a time; now let's see what we can look at through the window.

That worked for a while, now let's try something different. I'll watch and analyse the change in my arm and hand as the tourniquet continues to press tightly. Yes, there's some pain but it's interesting; my arm also feels numb. It seems a bit swollen. The colour is also different. It seemed rose pink in the beginning. Now it seems more white.

You can also deal with the pain by using imagery. Let's transform the pain. Imagine you're lying on a beach and the sun warms your arm, or that your arm is cold or numb after injection of a local anaesthetic.[25] 〝

Students were encouraged to choose from a 'cafeteria' of coping tactics whichever suited them best. They were to use these at times when the pain seemed most unbearable and they felt like giving up. The students thus developed individually tailored coping packages to employ in times of trouble. They role-played teaching these skills to the trainer, telling him what to do when he was in pain or frightened. After brief training in such stress immunisation, they endured a tourniquet on their arm for twice as long as other students who had no preparation in imagination. . . .

Meichenbaum's approach has elements in common with two other stress-reducing approaches. First, its focus on slow deep breathing, imagery and distancing is also used in mindfulness and other forms of meditation.[26] Second, it overlaps with cognitive therapy (restructuring) that teaches sufferers to identify the 'negative automatic thoughts' and catastrophic beliefs that many have when anxious, and to practise substituting more positive ideas. In cognitive therapy sufferers are also encouraged to carry out 'behavioural experiments' to test the validity of their negative thoughts and beliefs such as 'if I avoid going out alone I'll faint and attract attention from passers-by'. They are asked to test this out by actually going out and seeing if they really will faint. Such behavioural experiments are a form of exposure or paradoxical intention, so most cognitive therapy practised is in fact cognitive behaviour therapy (CBT). A few studies, however, have found that even pure cognitive therapy without behavioural experiments (exposure) can reduce anxiety disorders.[27] When the point was examined, oddly enough most negative beliefs which were worked on in treatment only improved after people's behaviour and other symptoms had improved, so perhaps pure cognitive therapy works as a form of stress immunisation, a way of distancing oneself from one's fear.

Let us look at how pure cognitive therapy is done[28] – we saw an earlier example with Jeff in Chapter 6, p. 81.

Cognitive restructuring for post-traumatic stress disorder

While driving a bus two years previously Tim had been stabbed, his arm was lacerated, and two of his fingers became permanently paralysed. He did not return to work. When assessed he had intrusive thoughts and images of the attack most of the day, nightmares about it several nights a week, and tried to avoid thinking about the trauma. He avoided knives, buses, raw meat, and going out alone. He only went by car if accompanied and all its doors were locked and windows closed. He was depressed, slept badly, and lost his temper easily, upsetting his parents and girlfriend. He felt guilty at not having prevented the assault and angry with colleagues for trivialising it and not contacting him after it.

Tim understood the rationale for cognitive restructuring and used daily thought records to identify negative automatic thoughts and irrational beliefs. From these and discussion he recognised many such thoughts and beliefs:

1 *Overestimation of danger*: that the chance of his being re-assaulted was 80%. His therapist asked him to estimate how often he had been out with friends in the three years before the attack (6912 times), compute the chance of a future assault (1/6912 = 0.0004 or 0.04%), and explain the difference between perceived and actual risk. He thus came to recognise that he exaggerated the danger, and challenged it with 'My chance of being attacked is no more than that of other people.' Belief in his negative automatic thought fell to less than 10%, and belief in his alternative thought was 90%. Without any exposure instructions, soon after this Tim began to go out with friends and then alone.

2 *Shame*: Tim began to recognise unhelpful shaming thoughts and beliefs e.g. 'I'm weak because after the attack I cried; I'm a coward because I cried; men don't cry', and rated their validity as 85%. These thoughts were challenged by asking him to identify evidence for and against them. He found much evidence against them, e.g. his father had been upset after the assault and cried on visiting Tim in hospital, yet Tim didn't believe his father was a weak coward. A few years before, he and friends had wept at a funeral; this was appropriate, not a sign of weakness or cowardliness. After this *reframing*, Tim challenged the negative thoughts with the alternative 'Crying is appropriate in stressful or sad situations.' His belief in this challenge was 100% and in his negative thoughts was now 0%.

3 *Disfigurement*: Tim's arm was scarred after the assault. His negative thoughts were: 'People with scars are assumed to be criminals. Anyone seeing this scar will think I'm a criminal.' Tim rated their validity as 85%. To explore this, he was asked to list what criminals looked like, e.g. hair

colour, height, and to compare these with his own features. The two lists did not match and his belief fell to 40%. He was asked to take home the audiotape of the session and

(a) think of people he knew with scars and how much he believed them to be criminals, and

(b) recognise the error he was making.

At a later session he said that during the first exercise he realised he knew many people with scars who were not criminals. From this he generated the alternative response: 'Acting suspiciously and having a criminal record suggest someone is a criminal, not scars.' He believed 100% in this thought and 0% in his negative thoughts. Tim correctly labelled his thinking error as *'mind reading'*.

The outcome was that soon after 10 treatment sessions Tim was sleeping much better with far fewer nightmares and intrusive thoughts. He was going out accompanied, travelling alone by car, less depressed, and oblivious of his scar. By the one-year follow-up he was almost symptom free and working again as a bus driver.

Can I carry out my own treatment?

Yes indeed. Self-help by doing your own exposure therapy is often effective without professional guidance, and Chapter 12 shows you how to do this in detail.

Many sufferers found that they felt better after exposing themselves to their feared situation when a chance change in their lives gave them a fillip to do so. The woman who described her agoraphobia on p. 57 found the impetus to change one day when

❝my husband came flying home and said 'I've found the very place; it's a nice shop for you and it's a Post Office for me but there's only one thing; it's in the open – open spaces.' And I said 'I'll try, I'll go, because anything is better than this.' When we settled in this shop, I made a list of everything I wanted to do and ticked off when I'd done it. I couldn't go up the garden when I first came, but now I go all around the garden, and ticked that off. I go on long walks with the dog. I go on car rides. So my husband and I again had a talk and he said: 'I'll enrol you at a driving school.' To me that was a panic again. I just couldn't do it, but he enrolled me and the first three times were terrible. I was so tense that I was away from home and with a strange person and in a strange village that I couldn't concentrate on driving, but he encouraged me, saying 'Don't worry. Just for today we'll go in small circles' and the circles got bigger and bigger. We went one mile, two miles, three miles, and now it's 40 miles and I don't care if it was 50 miles. I'd go.[29]❞

Beth's compulsive washing rituals concerning her baby's nappies were treated by accident, so to speak. When her daughter was sexually assaulted she had to leave her baby boy at home unattended to deal with the emergency.[30] On returning Beth found he had peed all over the carpet and elsewhere, but was so agitated about the other matter that she didn't carry out her usual cleaning ritual. Shortly after this she was again unable to do the cleaning and had to remain exposed to urine. After these events her compulsive ideas and rituals reduced so much that she could come off a treatment waiting list.

Successful self-help to master fears

Max had feared lifts since age 11 when he was stuck in one for three hours. 'I'm quite restricted at work since my fear forced me to work on the building's lower floors. Whenever I have to go to the top I use the stairs – walking up 15 storeys can take a long time! Luckily my bosses know about my problem and are sympathetic so they know I'm not a time waster.' Max decided his problem was 'I avoid all lifts for fear I might get stuck in one', and to start to overcome it set the goal 'Go five floors up in a lift at least five times every day'. He arranged to use a lift after office hours first, when it was quiet. Within three days he had got used to this goal. He then set a further goal: 'Go in a lift up five floors five times every day when it's crowded'. Max practised his goals daily using coping tactics to help (see Chapter 12, p. 187) and within two months asked his boss to transfer him to an office on the 14th floor so he could use the lift every day.

Effective self-help was also described by Harriett who wrote (on p. 57) about her acute anxiety and depression years before:

> 66 For three years I'd been unable to make a train journey alone. I now felt it was essential to my self-esteem to do so successfully. I arranged the journey carefully from one place of safety to another, had all my terrors beforehand, and travelled as if under light anaesthesia. I can't say I lost my fears as a result, but I realised I could do what I'd been unable to do. Soon after this I had to learn to drive. I passed the driving test without difficulty. . . . Waiting in traffic blocks brought at first a return of panics – and there was no running away. . . .
>
> Now I have my methods. The essentials are my few safety depots – people or places. The safety radius from them grows longer and longer. I'm still claustrophobic; that rules out tube trains for me, and I use the surface train. I find it difficult to meet relations and childhood friends, and to visit places where I lived or worked when I was very ill. But I've learned to make short visits to give me a sense of achievement and to follow them when I'm ready for it by a longer visit. People and places are shrinking to their normal size. Depression usually returns about a week before menstruation, and I've learned to remind myself that life will look different when my

period begins. . . . I'm also learning that it's permissible to admit to anxiety about things I've always sternly told myself are trifles to be ignored. Many of them, I find, are common fears.

If I'm fearful of going anywhere strange to meet my friends, I invite them home instead, or meet them at a familiar restaurant. . . I've used strangers deliberately; a cheerful bus conductor, a kindly shop assistant, can help me to calm a mounting panic and bring the world into focus again. If I have something difficult to do – to make a journey alone, sit trapped under the drier in a hairdresser's, or make a public speech – I know I'll be depressed and acutely afraid beforehand. I avoid trying myself too high meanwhile. When the time comes I fortify myself by recalling my past victories, remind myself that I can die only once and that it probably won't be so bad as this. The actual experience now is not much worse than severe stage fright, and if someone sees me to the wings I totter on. Surprisingly, no one seems to notice. . . .

I dare not accept my sickness – fear – because it never stays arrested. My very safety devices become distorted and grow into symptoms themselves. I must, therefore, as I go along, break down the aids I build up; otherwise the habits of response to fear, or avoidance of occasions of fear, can be as inhibiting as the fear itself. **"**

Harriett treated herself long before exposure principles were worked out. Now that these are known, many others can follow suit more easily.

Computer-guided self-help

Recent aids include computer-guided self-help systems for sufferers from anxiety disorders.[31] After a brief interview by a doctor or nurse to check that they are suitable for the system, sufferers are guided by a computer to do whatever self-exposure and/or cognitive therapy are needed to overcome their problem. Sufferers can interact with the computer either by sitting at a computer screen and typing on a keyboard and moving a mouse, or by phoning the computer from home and pressing keys on their telephone keypad to drive an interview – the key presses select what message to hear out of hundreds of natural voice messages stored in the computer – this is called interactive voice response (IVR). Computer-guided self-help systems enable sufferers to access expert help with a minimum of contact with a clinician and have yielded promising results in early trials. Many users confide more sensitive information to a computer-guided self-help system than in a face-to-face consultation with a clinician. Such systems are likely to come into increasing use in the next few years, enabling many more sufferers to get help than ever before, though of course some will still prefer to get help directly from a clinician.

A proven example of a computer-screen self-help system for phobia and panic is *FearFighter*. Proven examples of IVR self-help systems you can phone are *BTSteps* (BT = behaviour therapy) for obsessive-compulsive disorder (OCD), and *Cope* which teaches cognitive behaviour therapy for depression. A grateful phobic who improved under guidance of the *FearFighter* system brought Belgian chocolates in gratitude to the nurse who started her on the system. A *BTSteps* user with OCD told a newspaper that '*BTSteps* forces me to face my fears one at a time by telling me to do a task I usually find impossible. If I'm having a panic I ring the computer, which advises me over the phone how to cope with the situation. It's been five months now and I'm feeling loads better. I've even stopped collecting and I've thrown loads of things out. I'm not having seven baths a day any more and I'm tackling my strange compulsions. It's not an overnight cure but every day is getting better.'

In very recent research, when doing self-exposure therapy phobics guided by *FearFighter* and OCD sufferers guided by *BTSteps* improved almost as much as sufferers guided by clinicians. Moreover, a neuroimaging study found the brain blood flow changes which are expected with improvement in OCD sufferers who do self-help guided by *BTSteps*; the brain blood flow changes resembled those found in OCD sufferers who had improved with clinician-guided exposure therapy or with fluoxetine. You can enquire about all three self-help systems (*FearFighter*, *BTSteps* and *Cope*) at the Stress Self-Help Clinic, 303 North End Rd, London W14 9NS (tel: 0207 610 2594, fax: 0207 385 7471).

Daisy's improvement with computer-guided self-help

Daisy's experience with *BTSteps* at nearly age 70 gives a more detailed idea of how it works.[32] She had OCD for 50 years, keeping it secret from friends and employers, and due to shame only sought help after decades of suffering. She worried that harm would befall herself or others unless she checked and washed for hours and avoided contaminating situations and substances. She had been treated unsuccessfully by medication, electroconvulsive therapy and 12 years of Freudian psychoanalysis until she eventually improved for 10 years after nine weeks of exposure therapy. When her OCD recurred she had exposure and ritual prevention therapy guided by *BTSteps*. She never saw a therapist face-to-face. First a doctor interviewed her on the phone. Daisy was then posted the *BTSteps* self help manual and an ID number to phone *BTSteps*' computer-guidance system from her home at any time of day or night that she wanted. After reading each step in the manual she phoned to consult the *BTSteps* computer-guidance system repeatedly for a total of 13 hours over five months, and also phoned for brief advice from a clinician. He advised her to allow herself to experience repeatedly and *ad nauseam* her terrible thoughts and the chance that they might have ghastly consequences until her thoughts became boring, showing that she was then habituated and could think whatever she wanted. Daisy improved by 67% on OCD measures and 58% on work and social adjustment measures, allowing her to do much more ambitious professional work. She stays well by doing relapse prevention exercises suggested by the computer involving exposure and ritual prevention homework, by facing things she would rather avoid and the feared consequences of such avoidance.

Chapter 12 of this book will show you in more detail how to help yourself, or co-operate better with a therapist. Meanwhile, we will look at other methods professionals have used to reduce anxiety.

Abreaction

Abreactive treatments are uncertain in their effects although, rarely, they can be surprisingly helpful. They are designed to help people express their feelings freely with much emotion, after which their tension abates. Many religious ceremonies have abreactive features such as talking in tongues during voodoo sessions, or confessing to a priest. Certain drugs used to be injected intravenously to aid the process of talking, but this is no longer necessary.

Another past method is *induced anxiety*. The patient is relaxed and asked to concentrate inwardly, forget everything outside himself, and let a small feeling way down inside start to grow. Continued suggestions are made that the feeling is growing ever stronger. The therapist sits on a chair next to the patient's couch with one hand on the patient's wrist and one hand on his other arm, monitoring his tension. When the patient contracts his muscles, the therapist says 'Good, let it out' and so on. Gradually intense emotion develops along with muscular tension, rapid breathing, and sobbing, sometimes with intense anger, fear, and even laughter. The patient will remember past events associated with the emotion and is encouraged to talk about them. This method relieved some people's anxiety.

In wartime, soldiers who developed shell-shock (a form of post-traumatic stress disorder) were encouraged to describe their bad experiences and often felt better thereafter. Hypnosis helped some to recover the experiences. In 'primal scream therapy' people were encouraged to relieve tension by screaming.

Relaxation

Anxiety is occasionally helped, at least briefly, by relaxation exercises, though they are unnecessary to overcome phobias or obsessions. You can learn to relax by listening to an audiotape (which you could buy or prepare yourself) for 15 minutes or more daily. On the tape you might hear:

❝Settle back comfortably. Let yourself relax as best you can. Now, as you relax like that, clench your right fist, just clench it tighter and tighter, and study the tension as you do so. Keep it clenched and feel the tension in your right fist, hand, and forearm . . . now relax. Let the fingers of your right hand become loose, and watch the contrast of feeling in your muscles. Let those muscles just relax completely. . . . Once more, clench your right fist really tight . . . hold it, and notice the tension again . . . now let go, relax; your fingers straighten out, and you notice the difference once more. . . . Now repeat this with your left fist. Clench your left fist while the rest of your body relaxes; clench that fist tighter and feel the tension. Relax and feel the difference. Continue relaxing like that for a while. . . . Clench both fists tighter and tighter, both fists tense, forearms tense, study the sensations . . . and relax. Straighten your fingers and feel that relaxation in your hand and forearm muscles. Continue relaxing your hands and forearms more and more. . . . Now bend your elbows and tense your biceps. . . .[33]❞

Autogenic training is another way to relax. Here you visualise one part of your body, hold that image, and then relax that part. For example: 'Get a clear picture of your right hand, see the outline of the fingers, the colour of the skin and nails, the wrinkles on your knuckles. Now relax your right hand as you think about it, keeping the image in your mind all the time. Now try to see your right forearm in your mind's eye . . . , etc.'

Which mode of relaxation you use doesn't seem to matter much, provided you attain complete muscular and mental relaxation. Relaxation is also used in *meditational methods*. Mantra meditation involves thinking about a secret word and holding that in mind while sitting motionless and excluding all other thoughts. Yoga, Zen and mindfulness meditation employ further strategies, some of which are mastered in a couple of months, while others take years to perfect. Research on how effective meditational approaches are for anxiety disorders is in its infancy.

Hypnosis is another way of inducing relaxation in some people by a variety of means. Only a minority are good hypnotic subjects. In them hypnosis may be a good way to achieve relaxation in the face of panic, but hypnosis is not a reliable way to lastingly overcome fear in most people.

Medications and other physical treatments for anxiety

Medications

Sedative drugs

These are widely used to damp down anxiety as long as the drug is in the body, but the effect disappears when the drug is excreted. The drugs can produce side effects such as drowsiness and can also affect one's judgement and concentration. Sedative benzodiazepines include diazepam (*Valium*), lorazepam (*Atavan*) and alprazolam (*Xanax*). Another class of sedative is buspirone (*Buspar*). Such drugs are usually given by mouth. Their use by injection or suppository is rarely necessary. Barbiturates are no longer used as sedatives because they can be less safe.

The most widely used sedative of all is freely available without prescription. Alcohol has, since time immemorial, been used to relieve tension. When used socially it loosens the tongue and helps people to mix better in potentially awkward situations. Many people who have mild phobias find alcohol useful but, as with sedative drugs, its value does not last long, and paradoxically taking alcohol repeatedly might actually increase rather than reduce tension.

A few people go on to drink or take sedatives so much that they become alcohol or drug dependent. They can be treated successfully if they slowly come off their drug or drink and then do self-exposure therapy for their fears. Sedatives help us *temporarily* over times of tribulation and are not to be scorned for such purposes, but they do not help us get over anxiety disorders enduringly, unlike exposure therapy. Taking a sedative before doing exposure therapy is not a good idea, since what is learned while on the drug or alcohol is not retained well after one stops taking the sedative.

Antidepressant drugs

Antidepressant drugs are of most value in anxiety disorders complicated by depression. Depression occurs from time to time in about a third of people with anxiety disorders other than specific phobias, where it is uncommon. It usually takes two to four weeks to improve with antidepressant medication, and anxiety lessens along with the depression. After depressed patients have improved, they may need to continue taking their drugs for several months, or rarely even years, to prevent relapse. Whether the drugs are still needed can be decided by slowly withdrawing the tablets over several months. If the depression shows signs of returning, the previous dose needs to be restored.

A word of caution – in a recent study, at drug-free follow-up, panic disorder patients who had been on imipramine six months earlier were *worse* off than those who had been on a placebo six months earlier,[34] just as was found with benzodiazepine drugs such as alprazolam,[35] and midazolam.[36] This issue of being worse at follow-up after stopping medication than after stopping placebo remains to be studied with further antidepressants and anxiety disorders. Perhaps depression which complicates anxiety disorders can be treated by the brief psychological treatments that improve depression – interpersonal, cognitive-behavioural and problem-solving therapies – but that issue too is unstudied.

Table 11.1 shows the main forms of antidepressant drugs used today – their number has grown steadily over the years. Various manufacturers claim that one or other antidepressant is better for particular problems, say social phobia or OCD, though the evidence for this is disputed. Side effects such as inability to reach sexual climax are common with many of the drugs; they may be less common with SSRIs (specific serotonin reuptake inhibitors). Despite drug side effects, a minority of sufferers from anxiety disorders even without depression remain well for years on a modest dose of an antidepressant drug and worsen if they come off it, in which case it is beneficial to stay on the medication.

Medication for impotence

The main drug for failure to get an erection due to sexual anxiety is sildenafil, famous under the name of *Viagra*.[37,38] From an hour after taking a single dose of sildenafil (50–100 mg), an erection is enabled by sexual stimulation but not without it. Sildenafil improves the quality and frequency of erections by about 30%, but does not stimulate sexual desire. It may cause headaches, facial flushing, stuffy nose, low blood pressure, indigestion and a blue tinge to the vision. It must be prescribed by a doctor. You should not take sildenafil with grapefruit juice or if you're on nitrates, amyl nitrite, some other drugs, or have heart, liver, or bleeding disorders, or peptic ulcer, or certain eye disorders. The dose should be reduced to 25 mg if you are on cimetidine, or erythromycin, or have impaired kidney function.

Physical treatments

Electroconvulsive therapy (ECT) sounds more awful than it actually is, and helps a few people with agitated depression who fail to improve with anti-depressant drugs. Such depression very rarely complicates anxiety disorders and so will not be considered further here.

Surgical treatments for anxiety used to include leucotomy to destroy a small part of the white matter of the brain in the frontal lobes. The operation done in the 1940s got a bad name because it could cause undesirable personality changes. After it was modified to destroy less brain tissue, fewer undesirable side effects appeared. More recently other areas of the brain have been operated on, for example, by cingulotomy. These later operations cause far less change to patients' personality and help a tiny number of severely disabled sufferers with long-standing chronic anxiety in whom all other methods have failed.

Table 11.1: Antidepressant medications

	Generic name	Brand name in:		Usual daily dose (mgs.)	
		UK	USA	Starting	Effective
Selective	Citalopram	*Cipramil*	*Celexa*	20	20–60
Serotonin	Fluoxetine	*Prozac*	*Prozac*	20	20–80
Reuptake	Fluvoxamine	*Faverin*	*Luvox*	50	75–150
Inhibitors	Paroxetine	*Seroxat*	*Paxil*	20	20–50
(SSRIs)	Setraline	*Lustral*	*Zoloft*	50	50–200
Tricyclics	Amitriptyline	*Lentizol, Triptafen*	*Elavil, Ende*	50–75	75–300
	Amoxapine	*Asendis*	*Asendin*	100–150	200–400
	Clomipramine	*Anafranil*	*Aafranil*	25	100–250
	Desipramine	–	*Norpramin, Petrofrane*	50	100–300
	Doxepin	*Sinequan*	*Sinequan, Adapin*	50–75	75–300
	Imipramine	*Tofranil*	*Tofranil*	50–75	100–300
	Nortriptyline	*Allegron, Motipress, Motival*	*Pamelor*	25–50	100–150
	Protriptyline	*Concordin*	*Vivactil*	15	15–60
	Trimipramine	*Surmontil*	*Surmontil*	50–75	100–300
Tetracyclic	Maprotiline	*Ludiomil*	*Ludiomil*	50–75	100–150
	Mirtazapine	*Zispin*	*Remeron*	15	15–45
Novel	Bupropion	–	*Wellbutrin*	200	200–450
	Nefazodone	*Dutonin*	*Serzone*	200	300–600
	Trazodone	*Molipaxin*	*Desyrel*	150	150–400
	Venlafaxine	*Efexor*	*Effexor*	75	75–375
Monamine	Phenelzine	*Nardil*	*Nardil*	30	60–90
Oxidase	Tranylcypromine	*Parnate*	*Parnate*	20	30–60
Inhibitors	Moclobemide	*Manerix*	–	300	300–600
(MAOIs)					

summary

Do not try to abolish normal anxiety, which is helpful. Instead, try to put anxiety in perspective and welcome it as a spur to necessary action. Discussion of our troubles with other people can help to put them in a new light and suggest possible solutions. Where this approach alone does not help, behavioural and cognitive treatments do.

Exposure therapy is effective for persistent phobias, panic, obsessive-compulsive and post-traumatic stress disorders, and can work within a few days or weeks or months at most. It reduces the anxiety problems directly, by the sufferer learning how to face the situations which trigger discomfort so that they gradually become tolerated. This approach works in most cases, even if the problems have been present for many years.

If we deliberately expose ourselves to the things that frighten us we eventually get used to them instead of being afraid of them. On confronting our fear determinedly it will diminish. Longer exposure lasting several hours is better than shorter exposure for a few minutes at a time. The more rapidly you tackle your worst fears, the more quickly you will recover. You will feel panic early in exposure treatment, but nervousness is not generally harmful and soon dies down. After accidents, in order to prevent phobias developing, the golden rule is to nip them in the bud – avoid escape and encourage the facing of fear by re-entering the traumatic situation immediately after the original accident.

You should leave enough time in your self-exposure sessions (at least an hour) to allow yourself slowly to get used to whatever triggers your panic. Determination and patience are essential to accomplish your goal. Failure is likely if you feel that treatment is unnecessary and embark on it in a half-hearted way.

There are many forms of exposure therapy ranging from very slow, gradual methods called desensitisation to the more rapid approaches of flooding. The frightening situations to which you expose yourself can be purely in your mind's eye (in fantasy), on slides, pictures, videos or visual reality, or in real life. Real-life exposure hastens eventual reduction of phobias. The usual approach is to enter the phobic situation in real life and stay there up to several hours until one feels better. Exposure treatment can be carried out with groups of phobics at a time. Nightmares, too, can be treated like phobias; reliving them in a deliberate, masterful fashion can lead to their disappearance. You can carry out your own exposure treatment by yourself with the aid of a suitable manual or computer-guidance system. For self-help to be successful, it needs to be seriously structured and completed along the lines described in the Chapter 12.

Stress immunisation involves preparing for difficulties, learning what these will be, what can be done to overcome or reduce them, and rehearsing possible solutions.

This can help when the real time of trouble arrives. In this way people have dealt better with stressful situations such as surgical operations. In cognitive therapy you identify negative automatic thoughts and beliefs that accompany anxiety and substitute more positive ones instead.

Antidepressant medications can help the depression that complicates anxiety disorders in perhaps a third of cases. Neither sedative drugs nor alcohol give long-term benefit for anxiety.

chapter 2

self-help for your fears and anxiety

We all know that exercise is healthy, but few of us take enough exercise. Yet if a dog needs to be taken for regular walks, we might walk the soles off our shoes for its sake. Many people are terribly lonely only yards away from others longing for their company but cannot push themselves to make the first approach. Yet provide their block of flats with a communal room with washing machines and they meet and gradually develop friendships. We know we should go for walks or arrange social contacts, but we often do not act on common sense until a suitable framework is provided.

Much behavioural and cognitive therapy is a framework for applying common sense to problems. You can overcome your anxiety more effectively within such a framework than by a simple command to 'pull yourself together' or 'use your will-power' which we hear all too often. Behavioural and cognitive treatment can do for your conquest of fear what the dog does for exercise and the communal laundry does for socialising. Before you read the steps in self-treatment, first determine whether it is likely to ease your problem.

Will it benefit me? – ten tests

Self-management is worth considering when professional therapists are unavailable or you want to see what you can do by yourself anyway without the bother of, or potential stigma or loss of confidentiality entailed in, consulting a professional. Certain conditions are necessary to increase the chances of self-help being successful. Before you put yourself to trouble which might not be worthwhile in the end, work through the next ten tests. They are questions therapists might ask you in order to decide whether you could benefit from behavioural or cognitive treatment.

First, two complications that may accompany an anxiety disorder indicate that you should see a doctor rather than treat yourself:

Test 1: Are you so depressed that you are seriously thinking of suicide?

If yes: Ask a doctor for help. Severe depression together with suicidal plans will probably stop you completing a self-management programme, and requires prompt medical treatment, which can be very effective. **Do not proceed to Test 2**.

If no: Proceed to Test 2.

Test 2: Do you often drink alcohol to the point of being drunk and/or take more than two tablets a day of a sedative such as diazepam, lorazepam or alprazolam?

If yes: Either come down to less than three drinks a day or less than two sedative tablets a day, or consult a doctor. Self-management is likely to fail if you are drunk with alcohol or sedated by drugs during your exercises. **Do not proceed to Test 3**.

If no: Proceed to Test 3.

You may need medical advice about disease before carrying out self-management.

Test 3: Do you have physical disease such as heart trouble, asthma, peptic ulcer, or ulcerative colitis?

If yes or unsure: Ask your physician whether severe panic can complicate your condition. If he does not think it will, proceed to Test 4.

If he thinks it is safe for you to tolerate some anxiety, you can do exposure treatment *slowly*. Remember this when doing exposure exercises (pp. 182–3).

Proceed to Test 4.

If he thinks any anxiety at all might be harmful, **exposure treatment is not indicated**.

If no: Proceed to Test 4.

Your anxiety needs to be of a certain kind for your programme to succeed.

Test 4: Is your anxiety triggered by specific situations, people, or objects?

Answer *Yes* if your fears are set off by particular events such as parties, crowded shops, getting your hands dirty, going out alone, dogs, sexual intercourse, meeting someone in authority, etc. (If you can't think of any, then to jog your memory you can go through lists of common triggers on p. 175–6.) Anxiety related to particular situations can subside with self-help.

If yes: Proceed to Test 5.

Answer *No* if you can't think of anything that repeatedly starts off your anxiety.

If no: **Exposure treatment is not indicated**.

If you wish to try a more general approach to anxiety *proceed to relaxation* (p. 161) or to *coping tactics* (Step 5, p. 187).

Test 5: Can you define your problems in precise, observable terms?

If yes: My problems in order of importance are (write in pencil so you can amend them later if necessary):

1 _____

2 _____

3 _____

Compare your answers with the following examples of *precise* definitions of problems you can overcome:

Problem **1** : I panic whenever I go out of doors alone, so I stay indoors unless I have an escort.

2 : I can't bear people looking at me, so I avoid friends, parties, and social receptions.

3 : I'm terrified of aeroplanes and always avoid air travel.

4 : I worry about dirt and germs so I wash my hands all day and can't work.

5 : I tense up as soon as my husband wants sex and find it painful.

Examples of *general* statements which don't lend themselves to self-help:

I want to be cured, to get better.
I'm a bundle of nerves.
I just feel miserable all day.
I want to know what sort of person I am.
I want to have a purpose and meaning in life.

General statements may be meaningful but do not allow you to work out steps by which such problems can be solved. Self-treatment works best when you describe what you want clearly in observable terms.

If you wish, amend the problem definitions you wrote down earlier to make them more precise.

If you can now say 'Yes, my problems are precise and observable', proceed to Test 6.

If your answer is 'No, my problems are too general to be defined', **self-management is not indicated**. You can try *relaxation* (p. 161) or *coping tactics* (Step 5, p. 187).

Test 6: For each precise problem you wrote down in *Test 4*, can you name a specific goal you wish to achieve in treatment?

Before doing so, read examples of more and less useful goals for Problems 1 to 5 above.

Problem	Well-defined goal	Less preferable goal
1	Spend two hours a week shopping in the nearest shops or mall.	Get out and about by myself.
2	At least once a week, visit friends or go to a party and stay to the end.	Become more sociable.
3	Fly from London to Rome and back.	Lose my fear of air travel.
4	Touch the floor, my shoes and rubbish every day without washing hands afterwards.	Get over my hang-up about dirt.
5	Have sex with my spouse twice a week with satisfactory orgasm.	I want my sex life to improve.

Can you now write down tangible goals for your particular problems?

If yes: The goals for my problems are:

Problem 1 : _____

2 : _____

3 : _____

Proceed to Test 7.

If no: I'm not sure what I want to achieve in treatment.

Until you have clarified what you want in tangible terms, self-help is unlikely to succeed.

Test 7: Will it really make a difference to your life if you overcome these problems?

Before listing what you, your family, or friends might gain if you lose your worry, read the examples below:

Agoraphobia: We'll be able to go on holiday together for the first time in five years.
I'll be able to take a job again.

School phobia: My child will resume attending school.
There won't be arguments every morning at breakfast.

Compulsive rituals: I'll be able to hug my children again without worrying that I'm infecting them with germs.
I'll be able to help run our home and spend time with my family.

Sex dysfunction: My spouse and I will have regular good sex.
We won't talk endlessly about divorce.

If overcoming your problem really will make a difference, write your gains below:

Yes, the gains from losing my worry will be:

1. _____

2. _____

3. _____

Proceed to Test 8.

If your answer is No, I can't think of any way in which my life or my family's life would benefit if treatment were successful **then it may not be worth the trouble of a self-management programme**.

Test 8: Will you invest the time and effort necessary to overcome your worry?

Will you set aside a regular time to do your homework, promise to stand your ground and not run away when you feel fear, record what you have done, and work out what you need to do next time to overcome even more of your anxiety? Daily practice is preferable, and if your timetable is already over-crowded you may have to give up some other activity to free time to deal with your problem.

If Yes, I promise to follow my programme diligently: proceed to Test 9.

If No, I don't really have the time or inclination, **your self-management program is less likely to work well**. But you may improve a bit with only limited practice if you are lucky.

If you fail to improve, don't be disappointed, just wait until you really have the time and energy to carry out your programme fully, and the chances are that you'll then achieve the goals you wrote down in Test 4.

Test 9: Would your self-management programme need relatives or friends involved as your co-therapist(s)?

The answer is probably *Yes*:

If you hate keeping appointments even with yourself, and dislike recording your activities and planning ahead. A friend or relative can be your co-therapist and help you devise the framework of your treatment and stick to the detailed work necessary to get over your difficulties. Your co-therapist could regularly sign the diaries you keep, praise you for progress you have made, and help you plan each step in turn.

If you are so frightened of going out that your family or friends must accompany you everywhere.

If you persuade your family to wash or check things for you or take over your role in the home, or to give you repeated reassurance about whether you are clean, safe, healthy, etc. Whoever you involve in your rituals needs to help as your co-therapist, whether spouse, parent, child, or other relative or friend.

If you are a parent trying to help your child over worry, your spouse would be useful as a co-therapist. It is easier if *both* parents co-operate in working out and implementing the child's programme so as not to get at odds with each other or have the child playing one parent off against the other.

If your problem is sexual, your partner should be involved in your treatment programme.

Question: What if my partner isn't interested?
Answer: Treatment is unlikely to help until your partner can be persuaded to join in.
Question: What if I don't have a partner?
Answer: You need to get one.

Question: What if I'm too shy to get one?

Answer: You need to restructure your self-treatment programme with the goal of overcoming your social fears and establishing a friendship with someone who could become a partner.

If 'Yes, I need a co-therapist': proceed to Test 10.

The answer to Test 9 is probably *No*:

If your problem concerns only your own lifestyle, doesn't interfere with anyone else's activities, and you don't mind working out and monitoring your own treatment programme, for example:

If your checking or washing rituals keep only you awake at night.

If your travel phobia restricts only your, not other people's, movements.

If your dread of dogs inconveniences only you, not your friends or relatives.

If no: Proceed to 'strategy for treatment' below.

Test 10: Can you enlist the help of a co-therapist where this is needed?

If yes: Proceed to 'strategy for treatment' below.

If no: Absence of a co-therapist may make your self-treatment less likely to succeed, but it might be worth a try.

Proceed to 'strategy for treatment' below.

Strategy for self-help: five steps

Step 1: Work out exactly what you fear; don't waste time treating the wrong thing.

In your self-management programme you will make yourself gradually face all those things that upset you, and stay with them until you feel better about them. Tailor your treatment plan to your own needs. If you hate going alone into public places, is it because you are afraid that you will look foolish, or because you are scared that you will have a heart attack, or because you get dizzy in crowds? If you are upset by dirt, is it just ordinary dirt from the floor or rubbish bin, or that you fear catching or transmitting certain diseases, and if so which ones? If an attractive person makes you go weak at the knees, is it because s/he might look down on you or find you ugly or smelly, or that you feel sexual attraction with which you can't cope?

When planning your self-exposure treatment it's easy to overlook things that bother you. Among thousands of sufferers round the world, their most common triggers for fear, panic, rituals, obsessions and/or other worries were things in the long lists below.

With a pen or pencil in hand, read through these lists carefully and *highlight*, *underline*, *circle* or *tick* any items that trouble you more than they do most people.

It might take an hour or two to do this properly if you have OCD involving lots of things. When you have finished, you can show the lists to family or friends who might have noticed further things you do that you have forgotten most people don't do.

Triggers for phobias, panic, and other worries

Leaving home, going far from home
Being alone at home
Open spaces, parks
Walking in the street, crossing roads
Crowds, queues
Market, supermarket
Shop, department store, shopping centre, hairdresser
Bank, post office
Transport: bus, coach, car, taxi, train (slow, fast, underground), boat/ship, plane, helicopter
Sports ground, stadium
Enclosed places, lifts, tunnels
Motorways, bridges
Heights, high buildings, ledges, platforms, stairs, escalators
Injections, minor surgery
Hospital, doctor, dentist
Sight of blood
Thought of injury or illness
Violence, reminders of past trauma
Being criticised
Talking to people in authority
Restaurant, eating/drinking with others, pub, bar, café, night club, disco, parties, receptions
Wedding, funeral, church, cinema, concert hall, theatre
Speaking/acting to an audience
Being watched or stared at
Darkness

Noise, storms, thunder, lightning
Dogs, cats, birds, spiders, worms, other beasties (specify) . . .

Triggers for washing, cleaning, checking, other rituals, obsessions, other worries

Some of the triggers above may bring on not phobias or panic but rather rituals, obsessions or other worries. If so, go back and *highlight, underline, circle* or *tick* them if you haven't already done so. Many other things, too, may bring on rituals such as washing, checking, repeating, tidying or doing things slowly.

Things at or outside home

Toilets, toilet seats
Shower/bathroom
Soap, deodorant, toothbrush
Doorknobs
Floor, ground
Clothes
Underwear
Socks
Shoes/slippers
Handkerchiefs, tissues
Nappies
Laundry room/basket
Sheets
Towels
Cooking, pots, pans
Cutlery, dishes/plates, glasses
Kitchen, loft, garage
Rubbish, bin
Taps, switches, appliances (kettle, cooker, TV), tools
Chairs others have sat in
Beds, furniture
Deliveries of letters, newspapers, packages, flyers, flowers
Telephones
People entering my home
Lawn, garden, plants
Laundrette, public bath/toilet
Swimming pool, beach
Closing/locking doors/windows
Checking when going to bed, leaving home, at work, in the car, going on
   holiday

Body parts or fluid of myself, other people or animals

Saliva, mouth, vomit, breath
Blood
Urine, faeces, anus, flatus (fart)
Semen
Genitals, sex, contraceptives
Sweat
Handshakes
Nose
Armpits
Hair
Sanitary towels, tampons

Chemicals and/or dangerous substances

Insecticides, weed killers
Poisons
Mothballs
Petrol, petrol caps
Asbestos
Radon
Cleaning fluids/powders
Medications

Other things bringing on washing

Stains, specks
Grease, sticky things
Dust, dirt
Bird/animal droppings
Animals/birds/insects
Death, funeral, cemeteries
Illness
Particular people, colours
Homosexuality
Money
Smelling/touching foods (meat, chicken, eggs, fat)
Food or drink containers
Medicine containers

Sharp/dangerous things or substances, or vulnerable people

Knives, forks, razor, scissors, staplers, screwdrivers
Pins
Fans
Broken glass
Fragile objects
Babies or old people

Other things bringing on checking

Getting dressed or undressed, bathing, brushing teeth
Brushing/styling hair
Left/right side of my body
Examining/looking at myself or part of my body in the mirror or other
    reflecting surface
Driving a car (bumps, pot holes, near pedestrians, reversing)
Walking on pavement, lines
Crossing the street
Going into/out of rooms
Looking at a clock, seeing numbers
Being around others I feel I may have harmed
Saying/writing/thinking embarrassing/hurtful/wrong things
Writing/signing my name (completing forms, signing cheques)
Paying bills
Posting letters, putting letters in envelopes
Reading
Seeing/touching/buying things (coupons, money)
Working
Sitting on/getting up from a chair
Looking at a series of things (fence, railings, row of books)
Using/seeing a wallet, purse, bag, pocket or keys
Calculating numbers or change, doing accounts
Odd/even/other numbers
Not doing things a certain number of times or in a certain order

Ordering or hoarding rituals or obsessive thoughts (ruminations)

Ordering/arranging/straightening/tidying things that seem out of order, out of
    place, imperfect, untidy, asymmetrical, not straight
Can't throw things away (rubbish, papers, food, mail or hair clippings, urine,
    faeces)

Repetitive intrusive thoughts (religious, blasphemous, aggressive, sexual) or
  trying to ignore them

Other triggers not listed above (describe): _____

_____

_____

You and a relative or friend might go through the lists above a second time to
ensure you have not forgotten bothersome things that you need to deal with
if you are to overcome your problem properly. But do not go through the lists
more than twice, to stop it becoming a ritual!

If your anxieties are about **sex**, *tick* whatever below describes your or your
partner's problem:

Women:

  1 I can't bear having my body touched.

  2 My vagina gets so tight that my partner can't insert his penis.

  3 I have pain during intercourse.

  4 I don't have orgasm as often as desired.

Men:

  1 I don't get an erection.

  2 I can't maintain an erection long enough during intercourse to achieve
      orgasm myself or allow my partner to climax.

  3 I maintain my erection but don't ejaculate.

  4 I ejaculate sooner than desired.

Women and men:

  1 I'm on medication that may interfere with sexual function (most drugs
      for high blood pressure, depression or psychosis, and some to suppress
      epilepsy or stimulate urine production). Such drugs make self-help more
      difficult. You can ask your doctor if you can take an alternative that
      interferes less with sex.

Step 2: Write down the specific problems and goals you definitely want to
work with now:

You did this earlier on pp. 171–2, but may wish to amend what you wrote, now
that you've completed Step 1 and the lists.

My problems and goals, in order of priority, are:

Problem 1:   Goal 1:

Problem 2:   Goal 2:

Problem 3:   Goal 3:

Step 3: Prepare your timetable to face what frightens you, and record what happened immediately after each session (see the accompanying table). Revise your plans each week in the light of your progress.

How many practice sessions a week can you promise yourself? When will they be, and for how long? Remember that one session of two hours of exposure helps more than four half-hour sessions. Allow enough time to complete your session properly. Immediately after completing it, rate the maximum anxiety you felt on a scale where 0 is complete calm and 100 is absolute panic, and 25, 50, and 75 represent mild, moderate and severe anxiety respectively. Write down your plans for the coming week and record what you did on your diary record of exposure tasks (see p. 184–5).

It might help to discuss your programme with a friend or relative who can be a co-therapist, monitor your progress, sign your records, praise your progress, and advise on the next step.

Proceed to Step 4.

Step 4: What feelings or thoughts do you have when you are frightened?

Underline which of the following feelings or thoughts most bother you:

I want to scream or run away.
My heart pounds and beats fast.
I freeze in my tracks
I feel dizzy, faint, light-headed, about to fall.
I tremble and shake.
I can't breathe properly.
I feel nauseous.
I break into a cold sweat.
My stomach gets churned up or tight.
I feel I'm going crazy.
I feel I'm dying.
I feel I'm losing control.
I feel I'm looking ridiculous to other people. Other feelings or thoughts (write
    down):

Read what you have just underlined, and whenever you are facing what you fear, remember to use these feelings or thoughts as signals to employ the coping devices you will now decide on.

Proceed to Step 5.

Step 5: From the following list of tactics, choose three you might find useful to do or say to cope with your anxiety while carrying out your exposure tasks.

Circle those you would prefer to use.

Remember to *use those tactics as soon as you are aware of the frightening feelings or thoughts* you just identified in Step 4, because that is when the tactics are easiest to bring into play. Write your chosen tactics on small cards which you keep in your pocket. Take them out and read them aloud to yourself the moment anxiety strikes.

(a) I must breathe slowly and steadily in – and out, in – and out, and gradually learn to deal with this situation. I feel terrible at the moment, but it will pass. I'll put my hand on my tummy to make sure I'm breathing slowly, in – and out, in – and out.

(b) I feel horribly tense. I must tense all my muscles as much as I possibly can, then relax them, then tense them again, then relax them, until slowly I feel easier in myself.

(c) I'm thinking of the worst possible things that might happen to me. Let's see if they are so bad after all. Let me imagine myself actually going crazy and being carted off to a mental hospital or fainting on the pavement, or just dropping dead. How vividly can I paint those scenes to myself? Let me start with the ambulance taking me away while I froth at the mouth and spectators laugh at me in the street . . . or (make up your own scene of horror).

(d) What can I do? I have to stay here until I can tolerate this panic, even if it takes an hour. Meanwhile let me feel the fear as deliberately and fully as possible.

(e) I feel I have to get away, but I know I must remain here.

(f) I feel awful. I'd feel better if I imagined something pleasant or positive. For me that might be lying in the warm sun, listening to the sound of the waves or (make up your own pleasant scene).

(g) My troublesome thoughts are just thoughts, only that, and I can get used to them.

(h) These sensations and thoughts are ghastly, but maybe I can change their meaning. Maybe my heart is pounding because I've just run a race and that is also why I'm breathing heavily now. My dizziness is because I got up suddenly a moment ago or (make up your own transformation).

(i) I'm so terrified but I'll get over this in time.

(j) I'll never get over this, I think, but that's just the way I feel, and in time I'll feel better.

(k) I'm so embarrassed, but it's something I'll have to get used to.

(l) I'll challenge my thoughts that I'm going mad or losing control and prove that I won't.

Decide now which three tactics you will use during your exercises, and the order in which you will bring them into play.

My coping tactics will be a b c d e f g h i j k l above (circle the appropriate letters and write 1, 2, 3 next to them to show which you'll try first, which second, and which third.)

Now for three minutes timed on your watch, imagine yourself in your most terrifying situation, and use one of your chosen tactics to deal with the fear. Repeat this at least three times so that you can employ these tactics *immediately* you feel anxious during your exposure exercises.

Ready? Now start your exposure tasks and record what happened. Remember, you will feel anxious and miserable at least some of the time during your exercises. Don't be put off by this, but press on until you have beaten your worry. If you have a physical disease which limits how much anxiety your doctor thinks you can safely experience, remember to pace your tasks slowly to the amount of fear you are allowed to tolerate.

Good luck. It's hard but worthwhile.

During exposure remember the rules for your sessions

1 Before starting each session plan exactly which goals you will definitely achieve this time to overcome your fear.

2 Leave enough time – up to several hours if need be – to reach these goals properly by the end of the session.

3 During the session use your frightened feelings and thoughts as reminders to practise the coping tactics you chose. Make sure they are written on cards in your pocket; be ready to take them out and read them at any time.

4 At the end of the session, record what you achieved each time, work out the next session's programme, and write down the date and time you plan to carry it out.

And the golden rules at all times

- Anxiety is unpleasant but rarely harmful.
- Avoid escape.
- Encourage the facing of fear.
- The longer you face it the better.
- The quicker you confront the worst, the quicker your fear will fade.

Repeat and repeat your appointment with fear

Take your first steps at a moderate but steady pace. Carry on relentlessly, confronting your fears, until those things that used to strike terror in you have become rather boring, and you have forgotten your past fear. Although you will have setbacks, these are part of the game, and constant repetition will make them less and less frequent. With repetition your coping tactics will become second nature and enable you to overcome your fear increasingly easily.

Helpful tips from a former agoraphobic

1. Arrange the expected phobic situations into groups according to the amount of distress which *you* anticipate in *your* particular case. An example may be:
   (a) Going into a quiet street – fairly easy
   (b) Going into a busy street – hard
   (c) Taking a ride on a bus – very hard
   (d) Shopping in a busy town centre – almost impossible.

2. Choose an easy situation, enter it, *and force yourself to remain there for as long as possible up to an hour or so.* It is most important not to run away from the phobic situation too soon.

3. Repeat exposure to the easy situation – the phobic reaction should not be less unpleasant.

4. Select a more difficult situation and repeat the procedure outlined in 2 and 3.

5. Carry on this process with progressively more difficult situations. This should generalise improvement so that work, etc, can be resumed. This approach to regaining mobility is very unpleasant and involves a lot of personal distress, but seems to be the most rapid treatment in existence where the patient can help himself. I have found it well worth the effort.

Diary record of exposure tasks

Day	Date	Began	Ended	The exposure task I performed was:	(0 = complete calm, 100 = absolute panic) My anxiety during the task was:	Comments including coping tactics I used	Name of co-therapist if any: (Co-therapist's signature that task was completed)
Sunday							
Monday							
Tuesday				*Example from an agoraphobic*			
Wednesday		2:30 pm	4:30 pm	Walked to local supermarket and surrounding shops, bought food and presents for family, had coffee at drug store	75	Felt worse when shops were crowded, practised deep-breathing exercises	J. Smith (husband)

| Thursday | 10 am | 11:30 am | Walked to local park, sat there for half an hour till I felt better, then caught a bus downtown and back home | 70 | Felt giddy and faint, practised imagining myself dropping dead | J. Smith |
| Friday | 2 pm | 4 pm | Rode a bus into town and back 3 times till I felt better about it | 60 | Worst when bus was crowded; did deep-breathing exercises | J. Smith |

Plan for next week: Repeat exposure exercises in bus, park and shops every day until my anxiety is no higher than 30. Thereafter start visits to my hairdresser, and short surface train journeys.

Saturday			
Sunday			
Monday			

If real life exposure is not possible, confront your fear in fantasy

Some phobic situations are not readily available for sufferers when they want to enter them. God does not provide thunderstorms on schedule for thunderstorm phobics. Those who are phobic of flying find it expensive to fly repeatedly. Instead you can try to rehearse facing your fear in fantasy, allowing plenty of time for your anxiety to fade. Do this at least 20 times, recording your practice in a log book, and when you encounter the real event, remember how you coped in your imagination.

Don't let setbacks set you back

Expect setbacks and be prepared to deal with them. You are bound to feel fresh panic and depression at some stage of your self-treatment. Just when you think you have conquered crossing a wide street in an agoraphobia programme, your next step fails. You stand at the kerb frightened and disappointed. Setbacks can last a minute or weeks. When they occur, you may feel dejected for days: 'I thought I'd conquered that phobia, that particular street, yet there were those feelings again, preventing me from crossing.' Realise that setbacks are part of the process of learning to over- come phobias. Don't dwell on why you can eat in a restaurant one day and not the next. Accept your bad days and rejoice in the good days. You can even welcome new panic as a fresh chance to practise mastering it yet again. Setbacks are especially likely to happen if for any reason you are unable to practise your exposure tasks for a while. If you are in bed for a few days because of 'flu or another illness, it will be more difficult to get started again, but perseverance will get you over the hump. Setbacks are signals for you to try again until you have conquered the situation where it occurred. Setbacks gradually fade once you tackle them systematically: 'Next week I'll cross that wide street – the one I couldn't cross this week. I'll have coffee in that shop on the other side.'

Although setbacks are inevitable, learn to cope with them. Don't be bluffed by strange new nervous feelings. What will be will be. It's no use being confident on Saturday, but being put out on Sunday when panic strikes out of the blue. You have to be ready for it and deal with it; try, try, and try again until you have reached the stage one phobic described after treatment: 'Yes, I still get panics from time to time now, but it's different, you know – now I don't have to run away from them. I can just experience them and let them pass while I carry on with whatever I happen to be doing at the time.' Recovery lies in meeting precisely those situations you fear; those are the ones you have to master.

As soon as you feel fear, use your coping tactics

Deal with your discomfort *early* in its development, before it becomes a runaway reaction. This principle holds not only for fear but for other problems too. Let us learn from Rex, a big Alsatian dog belonging to Don Meichenbaum.[1] Invariably when Don took Rex for a walk, Rex would fight other dogs. While walking at heel, Rex would see another dog approaching at a great distance. Without barking or giving any other sign he would suddenly bolt for the other dog, ignoring Don's shouts of 'down', 'come', 'heel' and worse. At other times, Rex would immediately obey any of the above commands. Through trial and error, Don found that if he spotted the other dog first, he could abort Rex's runaway reaction by saying 'No' firmly as soon as he could tell that Rex was about to shoot off. He thus became able to lead Rex completely calmly without incident right in front of other dogs. The impulse to attack that could not be inhibited when it was full-blown could easily be nipped in the bud when it was just starting.

A stitch in time saves nine. Just as Rex's aggression could be inhibited early, before it got intense, so your panic can be aborted by bringing in your preferred coping tactics as early as you possibly can – as soon as you feel a vague warning of dizziness, a faint flutter in your chest, or a hint of goose pimples on your skin.

Learn to live with fear and it will subside

You will obviously feel fear when you face frightening situations. Expect it. Try to experience it as fully as possible when it comes. Seize the opportunity to overcome it. Do not shut it out or run away. Remember, your sensations are normal bodily reactions. When fear appears, wait; concentrate on remaining where you are until it dies down. This it will do, though waiting for this to happen can seem like an eternity. Look at your watch to see that the fear usually starts to lessen within 20 to 30 minutes, and exceptionally within an hour, provided you remain in the situation and concentrate on feeling the fear instead of running away from it. If you do run away physically or mentally, your fear might actually increase. While waiting for the fear to pass, focus on where you happen to be. Just stay right where you are until you have calmed down. Learn to recognise and label your fear by rating your anxiety level on a 0 to 100 scale. Watch your fear slowly come down as time passes. Plan what to do next.

Take out your coping cards from your pocket, read them to yourself aloud (or silently if someone is nearby) and do what they say. Keep your fear level manageable, by very slow deep breathing with your hand on your tummy, or tensing and relaxing your muscles, or doing mental arithmetic, solving cross-word puzzles, counting the beads on a rosary, or whatever else you find useful. Gradually you will learn to reduce your anxiety to a reasonable level, although you will not eliminate it completely for a long time. Learn to carry on your normal activities even when you are a little frightened.

We cannot abolish fear, but we *can* learn to live with it as we do with any other emotion. We can face fear, accept it, float with it, and let time pass until it becomes manageable. We have to go along with the feelings without resistance. There is no need to be frightened of our heart beating loudly or of crying. After all, our heart beats and we cry when we are very happy as well as when we are anxious, and few of us run away from the tears and heartbeats of great joy. Feelings don't need to be feared. Flashes of intense panic are bound to come, but they will go away in time if our attitude is 'let it pass' and if we don't run away. Go with the tide, tread water until the worst is over. The flash experience of fright will eventually expend itself.

Welcome the worst and the present will feel better

Many people get relief by envisaging the most horrible consequences without flinching. If you have visions of going mad in the street, then deliberately imagine yourself screaming, frothing at the mouth, soiling yourself, running amok, until you can do this in a matter-of-fact way. Eventually these ideas will bore you utterly. If you are at the edge of a cliff and fear throwing yourself off, sit down at a safe distance from the edge and rehearse doing it in your mind's eye, time and time again until the idea loses its power over you. If you feel trapped in a car in a traffic jam, pull over to the side, continue sitting in the car, and see yourself all crowded in and suffocating. Resume your journey only when you can laugh at the whole idea.

I myself find this device useful on aeroplanes bumping through air pockets. I imagine the plane crashing and killing all its passengers, me included, see our bloody corpses dismembered on the ground, and think resignedly, 'Well, there's nothing more to be done, let's just get through this as best we can.' This exercise stills my anxiety about the journey.

The dramatic relief of anxiety through mental resignation was brought home vividly to me one night on a train nearing the end of its long journey. Standing near me at the door was a man waiting to rush off to catch a plane as soon as the train reached the station. The train stopped for ten minutes 300 metres before the station, and he couldn't jump out on to the electrified line. For the first five minutes he was intensely agitated, puffing furiously at his cigarette, fuming and fretting, swearing and looking at his watch repeatedly. Then suddenly he said, 'It's too late now, I've missed my plane, it's no use.' And with that all his anxiety ceased, and he relaxed completely. This transformation appeared as he abandoned hope of achieving his target, but it was the calm of resignation, not of despair.[2] This attitude can be very therapeutic in tense situations.

Special tactics for specific problems

Worry about sleeplessness

Maybe you have been lying awake at night worrying about all the beauty sleep you are missing; this builds up more tension and ensures that you don't fall asleep. One solution is to try and do the opposite. Try to stay awake as long as possible, repeatedly going over what you did during the day, or doing mental calculations, or reading boring books. Eventually, your body's natural controls will take over, your eyes will droop, and sleep will take over no matter how hard you struggle to keep awake.

As an alternative, close your eyes and imagine a pitch black window shade slowly unrolling downward.[3] On it you see in large letters the word SLEEP. Focus on this word on the shade as it gradually winds down. Feel yourself sinking steadily into sleep as the shade comes down.

Breathing difficulties from anxiety

If you feel that you can't catch your breath or breathe deeply, try this. Take a deep breath and hold it as long as you possibly can until you feel you are absolutely bursting. Don't cheat by taking little breaths. Time yourself. You will find that in about 60 seconds you can't keep from breathing any longer. Your body's reflexes will force you to take a deep breath. Repeat this exercise each time you feel you can't breathe properly.

Maybe your breathing problem is the opposite one – taking too many deep breaths. This washes out the carbon dioxide in one's blood and can lead to tingling in the fingers and painful contractions of the hands and feet. The remedy is simple. Continue breathing deeply but now hold a paper (*not* plastic) bag over your mouth so that you inhale back the carbon dioxide you've just breathed out. The overbreathing is also then likely to stop. Keep a paper bag in your pocket ready for use each time you catch yourself overbreathing.

Anxiety about swallowing

Perhaps your tension makes it hard for you to swallow solid food. Try to chew a dry biscuit. The idea is to chew, not swallow, it. Chew on and on until the biscuit is very soft and moist. Eventually after you chew for long enough you'll swallow the moist biscuit automatically without noticing. Just chew and the swallowing will look after itself.

Excessive tidiness

If your problem is excessive tidiness ensure that you untidy something in the house everyday. You can start by leaving a carpet askew on the floor in the living room. Tomorrow put a vase in the wrong place. The next day leave something unwashed in the kitchen sink. Expose yourself to increasing untidiness until you have reached the degree of untidiness you want to live with. Dr Leonard Cammer asked a tidy, clean woman to empty a full ashtray in the centre of her living room rug and leave it there for 48 hours. At intervals she'd return to glare at it, but gradually she felt less and less sore about it. Eventually, whenever she spotted something dirty or untidy, she would shrug and say 'Oh well, it can wait another 48 hours if need be.'[4]

Hoarding

If you are a hoarder, notice how the clutter in your house prevents you and others from moving about. Think what you can do with all the space that will become available to you when you throw away all your excess rubbish. Ask a spouse or friend to help you cart away your papers, tins, or whatever. A charity shop may want to buy some of your hoard. Don't buy back. Ensure you throw away things when you have finished with them or you will rekindle the hoarding habit. At first you will feel anxious when you have discarded surplus possessions, but after some days you will be relieved at the extra space you've cleared. Resolve to throw away something every day that previously you might have started to hoard.

List making

If making lists is your addiction, count how many items are on your list. Cross out two of those today, three tomorrow, four the next day, and so on until finally you have no more items on your list. You will worry about them for some days. Accept that you may in fact forget things and realise this won't be crucial, the world won't come to an end. If you want to be quick about it, tear up every list you have even if it convulses you and resolve never to make any others.

Intrusive obsessive thoughts

See p. 119–120.

Reread relevant earlier descriptions of treatment

In this book you have read descriptions of successful treatments. Where the problems treated resemble yours, reread those sections to find tips you can apply to your own treatment:

Agoraphobia, pp. 52–64, 153–4, 157, 183, 191–3

Anger, pp. 96–7

Anorgasmia, p. 125

Bird phobia, p. 87

Blood phobia, pp. 93–4

Body odour fears, pp. 77–9

Cat and dog phobias, pp. 146–8

Ejaculation failure, p. 126

Erection failure (impotence), p. 126

Examination anxiety, p. 145

Family problem-solving, pp. 110–11, 116–18, 193–7

Hoarding, p. 113

Illness worries, pp. 73–5

Nightmares, pp. 149–50

Obsessions and compulsions, pp. 107–21, 160–1, 176–81, 190, 193–7

Obsessive thoughts (ruminations), pp. 119–20, 179

Post-traumatic stress disorder, pp. 79–82, 156–7

Premature ejaculation, p. 126

Relatives as co-therapists, pp. 111, 116–18

Repeated requests for reassurance, pp. 76, 110–11, 116–18

Sexual problems, pp. 122–134, 179

Slowness, p. 113

Social anxieties, pp. 66–72, 125

Urinating in toilets outside one's home, phobia of, pp. 94–5

Vaginal spasm (vaginismus), p. 125

Examples of self-help

You may find it instructive to follow the progress of two people who largely carried out their own treatment.

Overcoming agoraphobia

Molly became agoraphobic during her pregnancy five years earlier at age 35.[5] Fears of leaving home made her give up her professional job. She had hardly been on a bus or train alone for four years and took the dog for a walk only around the corner. If accompanied she did more. She attended an outpatient department every day. Until five years previously she had led a busy social life and loved her work.

I saw Molly and her husband only once for an hour and explained that panic couldn't kill her. With prolonged exposure panic doesn't go completely but gradually lessens as one learns to tackle it without running away. One has to go out and meet the panic. She could overcome her phobia if she systematically exposed herself to whatever she feared. I showed her how to keep a diary of the exposure tasks she completed. Setbacks would come, but she must then go out again. As she lived far from London, no further appointments were arranged, further contact being by letter. The next week she wrote:

> ❝Since you saw my husband and me I've spent three days in the centre of Bristol travelling alone by bus. Today I walked around Bristol for three hours. I'm amazed how, faced with an open-ended cut-off from home or escape, I coped. I've achieved more in four days than during the last four years, and only feel afraid that I shall wake up and find it's a dream. I would never have thought it possible and it was only your reassurances, that fear will never kill you, that enabled me to take the first bus ride. I still don't really understand quite why the panics are diminished with the prospects of long exposure away from home, but they certainly are. It's incredible.[6]❞

With her letter, Molly enclosed a diary detailing the frightening situations she had been in over those four days (see pp. 184–5). Two months later Molly wrote again.

> ❝I've enclosed my schedule and hope you'll be as pleased with my progress as we are. I still run away from anxiety, especially in social situations, e.g. coffee mornings, dinners, and on the bus, where I feel panicking with its 'sweat, shake, and tears' routine would be hard to explain away. However, local shopping, walking with the dog, even going to the Zoo, are everyday events now and cause practically no trouble. This is wonderful to me. I rather clash with my phobic friends in hospital who are still undergoing gradual desensitisation (in fantasy). My husband is very pleased too with the way things are going.❞

After four more months Molly sent her up-to-date schedule showing she had been travelling freely everywhere and had increased her improvement. A year later she was still better.

> ❝Last Friday I travelled on my own to London on an express train to meet my husband and stay with friends for the weekend. You can imagine how thrilled we all are that my progress has allowed me to travel alone again.

Everyone says I'm better than I've been for years and I have to agree. My whole life style has changed since my visit to you. I lead quite a busy life now and rarely stay at home. I only visit the day hospital occasionally now but I do appreciate their help if I hit a bad patch, e.g. after 'flu, etc., as you warned. I still feel very uncomfortable at times but panics don't depress me like they used to. I can soon bounce back and have another go. I now belong to a badminton group, I have music lessons, take friends for music and movement, love taking the dog for walks, and go to parties with very little problem, quite a difference.

I know we have a little way before I completely disregard panics but I do feel well on the way. I enclose a copy of my diary, which I still like to keep up. Sometimes I think I've taken the easy way out again but I hope you'll agree that my horizons have widened. 🙶

I saw Molly and her husband only once, yet she grasped the self-help principles so well that without further ado, she did her necessary exercises and steadily overcame her fears, not by magic, but by systematically facing each one in turn. She wasn't cured overnight. It wasn't easy. She had setbacks which were to be expected, and dealt with them by renewed efforts at self-exposure. Her reward was freedom from the bonds of fear that had tied her for five years.

Molly sent me postcards annually from far-away places proving she was travelling freely. At about six years follow-up she wrote that recently she had become a bit depressed and her fears had returned. I invited her to see me again. She refused antidepressant medication. When asked what she needed to do to recover she said 'Do what I did before'. On my asking why she didn't just go ahead with a self-exposure programme she replied 'I need you to tell me to do so.' I said 'Go ahead'. Molly promptly did so, regained her previous improvement, and resumed sending me postcards annually about her many activities.

Overcoming obsessions and rituals about dirt

We turn to Sue, who had been terrified of dirt for 9 years.[7] Although a nurse helped her for a few days to get started, Sue did much of the treatment herself. Her programme gives you some idea of how to overcome OCD. Her description is long, showing how much you need to attend to detail. If rituals are not your problem, you may prefer to skip this section and go to p. 197.

First let's get an overview, and then look at her own description of what she did. Notice the principles of treatment. *Face up to precisely what you fear. Never avoid discomfort. Practise, practise, and practise doing what you are frightened of over and over again until it is second nature.* Sue had to practise facing situations she thought were connected with dirt, bacteria, or poison.

Sue's problem

Sue, now 37, was crippled for years with severe obsessive-compulsive dread. It began after she read of a local death from Weil's disease (transmitted by rats) and saw a dead rat in the road. Over the next few months she rapidly developed ruminations, rituals, and avoidance concerning imagined dirt, bacteria, and poison, and washed her hands 50 times a day. She was constantly preoccupied with 'germs' and what she might have touched ('Have I caught anything? Have I passed it on?'), particularly germs potentially connected with rats. She repeatedly threw away 'contaminated' articles, including a washing machine. Her husband and two teenage sons co-operated in carrying out rituals, reassuring her, and doing things she avoided due to her fears, for example, cooking, washing, and other household tasks. This led to many family quarrels. She held down a full-time unskilled job, her fears being less marked outside than at home. Over five years she benefited little from treatment, including hospital admission, antidepressant drugs, electro-convulsive therapy, tranquilisers, and supportive psychotherapy. With brief behavioural treatment that did not involve her family she improved somewhat but relapsed each time she ceased to contact her therapist.

Sue's therapist's description

During five days in hospital she was encouraged to 'contaminate' herself with 'germs' and refrain from washing her hands for increasingly long periods. Despite initial anxiety she persevered with the programme and quickly obtained relief. She transferred her improvement to her home, where she began to perform all the household duties she had previously avoided, and reduced handwashing to eight times per day. The family became co-therapists, each having specific roles to play, e.g. the children touched mum when entering the house and the husband had to stop doing the cooking and housework. Improvement continued until follow-up at one year.

From this summary you would not guess the hard work on so many details that Sue had to complete to get over her problem.

Sue's description of her treatment

    "When I came into hospital for five days my nurse wrote out a detailed treatment programme which we signed and stuck to my mirror above the washbasin.

Day 1. Programme for Monday, February 23.

1   Two handwashes allowed per day.

2   No soap allowed in bedroom except one dry bar, which is to remain unused.

3 Bedroom to be dirtied and not cleaned until further notice.

4 Prepare coffee and tea for several people after previously 'contaminating' cups.

5 'Contaminate' knives, forks, spoons by dropping them on the floor, picking them up and eating a meal with them.

6 Towel in room not to be changed.

7 Not allowed to wash clothes.

8 'Contaminate' hands at 9 am and not wash for at least 5 hours.

9 Bath allowed in late evening, but only if I keep to programme (an incentive to be diligent).

10 All visits to the toilet to be supervised. *No washes*.

I agree to keep to this programme   Signed   Sue

. . . We then carried out instructions on the programme. Soap and my towels were taken to the staff room. I was allowed one clean and one 'dirty' hospital towel ['dirty' here means simply used once by somebody else]. The 'dirty' towel was placed at the bottom of the bed and I had to sit on it. Then we took the wastepaper basket and went outside collecting muck from a drain cover in the road and long grass from under nearby huts. We returned to my room and threw the muck all round it. I threw my washing on the floor, and we both wiped our hands on the clean towel to dirty it. Without washing my hands I opened my suitcase, handled all my clean clothes and put them on coat hangers and in drawers. I went to the canteen and made tea, putting my hands in all the cups and the milk jug, rubbed the spoons in my hands, and then served tea which we all drank. Everyone knew what had happened and that I hadn't washed my hands. At supper time I rubbed my cutlery on the floor, touched my shoes and licked my fingers at every possible moment. I hadn't washed since 9 am. Before going to sleep I had a bath for 10 minutes.

Tuesday, February 24. I washed, dressed and made up my face, and made tea for the patients and staff, 'contaminating' the cups first. Using 'dirty' cloths, dustpan and broom I cleaned the cabins I'd dirtied the previous day with rubbish, grass and leaves. At 4 pm I touched toilet seats and then asked four people if I could clean their shoes for them. After cleaning their shoes I made four people some toast, found two people who wanted their beds made and tidied them. I touched a little girl I was afraid of, wrote a letter to my husband and children, telling them the letter was full of germs, and posted it. I went shopping after touching the toilet seats and bought grapes which I served at supper to unsuspecting patients. I bought a chemical toilet cleaner which I handled and sat with on my lap; I was terrified this would harm me. Before going to bed I had to put my arm round six people. I went to sleep with a 'contaminated' towel on my bedclothes, and wore someone else's nightdress.

Wednesday, February 25. After breakfast I went through my 'contaminating' exercises; going down corridors touching light switches, handles, phones, pictures, rubbish bins, soiled linen, urinal bottles, bedpans, basins containing unknown liquids, irons, ironing board, brooms, dusters, vacuum cleaner, mops, bleach bottles. As I was afraid of diseases which might be transmitted by rats I went to see rats in a cage and touched them, after which I made toast for the staff and touched a lady and her child. In the patients' toilets I touched the seats, made tea, served cakes and touched the cups. A nurse usually came with me to make sure I did everything and even woke me as I was sitting in a chair to remind me that I'd forgotten to make toast for patients. This I did. I read a magazine used by other patients, put on clothes I'd worn the previous day and practised touching other people's hair. I washed dirty underclothes in the bath before I could bathe in it. I resolved to let a rat run over me, and risk getting its disease.

Thursday, February 26. Completed the 'contaminating' exercises involving other people and myself. Bought a book to send my son, and on the walk back to the hospital touched several rubbish bins and every stationary car at the side of the road. Arrived back at the hospital really filthy and without washing I made tea for the patients.

Day 5, Friday, February 27. Completed my exposure routine, cleaned my bedroom, packed my clothes, mixing dirty with clean and avoided using plastic bags. Contaminated myself again before my husband arrived. Managed to pick up the little girl on the ward for a few moments and then went home with my husband. 〞

Self-management at home; general principle

❝ Touch whatever I'm scared of without washing afterwards. Instructions for my exposure exercises are on cards around the house and done every day.

1 'Contaminate' my hands by touching garbage can, toilet seat and brush, wheelbarrow with rubbish in it, bird aviary, bird droppings, raw meat. Touch laundry basket and clothes whenever I pass them. Hug my three sons regularly (previously avoided this completely). Fill the dog's waterbowl then touch taps in kitchen with unwashed hands.

2 'Contaminate' work surfaces, plates, cutlery, pots and all food before eating.

3 With unwashed hands lie on couch, answer phone and touch switches and door handles, television and curtains.

4 After touching the garbage cans tidy beds, lie on them and handle items on the dressing table.

5 Touch the toilet seat and thereafter towels, switches, medicine cabinet, my own hair.

Programme I devised for March 5. Got up and dressed, put on unwashed clothes which I'd worn yesterday, washed my hands and then contaminated myself and had breakfast after contaminating all the food. Completed my exposure routine, then cleaned the bathroom and toilet seat using a cloth usually reserved for the bath. Cleaned the bathroom cabinet with the cloth usually reserved for the bath, thereafter handled all medicines. Poured old medicines down the sink. Polished the floor using dirty cloth in bucket usually reserved for the kitchen, and made sure I trapped germs under the polish. Cleaned the toilet brush and holder using the floor cloth and poured dirty water down the bath. Picked up the ironing board and iron, rubbed them against the dirty clothes and with them ironed a 'clean' dress. Touched all my clean clothes. Went into town with dirty hands, tried on bras, bought one, walked home without checking where I was walking, and opened the door with the key (which previously I couldn't do). Without washing my hands then prepared lunch, hugged my sons, and went to the hairdresser with dirty hands. Had manicure with nail polish, came home and bathed without cleaning the bath first. Used a 'dirty' towel for drying, placed the used towel where the family could use it and put on the dress I'd previously ironed and ironed my husband's shirt. Then touched the rubbish bin and toilet. Went to the dance, shook hands with everyone. I came home, put the dress in the wardrobe next to all the other clothing rather than in the wash basket. Washed my hands and went to bed.[8] "

Does exposure treatment work? The scientific evidence

You may be getting impatient at patients' testimonials. 'That's all very well' you might think, and not without justice, 'but we all know about miracle cures which can't be repeated. Will it work for me? What's the scientific evidence that exposure and cognitive treatments work reliably for most people with my kind of trouble?'

The current yardstick of a treatment's value is a randomised controlled trial (RCT) in which sufferers draw either the treatment in question or an alternative procedure. Many RCTs have now found that exposure therapies were significantly more effective than other treatments in improving phobias, panic, OCD and post-traumatic stress disorder. They worked better than contrasting methods such as relaxation or refraining from exposure completely or analytic types of insight psychotherapy or being on a waiting list. This very book *Living With Fear* proved effective in a RCT of its first edition. Phobics who were asked by a psychiatrist to read *Living With Fear* and follow its self-exposure instructions improved as much as did phobics who did self-exposure therapy guided by a psychiatrist[9] and their gains persisted to the 6-month follow-up.

Moreover, improvement from exposure therapy is not a nine-day wonder that vanishes after a few weeks. Patients who improved after exposure therapy stayed that way over the two to eight *years* that they were followed up after discharge.[10] Improvement in their anxiety freed them and their families from the restrictions which formerly hemmed them in. Sufferers' moods improved somewhat too, though a few with a pre-existing tendency to recurrent depression continued to have that, which was managed by antidepressant medication during such episodes. Some sufferers increase their gains over the years. Others may relapse after a while, but brief booster treatment usually helps them improve again.

The evidence for exposure also applies to cognitive behaviour therapy, which usually includes exposure. In respect of cognitive restructuring on its own without exposure, this benefited PTSD and OCD in recent RCTs. Cognitive restructuring without exposure involves identifying and listing automatic negative thoughts and beliefs, challenging them, and substituting positive thoughts. Research may well develop further valuable techniques along these lines. Details of how cognitive restructuring is done are on pp. 81 and 156 in Chapter 11.

You can find a few more references to the research literature on p. 201. Hundreds of scientific papers on the subject appear every year and it would take a whole book just to list them.

Self-help organisations

Sufferers from many kinds of disorder find it helpful to join lay groups concerning their disorder so that they can share common experiences, learn helpful tips about how to cope, and have an additional social outlet. Anxiety sufferers are no exception. A UK correspondence club once had about 3,000 agoraphobic members. Similar organisations exist in several countries. Agoraphobics can club together for outings, help run children to and from school, arrange programmes to retrain themselves out of their phobias, and organise other activities. A few people are reluctant to join because they are afraid that listening to other people's troubles will worsen their own, but this is in fact a rare event.

The important point is not to make the club a grouse group just out to swap complaints, but a mutual aid society devoted to overcoming problems. This has been done in many ways. People who feared eating in restaurants went to lunch together, supporting and encouraging one another as the group ventured out. Flying phobics banded together to charter an aeroplane, and after preliminary instruction went for a group flight together. Club members can help one another even if their phobias are not the same. A driving phobic and a walking phobic joined forces to drive on roads and walk in stores together, thus helping themselves and each other.

Remember that:

- treating yourself is hard work but well worthwhile
- panic during self-treatment shows that you're really starting to confront your fear
- anxiety is not harmful.

Your efforts will be well rewarded once you confront your fears systematically.

Good luck with your self-help programme! You have nothing to lose but your fear.

List of self-help organisations, newsletters and websites for anxiety disorders

The list below is necessarily incomplete as many wax and wane over the years. In the year 2001 they include:

UK

NHS Stress Self-Help Clinic for anxiety disorders, 303 North End Rd, London W14 9NS. Tel: 0207 610 2594; Fax: 0207 385 7471.

TOP (Triumph Over Phobia) UK began in 1987. It is a network of structured self-help groups in England and the Channel Islands. TOP-UK groups are run by trained lay volunteers, most of whom are ex-phobics or ex-OCD sufferers. They use *Living With Fear* as a self-help manual, and also provide other self-help material. TOP is a unique charity in its aim of helping sufferers from phobia, panic and OCD to become ex-sufferers. Attenders of TOP groups who do self-exposure achieve much improvement over a few months. Head office: TOP-UK, PO Box 1831, Bath BA2 4YW, UK. Tel: +44(0)1225 330353; Fax: 469212; E-mail triumphoverphobia@ compuserve.com

No Panic 93 Brands Farm Way, Randlay, Telford TF3 2JQ. Tel: 01952 590 005.

Open Door Association 447 Pensby Rd, Heswall, Wirral, Merseyside LR1 9PQ.

Obsessive Action Aberdeen Centre, 22 Highbury Grove, London N5 2EA. Tel: 0207 226 4000.

First Steps to Freedom for OCD and other anxiety suffers. Helpline Tel: 01926 851608; Fax: 019206 864473 or 0870 1640567, E-mail: firststepstofreedom @compuserve.com and ljh@firststeps.demon.co.uk

Living with Spiders, Snakes and Birds Bristol Zoo Gardens, Clifton, Bristol BS8 3HA. Tel: 0117 970 6176 ext 229; fax 0117 973 6814; email: information @bristolzoo.org.uk; web site www.bristolzoo.org.uk

Luxembourg

LASH: Letzebuergesch Angscht Steierungen Hellef an Selwsthellef BP16 L-3205 Leudelange. Tel: 52 45 90 / 59 45 90.

The Netherlands

VALK for flying phobia. PO Box 110, 2300 AC Leiden. Tel: 071 527 37 33; Fax: 96.

USA has over 300 organisations. The following are some of the most well known.

Anxiety Disorders Association of America 11900 Parklawn Dr, Suite 100, Rockville, MD. Tel: 20852-2624.

Freedom From Fear 308 Seaview Ave, Staten Island, NY 10305. Tel: 718 351 1717.

Obsessive-Compulsive Foundation 337 Notch Hill Rd, North Branford, CT 06471. Tel: 203 315 2190.

Obsessive-Compulsive Information Center Madison Institute of Medicine, 7617 Mineral Point Rd, Suite 300, Madison WI 53717.

Tourette Syndrome Association 42 Bell Blvd, Bayside NY 11361. Tel: 713 224 2999.

Trichotillomania Learning Center 1215 Mission St, Suite 2, Santa Cruz CA 95060. Tel: 408 457 1004.

White Plains Hospital Center Anxiety and Phobia Clinic, Davis Ave, at Post Rd, White Plains NY10601. Tel: 914 681 0600.

Australia

TOP (Triumph Over Phobia)-NSW is affiliated with TOP-UK and runs TOP groups in New South Wales. PO Box 213, Rockdale, NSW 2216, Australia. Tel: 1800 626 077. Website: www.nswamh.org

OCD Information Lines. Tel: 1800 626 055.

Obsessive-Compulsive Disorders Support Service (OCDSS Inc) runs an Australia-wide newsletter. Room 318, Epworth Building, 33 Pirie St, Adelaide, South Australia 5000, Australia. Tel: +44 61 (0)8 8231 1588.

Recommended websites, apart from the e-mail addresses given above:

Phobia/panic computer-guided self-help system: www.fearfighter.com

OCD computer-guided self-help system: www.Copewithlife.com

OCD adolescent/child clinic in London: www.iop.kcl.ac.uk/main/Mhealth/OCDyoung

Social anxiety: www.factsforhealth.org

Post-traumatic stress disorder: www.factsforhealth.org

Depression computer-guided self-help system: www.Copewithlife.com

TOP-UK network of self-help groups: www.triumphoverphobia.com

Suggestions for further reading

Baer L., *Getting Control*, Penguin Plume, New York, 1992. Paperback self-help for OCD.

Baer L., *The Imp of the Mind*. Dutton, Penguin, London, 2000. Good paperback self-help for obsessive thoughts.

Cammer L., *Freedom from Compulsion*, Simon & Schuster, New York, 1976. Good description of OCD.

Kubler-Ross E., *On Death and Dying*, Macmillan, New York, 1975. Useful for medical staff and families of the terminally ill.

Marks I. M., *Fears, Phobias and Rituals*, Oxford University Press, New York, 1987. Detailed review of scientific evidence until 1987.

Ghosh A., Marks I. M. and Carr A., 'Therapist contact and outcome of self-exposure treatment for phobias'. *British Journal of Psychiatry*, 1988, **152**, 234–238. Controlled trial showing the value of *Living With Fear*.

Marks I. M., 'Computer aids to mental health care'. *Canadian Journal of Psychiatry*, 1999, **44**, 6, 548–555. Detailed review of computer-guided self-help.

Marks I., Lovell K., Noshirvani H., Livanou M. and Thrasher S., 'Treatment of PTSD by exposure and/or cognitive restructuring: a controlled study'. *Archives General Psychiatry*, 1998, **55**, 317–325. Evidence for the value of exposure and cognitive therapy for post-traumatic stress disorder.

Morrison A. L., *The Antidepressant Sourcebook: A User's Guide for Patients and Families*, Main Street Books Doubleday, London, 2000. For sufferers on antidepressant medication.

For information and self-help on sexual matters:

Comfort A., *The Joy of Sex*, Simon & Schuster, 1974. This manual has many illustrations and descriptions of normal sex.

Crowe M., Psychosexual Disorders, in Kerwin R. *et al.* (eds) *Psychopharmacology*, Sage, London, 1999. About drugs that interfere with or improve sexual function.

Kass D. J. and Stauss F. F., *Sex Therapy at Home*, Simon & Schuster, New York, 1975. A step-by-step approach to overcome sexual problems.

Yaffe, M. and Fenwick E., *Sexual Happiness*. Dorling Kindersley, 1986.

notes

Chapter 1

1. C. Darwin, *On the Expression of Emotions in Man and Animals*, John Murray, London, 1872.
2. Ibid.
3. D. Keltner and P. Ekman, 'Facial expression of emotion', in M. Lewis and J. Haviland-Jones (eds.) *Handbook of Emotions*, 2nd edn, Guilford Publications, New York, 2000.
4. For the three examples mentioned here, see M. H. Lader and I. M. Marks, *Clinical Anxiety*, Heinemann Medical, London, 1971.
5. Report of author's experience, 1966.
6. The two examples are contained in D. D. Bond, *The Love and Fear of Flying*, International Universities Press, New York, 1952.
7. Patient's report to author.
8. Ibid.
9. Ibid.
10. Ibid.
11. F. Kraupl Taylor, *Psychopathology, its Causes and Symptoms*, Butterworths, London, 1966, pp. 156–159.
12. J. Price and J. Kasriel, lecture to the Indian Psychiatric Society Silver Jubilee meeting, Chandigarh, India, June 1973.
13. Ibid.
14. Ibid.
15. Ibid.
16. Ibid.
17. Ibid.
18. Ibid.
19. Ibid.
20. Ibid.
21. Ibid.
22. Ibid.
23. Ibid.
24. R. Burton, *The Anatomy of Melancholy*, 11th edn, London, 1813; first published in 1621.
25. Ibid.
26. I. MacAlphine, 'Syphilophobia', *British Journal of Venereal Disease*, vol. 33, 1957, pp. 92–99.
27. A. Le Camus, *Médicine de l'Esprit*, rev. edn, vol. 1, pp. 259–265.

Chapter 2

1. M. Cook and S. Mineka, 'Selective associations in the origins of phobic fears and their implications for behavior therapy', in P. Martin (ed.) *Handbook of Behavior Therapy and Psychological Science*, Pergamon Press, 1991, pp. 413–434.

2. I. M. Marks.

3. M. Daly and M. I. Wilson, 'Some differential attributes of lethal assaults on small children by stepfathers versus genetic Fathers', *Ethology and Sociobiology*, 1994, vol. 15, pp. 207–217.

4. Cited by I. M. Marks, *Fears and Phobias*, Heinemann Medical, London, 1969.

5. M. Cook and S. Mineka, 'Selective associations in the origins of phobic fears and their implications for behavior therapy', in P. Martin (ed.) *Handbook of Behavior Therapy and Psychological Science*, Pergamon Press, 1991, pp. 413–434.

6. C. W. Valentine, 'The Innate Bases of Fear', *Journal of Genetic Psychology*, vol. 37, 1930, pp. 394–419.

7. *The Observer*, London, Feb. 18, 1968, p. 21.

8. Ibid.

Chapter 3

1. Cited by J. Hinton, *Dying*, Pelican Books, London, 1967.

2. Ibid.

3. Ibid.

4. C. Parkes, 'The First Year of Grief', *Psychiatry*, vol. 33, 1970, pp. 444–467.

5. Ibid.

6. Ibid.

7. Ibid.

8. Ibid.

9. Ibid.

10. Ibid.

11. Ibid.

12. Ibid.

13. E. Lindemann, 'The Symptomatology and Management of Acute Grief', *American Journal of Psychiatry*, vol. 101, 1944, pp. 141–148.

14. Parkes, op. cit.

15. Ibid.

16. Ibid.

17. Ibid.

18. Ibid.

19. Ibid.

20. Ibid.

21. Ibid.

22. Ibid.

23. Ibid.

24. Ibid.

25. Ibid.

26. Ibid.

27. Ibid.

28. Ibid.

29. L. Sireling, D. Cohen, and I. M. Marks, 'Guided mourning for morbid grief: a controlled replication', *Behavior Therapy*, vol. 19, 1988, pp. 121–132.

30. I. M. Marks and C. Wilks, 'Treatment of a dentist's phobia of practising dentistry', *British Dental Journal*, vol. 147, 1979, pp. 189–191.

31. Bond, *The Love and Fear of Flying*, International Universities Press, New York, 1952.

32. L. Eitinger, 'Anxiety in Concentration Camp Survivors', *Australia and New Zealand Journal of Psychiatry*, vol. 3, 1969, pp. 348–351.

Chapter 4

1. *Bethlem-Maudsley Gazette*, 1970.
2. I. M. Marks, *Fears and Phobias*, Heinemann Medical, London, 1969.
3. Ibid.
4. Cited by M. H. Lader and I. M. Marks, *Clinical Anxiety*, Heinemann Medical, London, 1971.
5. Ibid.
6. P. W. Ngui, 'The Koro Epidemic in Singapore', *Australia and New Zealand Journal of Psychiatry*, vol. 3, 1969, pp. 263–266.
7. Ibid.

Chapter 5

1. Cited by I. M. Marks, *Fears and Phobias*, Heinemann Medical, London, 1969.
2. Ibid.
3. Ibid.
4. Ibid.
5. Ibid.
6. 'Disabilities', Section 'Anxiety Neurosis', *Lancet*, 1952, pp. 79–83.
7. C. Westphal, 'Die Agoraphobie', *Archiv für Psychiatrie und Nervenkrankheiten*, vol. 3, 1871, pp. 138–171, 219–221.
8. F. Kraupl Taylor, *Psychopathology, its Causes and Symptoms*, Butterworths, London, 1966.
9. *Lancet*, op. cit.
10. I. M. Marks *et al.*, *Nursing in Behavioral Psychotherapy*, Royal College of Nursing, London, 1977, Appendix, patient 6.
11. Ibid., patient 3.

Chapter 6

1. I. M. Marks, *Fears and Phobias*, Heinemann Medical, London, 1969.
2. J. Greist in www.factsforhealth.org
3. Patient's report to author.
4. S. Mulkens, P. J. De Jong, A. Dobbelaar, *et al.*, 'Fear of blushing: Fearful preoccupation irrespective of facial coloration', *Behaviour Research and Therapy*, 1999, vol. 37, pp. 1119–1128.
5. Patient's report to author.
6. Ibid.
7. Phone call to BBC radio programme *Phone In*, 1974.
8. A. Stravynski, N. Arbel, J. Bounader *et al.*, 'Social phobia treated as a problem in social functioning, *Acta Psychiatria Scandinavica*, 2000, vol. 102, pp. 188–189.
9. R. Burton, *The Anatomy of Melancholy*, 11th edn, London, 1813, p. 272; first published in 1621.
10. Patient's report in author's unit.
11. Ibid.

12. Ibid.

13. Mary McArdle, 'Treatment of a Phobia', *Nursing Times*, 1974, pp. 637–639. This case was treated in the author's unit.

14. M. Basoglu, O. Parker, E. Ozmen *et al.*, 'Psychological effects of torture: Comparison of tortured with non-tortured political activists in Turkey', *American Journal of Psychiatry*, 1994, vol. 151, pp. 76–81.

15. A. Bystritsky, T. Vapnik, K. Maidment *et al.*, 'Acute responses of anxiety disorder patients after a natural disaster', *Depression and Anxiety*, 2000, vol. 11, pp. 43–44.

16. S. M. Thrasher, K. Lovell, H. Noshirvani *et al.*, 'Cognitive restructuring in the treatment of PTSD: two single cases', *Clinical Psychology and Psychotherapy*, 1996, vol. 3, pp. 137–148.

Chapter 7

1. Patients' reports to author.

2. S. Freud, *Totem and Taboo*, Hogarth, London, 1913, p. 127.

3. Phone calls to BBC radio programme *Phone In*, 1974.

4. Ibid.

5. Patient's report to author.

6. Ibid.

7. Phone calls to BBC radio programme *Phone In*, 1974.

8. Ibid.

9. I. M. Marks *et al.*, *Nursing in Behavioral Psychotherapy*, Royal College of Nursing, London, 1977, Appendix, patient 1.

10. Patient's report to author.

11. Phone calls to BBC radio programme *Phone In*, 1974.

12. Patient's report to author.

13. Ibid.

14. Ibid.

15. Ibid.

16. Ibid.

17. Ibid.

18. Patient seen in author's unit.

19. Bond, *The Love and Fear of Flying*, International Universities Press, New York, 1952.

20. Patient's report to author.

21. Ibid.

22. Ibid.

23. Ibid.

24. I. M. Marks *et al.*, *Nursing in Behavioral Psychotherapy*, op. cit., Appendix, patient 2.

25. Y. Lamontagne and I. M. Marks, 'Psychogenic Urinary Retention Treatment by Prolonged Exposure', *Behavior Therapy*, 1973, vol. 4, p. 581.

26. Patient's letter to author.

27. E. B. Blanchard, 'Brief Flooding Treatment for a Debilitating Revulsion', *Behavior Research and Therapy*, 1975, vol. 13, p. 193.

Chapter 8

1. A. A. Milne, *When We Were Very Young*, Methuen Paperbacks, London, 1975, pp. 12–13; first published 1924.

2. Patient's report to author.
3. Ibid.
4. Ibid.
5. M. R. Dadds, S. H. Spence, D. E. Holland, *et al.*, 'Prevention and early intervention for anxiety disorders: A controlled trial', *Journal of Consulting and Clinical Psychology*, 1997.
6. K. Stewart, 'Dream Theory in Malaya', in C. Tart (ed.), *Altered States of Consciousness*, Wiley, New York, 1969, ch. 9.
7. Ibid.

Chapter 9

1. E. Fenwick, *World Medicine*, 1972.
2. I. M. Marks, *Patterns of Meaning in Psychiatric Patients*, Oxford University Press, London, 1965, pp. 1–2.
3. Patients treated in author's unit.
4. Patients' reports to author.
5. Ibid.
6. Ibid.
7. Ibid.
8. Ibid.
9. Ibid.
10. L. Cammer, *Freedom from Compulsion*, Simon & Schuster, New York, 1976.
11. Ibid.
12. I. M. Marks *et al.*, *Nursing in Behavioural Psychotherapy*, Royal College of Nursing, London, 1977, Appendix, patient 5.
13. Patient seen by author.
14. Patient treated by author.
15. Ibid.
16. Ibid.
17. Ibid.

Chapter 10

1. Patient's report to author.
2. Ibid.
3. Ibid.
4. Ibid.
5. Couple treated by author.
6 Ibid
7. J. Lopiccolo, 'Direct Treatment of Sexual Dysfunction', in J. Money and H. Musaph (eds.), *Handbook of Sexology*, ASP Biological and Medical Press, Amsterdam, 1975.

Chapter 11

1. V. Frankl, personal communication.
2. K. Lovell, L. Fullalove, R. Garvey *et al.*, 'Telephone treatment of obsessive-compulsive disorder', *Behavioural and Cognitive Psychotherapy*, 2000, vol. 28, pp. 87–91.

3. 'Disabilities', Section 'Anxiety Neurosis', *Lancet*, 1952.

4. Letter from patient to author.

5. Ibid.

6. Ibid.

7. N. Malleson, 'Panic and Phobia: Possible Methods of Treatment', *Lancet*, 1959, vol. 1, p. 225.

8. V. Frankl, 'Paradoxical Intention', *American Journal of Psychotherapy*, 1960, vol. 14, pp. 520–535.

9. Report of patient in author's unit.

10. J. P. Watson, R. Gaind and I. M. Marks, 'Prolonged Exposure: A Rapid Treatment for Phobias', *British Medical Journal*, 1971, vol. 1, p. 13.

11. Patient treated by author.

12. I. Hand, Y. Lamontagne and I. M. Marks, 'Group Exposure (flooding) *in vivo* for Agoraphobics', *British Journal of Psychiatry*, 1974, vol. 125, pp. 588–602.

13. Ibid.

14. I. Silverman and J. H. Geer, 'The Elimination of Recurrent Nightmare by Densensitisation of a Related Phobia', *Behavior Research and Therapy*, 1968, vol. 6, pp. 109–112.

15. M. Burgess, M. Gill and I. M. Marks, 'Postal self-exposure treatment of recurrent nightmares: randomised controlled trial', *British Journal of Psychiatry*, 1998, vol. 172, pp. 257–262.

16. R. Surwit, unpublished PhD dissertation, McGill University, 1974.

17. R. S. Lazarus, *Psychological Stress and the Coping Process*, McGraw-Hill, New York, 1966.

18. Cited by D. Meichenbaum, *Cognitive Behavior Modification*, Plenum, New York, 1977.

19. Ibid.

20. Ibid.

21. Ibid.

22. Ibid.

23. Ibid.

24. C. Weekes, *Peace from Nervous Suffering*, Angus & Robertson, Sydney, 1962.

25. Meichenbaum, op. cit.

26. J. Kabat-Zinn, *Full Catastrophic Living: How to cope with stress, pain and illness using mindfulness meditation*. Piatkus, London, 1996.

27. I. M. Marks, K. Lovell, H. Noshirvani, M. Livanov and S. Thrasher, 'Treatment of post-traumatic stress disorder by exposure and/or cognitive restructuring: a controlled study', *Archives of General Psychiatry*, 1998, vol. 55, pp. 317–325.

28. Patient treated in author's unit by K. Lovell and S. Thrasher.

29. 'Disabilities', Section 'Anxiety Neurosis', *Lancet*, 1952.

30. Patient seen in author's unit.

31. I. M. Marks, 'Computer aids to mental health care', *Canadian Journal of Psychiatry*, 1999, vol. 44, 6, pp. 548–555.

32. I. M. Marks, 'Commentary on "OCD and Me"', by Daisy Fields, in *Light at the End of the Tunnel*, R. Ramsay (ed.), Gaskell, London, 2001.

33. I. M. Marks, *Fears and Phobias*, Heinemann Medical, London, 1969.

34. D. Barlow, J. M. Gorman, M. K. Shear, *et al.*, 'Randomized controlled trial of CBT vs imipramine and their combination for panic disorder: Primary outcome results', *Journal of American Medical Association*, 2000, May.

35. I. M. Marks, R. P. Swinson, M. Basoglu, *et al.*, 'Alprazolam and exposure alone and combined in panic disorder with agoraphobia. A controlled study in London and Toronto', *British Journal of Psychiatry*, 1993, vol. 162, pp. 776–787.

36. A. Thom, G. Sartory and P. Johren, 'Comparison between one-session psychological treatment and benzodiazepine in dental phobia', *Journal of Consulting and Clinical Psychology*, 2000, vol. 68.

37. H. D. Langtry and A. M. Markham, 'Sildenafil: Review of its use in erectile dysfunction', *Drugs*, 1999, vol. 57, pp. 967–989.

38. G. Williams, 'Male erectile dysfunction', *Prescribers Journal*, 2000, vol. 40, p. 52.

Chapter 12

1. D. Meichenbaum, *Cognitive Behavior Modification*, Plenum, New York, 1977.
2. Observation made by author.
3 L. Cammer, *Freedom from Compulsion*, Simon & Schuster, New York, 1976.
4 Ibid.
5. Patient seen by author.
6. Letter from patient to author.
7. Patient treated in author's unit.
8. Letter from patient to author.
9. A. Ghosh, I. M. Marks and A. Carr. 'Therapist contact and outcome of self-exposure treatment for phobias', *British Journal of Psychiatry*, 1988, vol. 152, 234–238
10. G. A. Fava, C. Rafanelli, S. Grandi, S. Conti, C. Ruini, L. Mangelli and P. Bellvardo, 'Long term outcome of panic disorder with agoraphobia treated by exposure', *Psychological Medicine*, 2001.

author index

subject index

Triumph Over Phobia (TOP U.K.) was started in 1987 under the auspices of Professor Isaac Marks by Celia Bonham Christie MBE, MA, who had recovered from a severe fear of flying by using the self-help programme in *Living with Fear*. Top U.K.'s mission is to help phobics to become ex-phobics by using this book as a self-help manual in a self-treatment group. The groups are run by lay people (mostly ex-phobics).

For more information, time and place of meetings contact

Head Office
Triumph Over Phobia (TOP U.K.) Registered Charity No. 1034932
PO Box 1831
Bath BA2 4YW
Tel: +44 (0) 1225 330353
Fax: +44 (0) 1225 469212
Website: www.triumphoverphobia.com

Affiliated to TOP U.K.
Triumph Over Phobia (TOP Jersey)
Tel: +44 (0) 1534 608080
e-mail: topjersey@freenet.co.uk

Triumph Over Phobia (TOP Sligo, Republic of Ireland)
Tel: +353 71 83962

Triumph Over Phobia (TOP New South Wales, Australia)
Tel: +61 295 793746

There will be 20+ groups in England in 2001. For more information about Triumph Over Phobia UK and TOP international groups, contact details are above.